Penguin Books
The Social Construction of Reality

Peter L. Berger is Professor of Sociology at Boston University and
Director of the Institute for the Study of Economic Culture. He
has previously been Professor of Sociology at Rutgers University,
New Jersey, and in the Graduate Faculty of the New School for
Social Research in New York. He is the author of many books
including *Invitation to Sociology*, *Pyramids of Sacrifice*, *Facing up
to Modernity* and *The Heretical Imperative*, and is co-author (with
Hansfried Kellner) of *Sociology Reinterpreted* and (with Brigitte
Berger) of *Sociology: A Biographical Approach* and *The War over
the Family*. His latest book is *The Capitalist Revolution*.

Thomas Luckmann is at present Professor of Sociology at the University of Constance, Federal Republic of Germany. Previously he
taught at the University of Frankfurt, at the Graduate Faculty of
the New School for Social Research in New York, and was fellow
at the Center for Advanced Study in the Behavioral Sciences in
Stanford. He has published widely, and his titles include *The
Invisible Religion*, *The Sociology of Language*, *Life-World and Social
Realities* and *The Structures of the Life-World* (with Alfred Schütz).
He is editor of *Phenomenology and Sociology* and *The Changing
Face of Religion* (with James A. Beckford).

Peter L. Berger
and Thomas Luckmann

The Social Construction of Reality

A Treatise in the Sociology
of Knowledge

Penguin Books

PENGUIN BOOKS

Published by the Penguin Group
Penguin Books Ltd, 27 Wrights Lane, London w8 5tz, England
Viking Penguin, a division of Penguin Books USA Inc.
375 Hudson Street, New York, New York 10014, USA
Penguin Books Australia Ltd, Ringwood, Victoria, Australia
Penguin Books Canada Ltd, 2801 John Street, Markham, Ontario, Canada l3r 1b4
Penguin Books (NZ) Ltd, 182–190 Wairau Road, Auckland 10, New Zealand

Penguin Books Ltd, Registered Offices: Harmondsworth, Middlesex, England

First published in the USA 1966
Published in Great Britain by Allen Lane
The Penguin Press 1967
Published in Penguin University Books 1971
Reprinted in Peregrine Books 1979
Reprinted in Pelican Books 1984
Reprinted in Penguin Books 1991
10 9 8 7 6 5 4 3

Printed in England by Clays Ltd, St Ives plc
Set in Monotype Plantin

Contents

CONTENTS

Preface

The present volume is intended as a systematic, theoretical treatise in the sociology of knowledge. It is not intended, therefore, to give a historical survey of the development of this discipline, or to engage in exegesis of various figures in this or other developments in sociological theory, or even to show how a synthesis may be achieved between several of these figures and developments. Nor is there any polemic intent here. Critical comments on other theoretical positions have been introduced (not in the text, but in the Notes) only where they may serve to clarify the present argument.

The core of the argument will be found in Sections Two and Three ('Society as Objective Reality' and 'Society as Subjective Reality'), the former containing our basic understanding of the problems of the sociology of knowledge, the latter applying this understanding to the level of subjective consciousness and thereby building a theoretical bridge to the problems of social psychology. Section One contains what might best be described as philosophical prolegomena to the core argument, in terms of a phenomenological analysis of the reality of everyday life ('The Foundations of Knowledge in Everyday Life'). The reader interested only in the sociological argument proper may be tempted to skip this, but he should be warned that certain key concepts employed throughout the argument are defined in Section One.

Although our interest is not historical, we have felt obliged to explain why and in what way our conception of the sociology of knowledge differs from what has hitherto been generally understood by this discipline. This we do in the Introduction. At the end, we make some concluding remarks to indicate what we consider to be the 'pay-off' of the present enterprise for sociological theory generally and for certain areas of empirical research.

The logic of our argument makes a certain measure of repetitiveness inevitable. Thus some problems are viewed within phenomenological brackets in Section One, taken up again in Section Two with these brackets removed and with an interest in their empirical genesis, and then taken up once more in Section Three on the level of subjective consciousness. We have tried to make this book as readable as possible, but not in violation of its inner logic, and we hope that the reader will understand the reasons for those repetitions that could not be avoided.

Ibn ul-'Arabi, the great Islamic mystic, exclaims in one of his poems – 'Deliver us, oh Allah, from the sea of names!' We have often repeated this exclamation in our own readings in sociological theory. We have, in consequence, decided to eliminate all names from our actual argument. The latter can now be read as one continuous presentation of our own position, without the constant intrusion of such observations as 'Durkheim says this', 'Weber says that', 'We agree here with Durkheim but not with Weber', 'We think that Durkheim has been misinterpreted on this point', and so forth. That our position has not sprung up *ex nihilo* is obvious on each page, but we want it to be judged on its own merits, not in terms of its exegetical or synthesizing aspects. We have, therefore, placed all references in the Notes, as well as (though always briefly) any arguments we have with the sources to which we are indebted. This has necessitated a sizeable apparatus of notes. This is not to pay obeisance to the rituals of *Wissenschaftlichkeit*, but rather to be faithful to the demands of historical gratitude.

The project of which this book is the realization was first concocted in the summer of 1962, in the course of some leisurely conversations at the foot of and (occasionally) on top of the Alps of western Austria. The first plan for the book was drawn up early in 1963. At that time it was envisaged as an enterprise involving one other sociologist and two philosophers. The other participants were obliged for various biographical reasons to withdraw from active involvement in the project, but we wish to acknowledge with great appreciation the continuing critical comments of Hansfried Kellner (currently at the University of Frankfurt) and Stanley Pullberg (currently at the École Pratique des Hautes Études).

How much we owe to the late Alfred Schutz will become clear in various parts of the following treatise. However, we would like to acknowledge here the influence of Schutz's teaching and writing on our thinking. Our understanding of Weber has profited immensely from the teaching of Carl Mayer (Graduate Faculty, New School for Social Research), as that of Durkheim and his school has from the interpretations of Albert Salomon (also of the Graduate Faculty). Luckmann, recollecting many fruitful conversations during a period of joint teaching at Hobart College and on other occasions, wishes to express his appreciation of the thinking of Friedrich Tenbruck (now at the University of Frankfurt). Berger would like to thank Kurt Wolff (Brandeis University) and Anton Zijderveld (University of Leiden) for their continuing critical interest in the progress of the ideas embodied in this work.

It is customary in projects of this sort to acknowledge various intangible contributions of wives, children and other private associates of more doubtful legal standing. If only to contravene this custom, we have been tempted to dedicate this book to a certain *Jodler* of Brand/Vorarlberg. However, we wish to thank Brigitte Berger (Hunter College) and Benita Luckmann (University of Freiburg), not for any scientifically irrelevant performances of private roles, but for their critical observations as social scientists and for their steadfast refusal to be easily impressed.

Peter L. Berger
GRADUATE FACULTY
NEW SCHOOL FOR SOCIAL RESEARCH
NEW YORK

Thomas Luckmann
UNIVERSITY OF FRANKFURT

Introduction

The Problem of the Sociology of Knowledge

The basic contentions of the argument of this book are implicit in its title and sub-title, namely, that reality is socially constructed and that the sociology of knowledge must analyse the process in which this occurs. The key terms in these contentions are 'reality' and 'knowledge', terms that are not only current in everyday speech, but that have behind them a long history of philosophical inquiry. We need not enter here into a discussion of the semantic intricacies of either the everyday or the philosophical usage of these terms. It will be enough, for our purposes, to define 'reality' as a quality appertaining to phenomena that we recognize as having a being independent of our own volition (we cannot 'wish them away'), and to define 'knowledge' as the certainty that phenomena are real and that they possess specific characteristics. It is in this (admittedly simplistic) sense that the terms have relevance both to the man in the street and to the philosopher. The man in the street inhabits a world that is 'real' to him, albeit in different degrees, and he 'knows', with different degrees of confidence, that this world possesses such and such characteristics. The philosopher, of course, will raise questions about the ultimate status of both this 'reality' and this 'knowledge'. *What is real? How is one to know?* These are among the most ancient questions not only of philosophical inquiry proper, but of human thought as such. Precisely for this reason the intrusion of the sociologist into this time-honoured intellectual territory is likely to raise the eyebrows of the man in the street and even more likely to enrage the philosopher. It is, therefore, important that we clarify at the beginning the sense in which we use these terms in the context of sociology, and that we immediately disclaim any pretension to the effect that sociology has an answer to these ancient philosophical preoccupations.

If we were going to be meticulous in the ensuing argument, we would put quotation marks around the two aforementioned terms every time we used them, but this would be stylistically awkward. To speak of quotation marks, however, may give a clue to the peculiar manner in which these terms appear in a sociological context. One could say that the sociological understanding of 'reality' and 'knowledge' falls somewhere in the middle between that of the man in the street and that of the philosopher. The man in the street does not ordinarily trouble himself about what is 'real' to him and about what he 'knows' unless he is stopped short by some sort of problem. He takes his 'reality' and his 'knowledge' for granted. The sociologist cannot do this, if only because of his systematic awareness of the fact that men in the street take quite different 'realities' for granted as between one society and another. The sociologist is forced by the very logic of his discipline to ask, if nothing else, whether the difference between the two 'realities' may not be understood in relation to various differences between the two societies. The philosopher, on the other hand, is professionally obligated to take nothing for granted, and to obtain maximal clarity as to the ultimate status of what the man in the street believes to be 'reality' and 'knowledge'. Put differently, the philosopher is driven to decide where the quotation marks are in order and where they may safely be omitted, that is, to differentiate between valid and invalid assertions about the world. This the sociologist cannot possibly do. Logically, if not stylistically, he is stuck with the quotation marks.

For example, the man in the street may believe that he possesses 'freedom of the will' and that he is therefore 'responsible' for his actions, at the same time denying this 'freedom' and this 'responsibility' to infants and lunatics. The philosopher, by whatever methods, will inquire into the ontological and epistemological status of these conceptions. *Is man free? What is responsibility? Where are the limits of responsibility? How can one know these things?* And so on. Needless to say, the sociologist is in no position to supply answers to these questions. What he can and must do, however, is to ask how it is that the notion of 'freedom' has come to be taken for granted in one society and not in another, how its 'reality' is maintained in the one society and how, even more interestingly, this 'reality' may once again be lost to an individual or to an entire collectivity.

Sociological interest in questions of 'reality' and 'knowledge' is thus initially justified by the fact of their social relativity. What is 'real' to a Tibetan monk may not be 'real' to an American businessman. The 'knowledge' of the criminal differs from the 'knowledge' of the criminologist. It follows that specific agglomerations of 'reality' and 'knowledge' pertain to specific social contexts, and that these relationships will have to be included in an adequate sociological analysis of these contexts. The need for a 'sociology of knowledge' is thus already given with the observable differences between societies in terms of what is taken for granted as 'knowledge' in them. Beyond this, however, a discipline calling itself by this name will have to concern itself with the general ways by which 'realities' are taken as 'known' in human societies. In other words, a 'sociology of knowledge' will have to deal not only with the empirical variety of 'knowledge' in human societies, but also with the processes by which *any* body of 'knowledge' comes to be socially established *as* 'reality'.

It is our contention, then, that the sociology of knowledge must concern itself with whatever passes for 'knowledge' in a society, regardless of the ultimate validity or invalidity (by whatever criteria) of such 'knowledge'. And in so far as all human 'knowledge' is developed, transmitted and maintained in social situations, the sociology of knowledge must seek to understand the processes by which this is done in such a way that a taken-for-granted 'reality' congeals for the man in the street. In other words, we contend that *the sociology of knowledge is concerned with the analysis of the social construction of reality*.

This understanding of the proper field of the sociology of knowledge differs from what has generally been meant by this discipline since it was first so called some forty years ago. Before we begin our actual argument, therefore, it will be useful to look briefly at the previous development of the discipline and to explicate in what way, and why, we have felt it necessary to deviate from it.

The term 'sociology of knowledge' (*Wissenssoziologie*) was

coined by Max Scheler.[1] The time was the 1920s, the place was Germany, and Scheler was a philosopher. These three facts are quite important for an understanding of the genesis and further development of the new discipline. The sociology of knowledge originated in a particular situation of German intellectual history and in a philosophical context. While the new discipline was subsequently introduced into the sociological context proper, particularly in the English-speaking world, it continued to be marked by the problems of the particular intellectual situation from which it arose. As a result the sociology of knowledge remained a peripheral concern among sociologists at large, who did not share the particular problems that troubled German thinkers in the 1920s. This was especially true of American sociologists, who have in the main looked upon the discipline as a marginal speciality with a persistent European flavour. More importantly, however, the continuing linkage of the sociology of knowledge with its original constellation of problems has been a theoretical weakness even where there has been an interest in the discipline. To wit, the sociology of knowledge has been looked upon, by its protagonists and by the more or less indifferent sociological public at large, as a sort of sociological gloss on the history of ideas. This has resulted in considerable myopia regarding the potential theoretical significance of the sociology of knowledge.

There have been different definitions of the nature and scope of the sociology of knowledge. Indeed, it might almost be said that the history of the sub-discipline thus far has been the history of its various definitions. Nevertheless, there has been general agreement to the effect that the sociology of knowledge is concerned with the relationship between human thought and the social context within which it arises. It may thus be said that the sociology of knowledge constitutes the sociological focus of a much more general problem, that of the existential determination (*Seinsgebundenheit*) of thought as such. Although here the social factor is concentrated upon, the theoretical difficulties are similar to those that have arisen when other factors (such as the historical, the psychological or the biological) have been proposed as determinative of human thought. In all these cases the general problem has been the extent to which thought reflects or is independent of the proposed determinative factors.

It is likely that the prominence of the general problem in recent German philosophy has its roots in the vast accumulation of historical scholarship that was one of the greatest intellectual fruits of the nineteenth century in Germany. In a way unparalleled in any other period of intellectual history the past, with all its amazing variety of forms of thought, was 'made present' to the contemporary mind through the efforts of scientific historical scholarship. It is hard to dispute the claim of German scholarship to the primary position in this enterprise. It should, consequently, not surprise us that the theoretical problem thrown up by the latter should be most sharply sensed in Germany. This problem can be described as the vertigo of relativity. The epistemological dimension of the problem is obvious. On the empirical level it led to the concern to investigate as painstakingly as possible the concrete relationships between thought and its historical situations. If this interpretation is correct, the sociology of knowledge takes up a problem originally posited by historical scholarship – in a narrower focus, to be sure, but with an interest in essentially the same questions.[2]

Neither the general problem nor its narrower focus is new. An awareness of the social foundations of values and world views can be found in antiquity. At least as far back as the Enlightenment this awareness crystallized into a major theme of modern Western thought. It would thus be possible to make a good case for a number of 'genealogies' for the central problem of the sociology of knowledge.[3] It may even be said that the problem is contained *in nuce* in Pascal's famous statement that what is truth on one side of the Pyrenees is error on the other.[4] Yet the immediate intellectual antecedents of the sociology of knowledge are three developments in nineteenth-century German thought – the Marxian, the Nietzschean, and the historicist.

It is from Marx that the sociology of knowledge derived its root proposition – that man's consciousness is determined by his social being.[5] To be sure, there has been much debate as to just what kind of determination Marx had in mind. It is safe to say that much of the great 'struggle with Marx' that characterized not only the beginnings of the sociology of knowledge but the 'classical age' of sociology in general (particularly as manifested in the works of Weber, Durkheim and Pareto) was really a struggle with a faulty interpretation of Marx by latter-day Marxists. This proposition gains plausibility when we reflect that it was only in 1932 that the very important *Economic and Philosophical Manuscripts of 1844* were rediscovered and only after the Second World War that the full implications of this rediscovery could be worked out in Marx research. Be this as it may, the sociology of knowledge inherited from Marx not only the sharpest formulation of its central problem but also some of its key concepts, among which should be mentioned particularly the concepts of 'ideology' (ideas serving as weapons for social interests) and 'false consciousness' (thought that is alienated from the real social being of the thinker).

The sociology of knowledge has been particularly fascinated by Marx's twin concepts of 'substructure/superstructure' (*Unterbau/Ueberbau*). It is here particularly that controversy has raged about the correct interpretation of Marx's own thought. Later Marxism has tended to identify the 'substructure' with economic structure *tout court*, of which the 'superstructure' was then supposed to be a direct 'reflection' (thus, Lenin, for instance). It is quite clear now that this misrepresents Marx's thought, as the essentially mechanistic rather than dialectical character of this kind of economic determinism should make one suspect. What concerned Marx was that human thought is founded in human activity ('labour', in the widest sense of the word) and in the social relations brought about by this activity. 'Substructure' and 'superstructure' are best understood if one views them as, respectively, human activity and the world produced by that activity.[6] In any case, the fundamental 'sub/superstructure' scheme has been taken over in various forms by the sociology of knowledge, beginning with Scheler, always with an understanding that there is some sort of relationship between thought and an 'underlying' reality other than thought. The fascination of the scheme prevailed despite the fact that much of the sociology of knowledge was explicitly formulated in opposition to Marxism and that different positions have been taken within it regarding the nature of the relationship between the two components of the scheme.

Nietzschean ideas were less explicitly continued in the sociology of knowledge, but they belong very much to its general intellectual background and to the 'mood' within which it arose. Nietzsche's anti-idealism, despite the differences in content not unlike Marx's in form, added additional perspectives on human thought as an instrument in the struggle for survival and power.[7] Nietzsche developed his own theory of 'false consciousness' in his analyses of the social significance of deception and self-deception, and of illusion as a necessary condition of life. Nietzsche's concept of 'resentment' as a generative factor for certain types of human thought was taken over directly by Scheler. Most generally, though, one can say that the sociology of knowledge represents a specific application of what Nietzsche aptly called the 'art of mistrust'.[8]

Historicism, especially as expressed in the work of Wilhelm Dilthey, immediately preceded the sociology of knowledge.[9] The dominant theme here was an overwhelming sense of the relativity of all perspectives on human events, that is, of the inevitable historicity of human thought. The historicist insistence that no historical situation could be understood except in its own terms could readily be translated into an emphasis on the social situation of thought. Certain historicist concepts, such as 'situational determination' (*Standortsgebundenheit*) and 'seat in life' (*Sitz im Leben*) could be directly translated as referring to the 'social location' of thought. More generally, the historicist heritage of the sociology of knowledge predisposed the latter towards a strong interest in history and the employment of an essentially historical method – a fact, incidentally, that also made for its marginality in the milieu of American sociology.

Scheler's interest in the sociology of knowledge, and in sociological questions generally, was essentially a passing episode during his philosophical career.[10] His final aim was the establishment of a philosophical anthropology that would transcend the relativity of specific historically and socially located viewpoints. The sociology of knowledge was to serve as an instrument towards this aim, its main purpose being the clearing away of the difficulties raised by relativism so that the real philosophical task could proceed. Scheler's sociology of knowledge is, in a very real sense, *ancilla philosophiae*, and of a very specific philosophy to boot.

In line with this orientation, Scheler's sociology of knowledge is essentially a negative method. Scheler argued that the relationship between 'ideal factors' (*Idealfaktoren*) and 'real factors' (*Realfaktoren*), terms that are clearly reminiscent of the Marxian 'sub/superstructure' scheme, was merely a regulative one. That is, the 'real factors' regulate the conditions under which certain 'ideal factors' can appear in history, but cannot affect the content of the latter. In other words, society determines the presence (*Dasein*) but not the nature (*Sosein*) of ideas. The sociology of knowledge, then, is the procedure by which the socio-historical selection of ideational contents is to be studied, it being understood that the contents themselves are independent of socio-historical causation and thus inaccessible to sociological analysis. If one may describe Scheler's method graphically, it is to throw a sizeable sop to the dragon of relativity, but only so as to enter the castle of ontological certitude better.

Within this intentionally (and inevitably) modest framework Scheler analysed in considerable detail the manner in which human knowledge is ordered by society. He emphasized that human knowledge is given in society as an *a priori* to individual experience, providing the latter with its order of meaning. This order, although it is relative to a particular socio-historical situation, appears to the individual as the natural way of looking at the world. Scheler called this the 'relative-natural world view' (*relativnatürliche Weltanschauung*) of a society, a concept that may still be regarded as central for the sociology of knowledge.

Following Scheler's 'invention' of the sociology of knowledge, there was extensive debate in Germany concerning the validity, scope and applicability of the new discipline.[11] Out of this debate emerged one formulation that marked the transposition of the sociology of knowledge into a more narrowly sociological context. The same formulation was the one in which the sociology of knowledge arrived in the English-speaking world. This is the formulation by Karl Mannheim.[12] It is safe to say when sociologists today think of the sociology of knowledge, *pro* or *con*, they usually do so in terms of Mannheim's formulation of it. In American sociology this is readily intelligible if one reflects on the accessibility in English of virtually the whole of Mannheim's work (some of which, indeed, was written in English, during the period Mannheim was teaching in England after the advent of Nazism in Germany, or was brought out in revised English versions), while Scheler's work in the sociology of knowledge has remained untranslated to date. Apart from this 'diffusion' factor, Mannheim's work is less burdened with philosophical 'baggage' than Scheler's. This is especially true of Mannheim's later writings and can be seen if one compares the English version of his main work, *Ideology and Utopia*, with its German original. Mannheim thus became the more 'congenial' figure for sociologists, even those critical of or not very interested in his approach.

Mannheim's understanding of the sociology of knowledge was much more far-reaching than Scheler's, possibly because the confrontation with Marxism was more prominent in his work. Society was here seen as determining not only the appearance but also the content of human ideation, with the exception of mathematics and at least parts of the natural sciences. The sociology of knowledge thus became a positive method for the study of almost any facet of human thought.

Significantly, Mannheim's key concern was with the phenomenon of ideology. He distinguished between the particular, the total and the general concepts of ideology – ideology as constituting only a segment of an opponent's thought; ideology as constituting the whole of an opponent's thought (similar to Marx's 'false consciousness'); and (here, as Mannheim thought, going beyond Marx) ideology as characteristic not only of an opponent's but of one's own thought as well. With the general concept of ideology the level of the sociology of knowledge is reached – the understanding that no human thought (with only the aforementioned exceptions) is immune to the ideologizing influences of its social context. By this expansion of the theory of ideology Mannheim sought to abstract its central problem from the context of political usage, and to treat it as a general problem of epistemology and historical sociology.

Although Mannheim did not share Scheler's ontological ambitions, he too was uncomfortable with the pan-ideologism into which his thinking seemed to lead him. He coined the term 'relationism' (in contradistinction to 'relativism') to denote the epistemological perspective of his sociology of knowledge – not a capitulation of thought before the socio-historical relativities, but a sober recognition that knowledge must always be knowledge from a certain position. The influence of Dilthey is probably of great importance at this point in Mannheim's thought – the problem of Marxism is solved by the tools of historicism. Be this as it may, Mannheim believed that ideologizing influences, while they could not be eradicated completely, could be mitigated by the systematic analysis of as many as possible of the varying socially grounded positions. In other words, the object of thought becomes progressively clearer with this accumulation of different perspectives on it. This is to be the task of the sociology of knowledge, which thus is to become an important aid in the quest of any correct understanding of human events.

Mannheim believed that different social groups vary greatly in their capacity thus to transcend their own narrow position. He placed his major hope in the 'socially unattached intelligentsia' (*freischwebende Intelligenz*, a term derived from Alfred Weber), a sort of interstitial stratum that he believed to be relatively free of class interests. Mannheim also stressed the power of 'utopian' thought, which (like ideology) produces a distorted image of social reality, but which (unlike ideology) has the dynamism to transform that reality into its image of it.

Needless to say, the above remarks can in no way do justice to either Scheler's or Mannheim's conception of the sociology of knowledge. This is not our intention here. We have merely indicated some key features of the two conceptions, which have been aptly called, respectively, the 'moderate' and 'radical' conceptions of the sociology of knowledge.[13] What is remarkable is that the subsequent development of the sociology of knowledge has, to a large extent, consisted of critiques and modifications of these two conceptions. As we have already pointed out, Mannheim's formulation of the sociology of knowledge has continued to set the terms of reference for the discipline in a definitive manner, particularly in English-speaking sociology.

The most important American sociologist to have paid serious attention to the sociology of knowledge has been Robert Merton.[14] His discussion of the discipline, which covers two chapters of his major work, has served as a useful introduction to the field for such American sociologists as have been interested in it. Merton constructed a paradigm for the sociology of knowledge, restating its major themes in a compressed and coherent form. This construction is interesting because it seeks to integrate the approach of the sociology of knowledge with that of structural–functional theory. Merton's own concepts of 'manifest' and 'latent' functions are applied to the sphere of ideation, the distinction being made between the intended, conscious functions of ideas, and the unintended, unconscious ones. While Merton concentrated on the work of Mannheim, who was for him the sociologist of knowledge *par excellence*, he stressed the significance of the Durkheim school and of the work of Pitirim Sorokin. It is interesting that Merton apparently failed to see the relevance to the sociology of knowledge of certain important developments in American social psychology, such as reference-group theory, which he discusses in a different part of the same work.

Talcott Parsons has also commented on the sociology of knowledge.[15] This comment, however, is limited mainly to a critique of Mannheim and does not seek an integration of the discipline within Parsons's own theoretical system. In the latter, to be sure, the 'problem of the role of ideas' is analysed at length, but in a frame of reference quite different from that of either Scheler's or Mannheim's sociology of knowledge.[16] We would, therefore, venture to say that neither Merton nor Parsons has gone in any decisive way beyond the sociology of knowledge as formulated by Mannheim. The same can be said of their critics. To mention only the most vocal one, C. Wright Mills dealt with the sociology of knowledge in his earlier writing, but in an expositional manner and without contributing to its theoretical development.[17]

An interesting effort to integrate the sociology of knowledge with a neo-positivist approach to sociology in general is that of Theodor Geiger, who had a great influence on Scandinavian sociology after his emigration from Germany.[18] Geiger returned to a narrower concept of ideology as socially distorted thought and maintained the possibility of overcoming ideology by careful adherence to scientific canons of procedure. The neo-positivist approach to ideological analysis has more recently been continued in German-speaking sociology in the work of Ernst Topitsch, who has emphasized the ideological roots of various philosophical positions.[19] In so far as the sociological analysis of ideologies constitutes an important part of the sociology of knowledge as defined by Mannheim, there has been a good deal of interest in it in both European and American sociology since the Second World War.[20]

Probably the most far-reaching attempt to go beyond Mannheim in the construction of a comprehensive sociology of knowledge is that of Werner Stark, another émigré continental scholar who has taught in England and the United States.[21] Stark goes furthest in leaving behind Mannheim's focus on the problem of ideology. The task of the sociology of knowledge is not to be the debunking or uncovering of socially produced distortions, but the systematic study of the social conditions of knowledge as such. Put simply, the central problem is the sociology of truth, not the sociology of error. Despite his distinctive approach, Stark is probably closer to Scheler than to Mannheim in his understanding of the relationship between ideas and their social context.

Again, it is obvious that we have not tried to give an adequate historical overview of the history of the sociology of knowledge. Furthermore, we have so far ignored developments that might theoretically be relevant to the sociology of knowledge but that have not been so considered by their own protagonists. In other words, we have limited ourselves to developments that, so to speak, sailed under the banner 'sociology of knowledge' (considering the theory of ideology to be a part of the latter). This has made one fact very clear. Apart from the epistemological concern of some sociologists of knowledge, the empirical focus of attention has been almost exclusively on the sphere of ideas, that is, of theoretical thought. This is also true of Stark, who sub-titled his major work on the sociology of knowledge 'An Essay in Aid of a Deeper Understanding of the History of Ideas'. In other words, the interest of the sociology of knowledge has been on epistemological questions on the theoretical level, on questions of intellectual history on the empirical level.

We would emphasize that we have no reservations whatsoever about the validity and importance of these two sets of questions. However, we regard it as unfortunate that this particular constellation has dominated the sociology of knowledge so far. We would argue that, as a result, the full theoretical significance of the sociology of knowledge has been obscured.

To include epistemological questions concerning the validity of sociological knowledge in the sociology of knowledge is somewhat like trying to push a bus in which one is riding. To be sure, the sociology of knowledge, like all empirical disciplines that accumulate evidence concerning the relativity and determination of human thought, leads towards epistemological questions concerning sociology itself as well as any other scientific body of knowledge. As we have remarked before, in this the sociology of knowledge plays a part similar to history, psychology and biology, to mention only the three most important empirical disciplines that have caused trouble for epistemology. The logical structure of this trouble is basically the same in all cases: How can I be sure, say, of my sociological analysis of American middle-class *mores* in view of the fact that the categories I use for this analysis are conditioned by historically relative forms of thought, that I myself and everything I think is determined by my genes and by my ingrown hostility to my fellowmen, and that, to cap it all, I am myself a member of the American middle class?

Far be it from us to brush aside such questions. All we would contend here is that these questions are not themselves part of the empirical discipline of sociology. They properly belong to the methodology of the social sciences, an enterprise that belongs to philosophy and is by definition other than sociology, which is indeed an object of its inquiries. The sociology of knowledge, along with the other epistemological troublemakers among the empirical sciences, will 'feed' problems to this methodological inquiry. It cannot solve these problems within its own proper frame of reference.

We therefore exclude from the sociology of knowledge the

epistemological and methodological problems that bothered both of its major originators. By virtue of this exclusion we are setting ourselves apart from both Scheler's and Mannheim's conception of the discipline, and from the later sociologists of knowledge (notably those with a neo-positivist orientation) who shared the conception in this respect. Throughout the present work we have firmly bracketed any epistemological or methodological questions about the validity of sociological analysis, in the sociology of knowledge itself or in any other area. We consider the sociology of knowledge to be part of the empirical discipline of sociology. Our purpose here is, of course, a theoretical one. But our theorizing refers to the empirical discipline in its concrete problems, not to the philosophical investigation of the foundations of the empirical discipline. In sum, our enterprise is one of sociological theory, *not* of the methodology of sociology. Only in one section of our treatise (the one immediately following this introduction) do we go beyond sociological theory proper, but this is done for reasons that have little to do with epistemology, as will be explained at the time.

We must also, however, redefine the task of the sociology of knowledge on the empirical level, that is, as theory geared to the empirical discipline of sociology. As we have seen, on this level the sociology of knowledge has been concerned with intellectual history, in the sense of the history of ideas. Again, we would stress that this is, indeed, a very important focus of sociological inquiry. Furthermore, in contrast with our exclusion of the epistemological/methodological problem, we concede that this focus belongs with the sociology of knowledge. We would argue, however, that the problem of 'ideas', including the special problem of ideology, constitutes only part of the larger problem of the sociology of knowledge, and not a central part at that.

The sociology of knowledge must concern itself with everything that passes for 'knowledge' in society. As soon as one states this, one realizes that the focus on intellectual history is ill-chosen, or rather, is ill-chosen if it becomes the central focus of the sociology of knowledge. Theoretical thought, 'ideas', *Weltanschauungen* are not *that* important in society. Although every society contains these phenomena, they are only part of the sum of what passes for 'knowledge'. Only a very limited group of people in any society engages in theorizing, in the business of 'ideas', and the construction of *Weltanschauungen*. But everyone in society participates in its 'knowledge' in one way or another. Put differently, only a few are concerned with the theoretical interpretation of the world, but everybody lives in a world of some sort. Not only is the focus on theoretical thought unduly restrictive for the sociology of knowledge, it is also unsatisfactory because even this part of socially available 'knowledge' cannot be fully understood if it is not placed in the framework of a more general analysis of 'knowledge'.

To exaggerate the importance of theoretical thought in society and history is a natural failing of theorizers. It is then all the more necessary to correct this intellectualistic misapprehension. The theoretical formulations of reality, whether they be scientific or philosophical or even mythological, do not exhaust what is 'real' for the members of a society. Since this is so, the sociology of knowledge must first of all concern itself with what people 'know' as 'reality' in their everyday, non- or pre-theoretical lives. In other words, common-sense 'knowledge' rather than 'ideas' must be the central focus for the sociology of knowledge. It is precisely this 'knowledge' that constitutes the fabric of meanings without which no society could exist.

The sociology of knowledge, therefore, must concern itself with the social construction of reality. The analysis of the theoretical articulation of this reality will certainly continue to be a part of this concern, but not the most important part. It will be clear that, despite the exclusion of the epistemological/ methodological problem, what we are suggesting here is a far-reaching redefinition of the scope of the sociology of knowledge, much wider than what has hitherto been understood as this discipline.

The question arises as to what theoretical ingredients ought to be added to the sociology of knowledge to permit its redefinition in the above sense. We owe the fundamental insight into the necessity for this redefinition to Alfred Schutz. Throughout his work, both as philosopher and as sociologist, Schutz concentrated on the structure of the common-sense world of everyday life. Although he himself did not elaborate a sociology of knowledge, he clearly saw what this discipline would have to focus on:

All typifications of common-sense thinking are themselves integral elements of the concrete historical socio-cultural *Lebenswelt* within which they prevail as taken for granted and as socially approved. Their structure determines among other things the social distribution of knowledge and its relativity and relevance to the concrete social environment of a concrete group in a concrete historical situation. *Here are the legitimate problems of relativism, historicism, and of the so-called sociology of knowledge.*[22]

And again:

Knowledge is socially distributed and the mechanism of this distribution can be made the subject matter of a sociological discipline. True, we have a so-called sociology of knowledge. Yet, with very few exceptions, the discipline thus misnamed has approached the problem of the social distribution of knowledge merely from the angle of the ideological foundation of truth in its dependence upon social and, especially, economic conditions, or from that of the social implications of education, or that of the social role of the man of knowledge. Not sociologists but economists and philosophers have studied some of the many other theoretical aspects of the problem.[23]

While we would not give the central place to the social distribution of knowledge that Schutz implies here, we agree with his criticism of 'the discipline thus misnamed' and have derived from him our basic notion of the manner in which the task of the sociology of knowledge must be redefined. In the following considerations we are heavily dependent on Schutz in the prolegomena concerning the foundations of knowledge in everyday life and greatly indebted to his work in various important places of our main argument thereafter.

Our anthropological presuppositions are strongly influenced by Marx, especially his early writings, and by the anthropological implications drawn from human biology by Helmuth Plessner, Arnold Gehlen and others. Our view of the nature of social reality is greatly indebted to Durkheim and his school in French sociology, though we have modified the Durkheimian theory of society by the introduction of a dialectical perspective derived from Marx and an emphasis on the constitution of social reality through subjective meanings derived from Weber.[24] Our social-psychological presuppositions, especially important for the analysis of the internalization of social reality, are greatly influenced by George Herbert Mead and some developments of his work by the so-called symbolic-interactionist school of American sociology.[25] We shall indicate in the footnotes how these various ingredients are used in our theoretical formation. We fully realize, of course, that in this use we are not and cannot be faithful to the original intentions of these several streams of social theory themselves. But, as we have already stated, our purpose here is not exegetical, nor even synthesis for the sake of synthesis. We are fully aware that, in various places, we do violence to certain thinkers by integrating their thought into a theoretical formation that some of them might have found quite alien. We would say in justification that historical gratitude is not in itself a scientific virtue. We may cite here some remarks by Talcott Parsons (about whose theory we have serious misgivings, but whose integrative intention we fully share):

The primary aim of the study is not to determine and state in summary form what these writers said or believed about the subjects they wrote about. Nor is it to inquire directly with reference to each proposition of their 'theories' whether what they have said is tenable in the light of present sociological and related knowledge. . . . It is a study in social *theory*, not *theories*. Its interest is not in the separate and discrete propositions to be found in the works of these men, but in a *single* body of systematic theoretical reasoning.[26]

Our purpose, indeed, is to engage in 'systematic theoretical reasoning'.

It will already be evident that our redefinition of its nature and scope would move the sociology of knowledge from the periphery to the very centre of sociological theory. We may assure the reader that we have no vested interest in the label 'sociology of knowledge'. It is rather our understanding of sociological theory that led us to the sociology of knowledge and guided the manner in which we were to redefine its problems and tasks. We can best describe the path along which we set out by reference to two of the most famous and most influential 'marching orders' for sociology.

One was given by Durkheim in *The Rules of Sociological Method*, the other by Weber in *Wirtschaft und Gesellschaft*. Durkheim tells us: 'The first and most fundamental rule is: *Consider social facts as things.*'[27] And Weber observes: 'Both for sociology in the present sense, and for history, the object of cognition is the subjective meaning-complex of action.'[28] These two statements are not contradictory. Society does indeed possess objective facticity. And society is indeed built up by activity that expresses subjective meaning. And, incidentally, Durkheim knew the latter, just as Weber knew the former. It is precisely the dual character of society in terms of objective facticity *and* subjective meaning that makes its 'reality *sui generis*', to use another key term of Durkheim's. The central question for sociological theory can then be put as follows: How is it possible that subjective meanings *become* objective facticities? Or, in terms appropriate to the aforementioned theoretical positions: How is it possible that human activity (*Handeln*) should produce a world of things (*choses*)? In other words, an adequate understanding of the 'reality *sui generis*' of society requires an inquiry into the manner in which this reality is constructed. This inquiry, we maintain, is the task of the sociology of knowledge.

Part One

The Foundations of Knowledge in Everyday Life

1. The Reality of Everyday Life

Since our purpose in this treatise is a sociological analysis of the reality of everyday life, more precisely, of knowledge that guides conduct in everyday life, and we are only tangentially interested in how this reality may appear in various theoretical perspectives to intellectuals, we must begin by a clarification of that reality as it is available to the common sense of the ordinary members of society. How that common sense reality may be influenced by the theoretical constructions of intellectuals and other merchants of ideas is a further question. Ours is thus an enterprise that, although theoretical in character, is geared to the understanding of a reality that forms the subject matter of the empirical science of sociology, that is, the world of everyday life.

It should be evident, then, that our purpose is *not* to engage in philosophy. All the same, if the reality of everyday life is to be understood, account must be taken of its intrinsic character before we can proceed with sociological analysis proper. Everyday life presents itself as a reality interpreted by men and subjectively meaningful to them as a coherent world. As sociologists we take this reality as the object of our analyses. Within the frame of reference of sociology as an empirical science it is possible to take this reality as given, to take as data particular phenomena arising within it, without further inquiring about the foundations of this reality, which is a philosophical task. However, given the particular purpose of the present treatise, we cannot completely by-pass the philosophical problem. The world of everyday life is not only taken for granted as reality by the ordinary members of society in the subjectively meaningful conduct of their lives. It is a world that originates in their thoughts and actions, and is maintained as real by these. Before turning to our main task we must, therefore, attempt to clarify the foundations of knowledge in everyday life, to wit, the objectivations of subjective processes (and meanings) by which the *inter*subjective common-sense world is constructed.

For the purpose at hand, this is a preliminary task, and we can do no more than sketch the main features of what we believe to be an adequate solution to the philosophical problem—adequate, let us hasten to add, only in the sense that it can serve as a starting point for sociological analysis. The considerations immediately following are, therefore, of the nature of philosophical prolegomena and, in themselves, pre-sociological. The method we consider best suited to clarify the foundations of knowledge in everyday life is that of phenomenological analysis, a purely descriptive method and, as such, 'empirical' but not 'scientific' – as we understand the nature of the empirical sciences.[1]

The phenomenological analysis of everyday life, or rather of the subjective experience of everyday life, refrains from any causal or genetic hypotheses, as well as from assertions about the ontological status of the phenomena analysed. It is important to remember this. Common sense contains innumerable pre- and quasi-scientific interpretations about everyday reality, which it takes for granted. If we are to describe the reality of common sense we must refer to these interpretations, just as we must take account of its taken-for-granted character – but we do so within phenomenological brackets.

Consciousness is always intentional; it always intends or is directed towards objects. We can never apprehend some putative substratum of consciousness as such, only consciousness of something or other. This is so regardless of whether the object of consciousness is experienced as belonging to an external physical world or apprehended as an element of an inward subjective reality. Whether I (the first person singular, here as in the following illustrations, standing for ordinary self-consciousness in everyday life) am viewing the panorama of New York City or whether I become conscious of an inner anxiety, the processes of consciousness involved are intentional in both instances. The point need not be belaboured that the consciousness of the Empire State Building differs from the awareness of anxiety. A detailed phenomenological analysis would uncover the various layers of experience, and the different structures of meaning involved in, say, being bitten by a dog, remembering having been bitten by a dog, having a phobia about all dogs, and so forth. What interests us here is the common intentional character of all consciousness.

Different objects present themselves to consciousness as constituents of different spheres of reality. I recognize the fellowmen I must deal with in the course of everyday life as pertaining to a reality quite different from the disembodied figures that appear in my dreams. The two sets of objects introduce quite different tensions into my consciousness and I am attentive to them in quite different ways. My consciousness, then, is capable of moving through different spheres of reality. Put differently, I am conscious of the world as consisting of multiple realities. As I move from one reality to another, I experience the transition as a kind of shock. This shock is to be understood as caused by the shift in attentiveness that the transition entails. Waking up from a dream illustrates this shift most simply.

Among the multiple realities there is one that presents itself as the reality *par excellence*. This is the reality of everyday life. Its privileged position entitles it to the designation of paramount reality. The tension of consciousness is highest in everyday life, that is, the latter imposes itself upon consciousness in the most massive, urgent and intense manner. It is impossible to ignore, difficult even to weaken in its imperative presence. Consequently, it forces me to be attentive to it in the fullest way. I experience everyday life in the state of being wide-awake. This wide-awake state of existing in and apprehending the reality of everyday life is taken by me to be normal and self-evident, that is, it constitutes my natural attitude.

I apprehend the reality of everyday life as an ordered reality. Its phenomena are prearranged in patterns that seem to be independent of my apprehension of them and that impose themselves upon the latter. The reality of everyday life appears already objectified, that is, constituted by an order of objects that have been designated *as* objects before my appearance on the scene. The language used in everyday life continuously provides me with the necessary objectifications and posits the order within which these make sense and within which everyday life has meaning for me. I live in a place that is geographically designated; I employ tools, from can-openers to sports cars, which are designated in the technical vocabulary of my society; I live within a web of human relationships, from my chess club to the United States of America, which are also ordered by means of vocabulary. In this manner language marks the coordinates of my life in society and fills that life with meaningful objects.

The reality of everyday life is organized around the 'here' of my body and the 'now' of my present. This 'here and now' is the focus of my attention to the reality of everyday life. What is 'here and now' presented to me in everyday life is the *realissimum* of my consciousness. The reality of everyday life is not, however, exhausted by these immediate presences, but embraces phenomena that are not present 'here and now'. This means that I experience everyday life in terms of differing degrees of closeness and remoteness, both spatially and temporally. Closest to me is the zone of everyday life that is directly accessible to my bodily manipulation. This zone contains the world within my reach, the world in which I act so as to modify its reality, or the world in which I work. In this world of working my consciousness is dominated by the pragmatic motive, that is, my attention to this world is mainly determined by what I am doing, have done or plan to do in it. In this way it is *my* world *par excellence*. I know, of course, that the reality of everyday life contains zones that are not accessible to me in this manner. But either I have no pragmatic interest in these zones or my interest in them is indirect in so far as they may be, potentially, manipulative zones for me. Typically, my interest in the far zones is less intense and certainly less urgent. I am intensely interested in the cluster of objects involved in my daily occupation – say, the world of the garage, if I am a mechanic. I am interested, though less directly, in what goes on in the testing laboratories of the automobile industry in Detroit – I am unlikely ever to be in one of these laboratories, but the work done there will eventually affect my everyday life. I may also be interested in what goes on at Cape Kennedy or in outer space, but this interest is a matter of private, 'leisure-time' choice rather than an urgent necessity of my everyday life.

The reality of everyday life further presents itself to me as an intersubjective world, a world that I share with others. This intersubjectivity sharply differentiates everyday life from other realities of which I am conscious. I am alone in the world of my dreams, but I know that the world of everyday life is as real to others as it is to myself. Indeed, I cannot exist in everyday life without continually interacting and communicating with others. I know that my natural attitude to this world corresponds to the natural attitude of others, that they also comprehend the objectifications by which this world is ordered, that they also organize this world around the 'here and now' of *their* being in it and have projects for working in it. I also know, of course, that the others have a perspective on this common world that is not identical with mine. My 'here' is their 'there'. My 'now' does not fully overlap with theirs. My projects differ from and may even conflict with theirs. All the same, I know that I live with them in a common world. Most importantly, I know that there is an ongoing correspondence between *my* meanings and *their* meanings in this world, that we share a common sense about its reality. The natural attitude is the attitude of common-sense consciousness precisely because it refers to a world that is common to many men. Common-sense knowledge is the knowledge I share with others in the normal, self-evident routines of everyday life.

The reality of everyday life is taken for granted *as* reality. It does not require additional verification over and beyond its simple presence. It is simply *there*, as self-evident and compelling facticity. I *know* that it is real. While I am capable of engaging in doubt about its reality, I am obliged to suspend such doubt as I routinely exist in everyday life. This suspension of doubt is so firm that to abandon it, as I might want to do, say, in theoretical or religious contemplation, I have to make an extreme transition. The world of everyday life proclaims itself and, when I want to challenge the proclamation, I must engage in a deliberate, by no means easy effort. The transition from the natural attitude to the theoretical attitude of the philosopher or scientist illustrates this point. But not all aspects of this reality are equally unproblematic. Everyday life is divided into sectors that are apprehended routinely, and others that present me with problems of one kind or another.

37

Suppose that I am an automobile mechanic who is highly knowledgeable about all American-made cars. Everything that pertains to the latter is a routine, unproblematic facet of my everyday life. But one day someone appears in the garage and asks me to repair his Volkswagen. I am now compelled to enter the problematic world of foreign-made cars. I may do so reluctantly or with professional curiosity, but in either case I am now faced with problems that I have not yet routinized. At the same time, of course, I do not leave the reality of everyday life. Indeed, the latter becomes enriched as I begin to incorporate into it the knowledge and skills required for the repair of foreign-made cars. The reality of everyday life encompasses both kinds of sectors, as long as what appears as a problem does not pertain to a different reality altogether (say, the reality of theoretical physics, or of nightmares). As long as the routines of everyday life continue without interruption they are apprehended as unproblematic.

But even the unproblematic sector of everyday reality is so only until further notice, that is, until its continuity is interrupted by the appearance of a problem. When this happens, the reality of everyday life seeks to integrate the problematic sector into what is already unproblematic. Common-sense knowledge contains a variety of instructions as to how this is to be done. For instance, the others with whom I work are unproblematic to me as long as they perform their familiar, taken-for-granted routines – say, typing away at desks next to mine in my office. They become problematic if they interrupt these routines – say, huddling together in a corner and talking in whispers. As I inquire about the meaning of this unusual activity, there is a variety of possibilities that my common-sense knowledge is capable of reintegrating into the unproblematic routines of everyday life: they may be consulting on how to fix a broken typewriter, or one of them may have some urgent instructions from the boss, and so on. On the other hand, I may find that they are discussing a union directive to go on strike, something as yet outside my experience but still well within the range of problems with which my common-sense knowledge can deal. It will deal with it, though, as a problem, rather than simply reintegrating it into the unproblematic sector of everyday life. If, however, I come to the conclusion that my colleagues have gone collectively mad, the problem that presents itself is of yet another kind. I am now faced with a problem that transcends the boundaries of the reality of everyday life and points to an altogether different reality. Indeed, my conclusion that my colleagues have gone mad implies *ipso facto* that they have gone off into a world that is no longer the common world of everyday life.

Compared to the reality of everyday life, other realities appear as finite provinces of meaning, enclaves within the paramount reality marked by circumscribed meanings and modes of experience. The paramount reality envelops them on all sides, as it were, and consciousness always returns to the paramount reality as from an excursion. This is evident from the illustrations already given, as in the reality of dreams or that of theoretical thought. Similar 'commutations' take place between the world of everyday life and the world of play, both the playing of children and, even more sharply, of adults. The theatre provides an excellent illustration of such playing on the part of adults. The transition between realities is marked by the rising and falling of the curtain. As the curtain rises, the spectator is 'transported to another world', with its own meanings and an order that may or may not have much to do with the order of everyday life. As the curtain falls, the spectator 'returns to reality', that is, to the paramount reality of everyday life by comparison with which the reality presented on the stage now appears tenuous and ephemeral, however vivid the presentation may have been a few moments previously. Aesthetic and religious experience is rich in producing transitions of this kind, inasmuch as art and religion are endemic producers of finite provinces of meaning.

All finite provinces of meaning are characterized by a turning away of attention from the reality of everyday life. While there are, of course, shifts in attention *within* everyday life, the shift to a finite province of meaning is of a much more radical kind. A radical change takes place in the tension of consciousness. In the context of religious experience this has been aptly called 'leaping'. It is important to stress, however, that the reality of everyday life retains its paramount status even as such 'leaps' take place. If nothing else, language makes sure of this. The common language available to me for the objectification of my experiences is grounded in everyday life and keeps pointing back to it even as I employ it to interpret experiences in finite provinces of meaning. Typically, therefore, I 'distort' the reality of the latter as soon as I begin to use the common language in interpreting them, that is, I 'translate' the non-everyday experiences back into the paramount reality of everyday life. This may be readily seen in terms of dreams, but is also typical of those trying to report about theoretical, aesthetic or religious worlds of meaning. The theoretical physicist tells us that his concept of space cannot be conveyed linguistically, just as the artist does with regard to the meaning of his creations and the mystic with regard to his encounters with the divine. Yet all these – dreamer, physicist, artist and mystic – *also* live in the reality of everyday life. Indeed, one of their important problems is to interpret the coexistence of this reality with the reality enclaves into which they have ventured.

The world of everyday life is structured both spatially and temporally. The spatial structure is quite peripheral to our present considerations. Suffice it to point out that it, too, has a social dimension by virtue of the fact that my manipulatory zone intersects with that of others. More important for our present purpose is the temporal structure of everyday life.

Temporality is an intrinsic property of consciousness. The stream of consciousness is always ordered temporally. It is possible to differentiate between different levels of this temporality as it is intrasubjectively available. Every individual is conscious of an inner flow of time, which in turn is founded on the physiological rhythms of the organism though it is not identical with these. It would greatly exceed the scope of these prolegomena to enter into a detailed analysis of these levels of intrasubjective temporality. As we have indicated, however, intersubjectivity in everyday life also has a temporal dimension. The world of everyday life has its own standard time, which is intersubjectively available. This standard time may be understood as the intersection between cosmic time and its socially established calendar, based on the temporal sequences of nature, and inner time, in its aforementioned differentiations. There can never be full simultaneity between these various levels of temporality, as the experience of waiting indicates most clearly. Both my organism and my society impose upon me, and upon my inner time, certain sequences of events that involve waiting. I may want to take part in a sports event, but I must wait for my bruised knee to heal. Or again, I must wait until certain papers are processed so that my qualification for the event may be officially established. It may readily be seen that the temporal structure of everyday life is exceedingly complex, because the different levels of empirically present temporality must be ongoingly correlated.

The temporal structure of everyday life confronts me as a facticity with which I must reckon, that is, with which I must try to synchronize my own projects. I encounter time in everyday reality as continuous and finite. All my existence in this world is continuously ordered by its time, is indeed enveloped by it. My own life is an episode in the externally factitious stream of time. It was there before I was born and it will be there after I die. The knowledge of my inevitable death makes this time finite *for me*. I have only a certain amount of time available for the realization of my projects, and the knowledge of this affects my attitude to these projects. Also, since I do not want to die, this knowledge injects an underlying anxiety into my projects. Thus I cannot endlessly repeat my participation in sports events. I know that I am getting older. It may even be that this is the last occasion on which I have the chance to participate. My waiting will be anxious to the degree in which the finitude of time impinges upon the project.

The same temporal structure, as has already been indicated, is coercive. I cannot reverse at will the sequences imposed by it – 'first things first' is an essential element of my knowledge of everyday life. Thus I cannot take a certain examination before I have passed through certain educational programmes, I cannot practise my profession before I have taken this examination, and so on. Also, the same temporal structure provides the historicity that determines my situation in the world of everyday life. I was born on a certain date, entered school on another, started working as a professional on another, and so on. These dates, however, are all 'located' within a much more comprehensive history, and this 'location' decisively shapes my situation. Thus I was born in the year of the great bank crash in which my father lost his wealth, I entered school just before the revolution, I began to work just after the Great War broke out, and so forth. The temporal structure of everyday life not only imposes prearranged sequences upon the 'agenda' of any single day but also imposes itself upon my biography as a whole. Within the coordinates set by this temporal structure I apprehend both daily 'agenda' and overall biography. Clock and calendar ensure that, indeed, I am a 'man of my time'. Only within this temporal structure does everyday life retain for me its accent of reality. Thus in cases where I may be 'disoriented' for one reason or another (say, I have been in an automobile accident in which I was knocked unconscious), I feel an almost instinctive urge to 'reorient' myself within the temporal structure of everyday life. I look at my watch and try to recall what day it is. By these acts alone I re-enter the reality of everyday life.

2. Social Interaction in Everyday Life

The reality of everyday life is shared with others. But how are these others themselves experienced in everyday life? Again, it is possible to differentiate between several modes of such experience.

The most important experience of others takes place in the face-to-face situation, which is the prototypical case of social interaction. All other cases are derivatives of it.

In the face-to-face situation the other is appresented to me in a vivid present shared by both of us. I know that in the same vivid present I am appresented to him. My and his 'here and now' continuously impinge on each other as long as the face-to-face situation continues. As a result, there is a continuous interchange of my expressivity and his. I see him smile, then react to my frown by stopping the smile, then smiling again as I smile, and so on. Every expression of mine is oriented towards him, and vice versa, and this continuous reciprocity of expressive acts is simultaneously available to both of us. This means that, in the face-to-face situation, the other's subjectivity is available to me through a maximum of symptoms. To be sure, I may misinterpret some of these symptoms. I may think that the other is smiling while in fact he is smirking. Nevertheless, no other form of social relating can reproduce the plenitude of symptoms of subjectivity present in the face-to-face situation. Only here is the other's subjectivity emphatically 'close'. All other forms of relating to the other are, in varying degrees, 'remote'.

In the face-to-face situation the other is fully real. This reality is part of the overall reality of everyday life, and as such massive and compelling. To be sure, another may be real to me without my having encountered him face to face – by reputation, say, or by having corresponded with him. Nevertheless, he becomes real to me in the fullest sense of the word only when I meet him face to face. Indeed, it may be argued that the other in the face-to-face situation is more real to me than I myself. Of course I 'know myself better' than I can ever know him. My subjectivity is accessible to me in a way his can never be, no matter how 'close' our relationship. My past is available to me in memory in a fullness with which I can never reconstruct his, however much he may tell me about it. But this 'better knowledge' of myself requires reflection. It is not immediately apprehended to me. The other, however, *is* so apprehended in the face-to-face situation. 'What he is', therefore, is ongoingly available to me. This availability is continuous and prereflective. On the other hand, 'What I am' is *not* so available. To make it available requires that I stop, arrest the continuous spontaneity of my experience, and deliberately turn my attention back upon myself. What is more, such reflection about myself is typically occasioned by the attitude towards me that *the other* exhibits. It is typically a 'mirror' response to attitudes of the other.

It follows that relations with others in the face-to-face situation are highly flexible. Put negatively, it is comparatively difficult to impose rigid patterns upon face-to-face interaction. Whatever patterns are introduced will be continuously modified through the exceedingly variegated and subtle interchange of subjective meanings that goes on. For instance, I may view the other as someone inherently unfriendly to me and act towards him within a pattern of 'unfriendly relations' as understood by me. In the face-to-face situation, however, the other may confront me with attitudes and acts that contradict this pattern, perhaps up to a point where I am led to abandon the pattern as inapplicable and to view him as friendly. In other words, the pattern cannot sustain the massive evidence of the other's subjectivity that is available to me in the face-to-face situation. By contrast, it is much easier for me to ignore such evidence as long as I do not encounter the other face to face. Even in such a relatively 'close' relation as may be maintained by correspondence I can more successfully dismiss the other's protestations of friendship as not actually representing his subjective attitude to me, simply because in correspondence I lack the immediate, continuous and massively real presence of his expressivity. It is, to be sure, possible for me to misinterpret the other's meanings even in the face-to-face situation, as it is possible for him 'hypocritically' to hide his meanings. All the same, both misinterpretation and 'hypocrisy' are more difficult to sustain in face-to-face interaction than in less 'close' forms of social relations.

On the other hand, I apprehend the other by means of typificatory schemes even in the face-to-face situation, although these schemes are more 'vulnerable' to his interference than in 'remoter' forms of interaction. Put differently, while it is comparatively difficult to impose rigid patterns on face-to-face interaction, even it is patterned from the beginning if it takes place within the routines of everyday life. (We can leave aside for later consideration cases of interaction between complete strangers who have no common background of everyday life.) The reality of everyday life contains typificatory schemes in terms of which others are apprehended and 'dealt with' in face-to-face encounters. Thus I apprehend the other as 'a man', 'a European', 'a buyer', 'a jovial type', and so on. All these typifications ongoingly affect my interaction with him as, say, I decide to show him a good time on the town before trying to sell him my product. Our face-to-face interaction will be patterned by these typifications as long as they do not become problematic through interference on his part. Thus he may come up with evidence that, although 'a man', 'a European' and 'a buyer', he is also a self-righteous moralist, and that what appeared first as joviality is actually an expression of contempt for Americans in general and American salesmen in particular. At this point, of course, my typificatory scheme will have to be modified, and the evening planned differently in accordance with this modification. Unless thus challenged, though, the typifications will hold until further notice and will determine my actions in the situation.

The typificatory schemes entering into face-to-face situations are, of course, reciprocal. The other also apprehends me in a typified way – as 'a man', 'an American', 'a salesman', 'an ingratiating fellow', and so on. The other's typifications are as susceptible to my interference as mine are to his. In other words, the two typificatory schemes enter into an ongoing 'negotiation' in the face-to-face situation. In everyday life such 'negotiation' is itself likely to be prearranged in a typical manner – as in the typical bargaining process between buyers and salesmen. Thus, most of the time, my encounters with others in everyday life are typical in a double sense – I apprehend the other *as* a type and I interact with him in a situation that is itself typical.

The typifications of social interaction become progressively anonymous the further away they are from the face-to-face situation. Every typification, of course, entails incipient anonymity. If I typify my friend Henry as a member of category X (say, as an Englishman), I *ipso facto* interpret at least certain aspects of his conduct as resulting from this typification – for instance, his tastes in food are typical of Englishmen, as are his manners, certain of his emotional reactions, and so on. This implies, though, that these characteristics and actions of my friend Henry appertain to *anyone* in the category of Englishman, that is, I apprehend these aspects of his being in anonymous terms. Nevertheless, as long as my friend Henry is available in the plenitude of expressivity of the face-to-face situation, he will constantly break through my type of anonymous Englishman and manifest himself as a unique and therefore atypical individual – to wit, as my friend Henry. The anonymity of the type is obviously less susceptible to this kind of individualization when face-to-face interaction is a matter of the past (my friend Henry, *the Englishman*, whom I knew when I was a college student), or is of a superficial and transient kind (the Englishman with whom I have a brief conversation on a train), or has never taken place (my business competitors in England).

An important aspect of the experience of others in everyday life is thus the directness or indirectness of such experience. At any given time it is possible to distinguish between consociates with whom I interact in face-to-face situations and others who are mere contemporaries, of whom I have only more or less detailed recollections, or of whom I know merely by hearsay. In face-to-face situations I have direct evidence of my fellowman, of his actions, his attributes, and so on. Not so in the case of contemporaries – of them I have more or less reliable knowledge. Furthermore, I must take account of my fellowmen in face-to-face situations, while I may, but need not, turn my thoughts to mere contemporaries. Anonymity increases as I go from the former to the latter, because the anonymity of the typifications by means of which I apprehend fellowmen in face-to-face situations is constantly 'filled in' by the multiplicity of vivid symptoms referring to a concrete human being.

This, of course, is not the whole story. There are obvious differences in my experiences of mere contemporaries. Some I have experienced again and again in face-to-face situations and expect to meet again regularly (my friend Henry); others I *recollect* as concrete human beings from a past meeting (the blonde I passed on the street), but the meeting was brief and, most likely, will not be repeated. Still others I *know of* as concrete human beings, but I can apprehend them only by means of more or less anonymous intersecting typifications (my British business competitors, the Queen of England). Among the latter one could again distinguish between likely partners in face-to-face situations (my British business competitors), and potential but unlikely partners (the Queen of England).

The degree of anonymity characterizing the experience of others in everyday life depends, however, upon another factor too. I see the newspaper vendor on the street corner as regularly as I see my wife. But he is less important to me and I am not on intimate terms with him. He may remain relatively anonymous to me. The degree of interest and the degree of intimacy may combine to increase or decrease anonymity of experience. They may also influence it independently. I can be on fairly intimate terms with a number of the fellow-members of a tennis club and on very formal terms with my boss. Yet the former, while by no means completely anonymous, may merge into 'that bunch at the courts' while the latter stands out as a unique individual. And finally, anonymity may become near-total with certain typifications that are not intended ever to become individualized – such as the 'typical reader of *The Times*'. Finally, the 'scope' of the typification – and thereby its anonymity – can be further increased by speaking of 'British public opinion'.

The social reality of everyday life is thus apprehended in a continuum of typifications, which are progressively anonymous as they are removed from the 'here and now' of the face-to-face situation. At one pole of the continuum are those others with whom I frequently and intensively interact in face-to-face situations – my 'inner circle', as it were. At the other pole are highly anonymous abstractions, which by their very nature can never be available in face-to-face interaction. Social structure is the sum total of these typifications and of the recurrent patterns of interaction established by means of them. As such, social structure is an essential element of the reality of everyday life.

One further point ought to be made here, though we cannot elaborate it. My relations with others are not limited to consociates and contemporaries. I also relate to predecessors and successors, to those others who have preceded and will follow me in the encompassing history of my society. Except for those who are past consociates (my dear friend Henry), I relate to my predecessors through highly anonymous typifications – 'my immigrant great-grandparents', and even more, 'the Founding Fathers'. My successors, for understandable reasons, are typified in an even more anonymous manner – 'my children's children', or 'future generations'. These typifications are substantively empty projections, almost completely devoid of individualized content, whereas the typifications of predecessors have at least some such content, albeit of a highly mythical sort. The anonymity of both these sets of typifications, however, does not prevent their entering as elements into the reality of everyday life, sometimes in a very decisive way. After all, I may sacrifice my life in loyalty to the Founding Fathers – or, for that matter, on behalf of future generations.

3. Language and Knowledge in Everyday Life

Human expressivity is capable of objectivation, that is, it manifests itself in products of human activity that are available both to their producers and to other men as elements of a common world. Such objectivations serve as more or less enduring indices of the subjective processes of their producers, allowing their availability to extend beyond the face-to-face situation in which they can be directly apprehended. For intance, a subjective attitude of anger is directly expressed in the face-to-face situation by a variety of bodily indices – facial mien, general stance of the body, specific movements of arms and feet, and so on. These indices are continuously available in the face-to-face situation, which is precisely why it affords me the optimal situation for gaining access to another's subjectivity. The same indices are incapable of surviving beyond the vivid present of the face-to-face situation. Anger, however, can be objectivated by means of a weapon. Say, I have had an altercation with another man, who has given me ample expressive evidence of his anger against me. That night I wake up with a knife embedded in the wall above my bed. The knife *qua* object expresses my adversary's anger. It affords me access to his subjectivity even though I was sleeping when he threw it and never saw him because he fled after his near-hit. Indeed, if I leave the object where it is, I can look at it again the following morning, and again it expresses to me the anger of the man who threw it. What is more, other men can come and look at it and arrive at the same conclusion. In other words, the knife in my wall has become an objectively available constituent of the reality I share with my adversary and with other men. Presumably, this knife was not produced for the exclusive purpose of being thrown *at me*. But it expresses a subjective intention of violence, whether motivated by anger or by utilitarian considerations, such as killing for food. The weapon *qua* object in the real world continues to express a general intention to commit violence that is recognizable by anyone who knows what a weapon is. The weapon, then, is both a human product and an objectivation of human subjectivity.

The reality of everyday life is not only filled with objectivations; it is only possible because of them. I am constantly surrounded by objects that 'proclaim' the subjective intentions of my fellowmen, although I may sometimes have difficulty being quite sure just what it is that a particular object is 'proclaiming', especially if it was produced by men whom I have not known well or at all in face-to-face situations. Every ethnologist or archaeologist will readily testify to such difficulties, but the very fact that he *can* overcome them and reconstruct from an artifact the subjective intentions of men whose society may have been extinct for millennia is eloquent proof of the enduring power of human objectivations.

A special but crucially important case of objectivation is signification, that is, the human production of signs. A sign may be distinguished from other objectivations by its explicit intention to serve as an index of subjective meanings. To be sure, all objectivations are susceptible of utilization as signs, even though they were not originally produced with this intention. For instance, a weapon may have been originally produced for the purpose of hunting animals, but may then (say, in ceremonial usage) become a sign for aggressiveness and violence in general. But there are certain objectivations originally and explicitly intended to serve as signs. For instance, instead of throwing a knife at me (an act that was presumably intended to kill me, but that might conceivably have been intended merely to signify this possibility), my adversary could have painted a black X-mark on my door, a sign, let us assume, that we are now officially in a state of enmity. Such a sign, which has no purpose beyond indicating the subjective meaning of the one who made it, is also objectively available in the common reality he and I share with other men. I recognize its meaning, as do other men, and indeed it is available to its producer as an objective 'reminder' of his original intention in making it. It will be clear from the above that there is a good deal of fluidity between the instrumental and the significatory uses of certain objectivations. The special case of magic, in which there is a very interesting merging of these two uses, need not concern us here.

Signs are clustered in a number of systems. Thus there are systems of gesticulatory signs, of patterned bodily movements, of various sets of material artifacts, and so on. Signs and sign systems are objectivations in the sense of being objectively available beyond the expression of subjective intentions 'here and now'. This 'detachability' from the immediate expressions of subjectivity also pertains to signs that require the mediating presence of the body. Thus performing a dance that signifies aggressive intent is an altogether different thing from snarling or clenching fists in an outburst of anger. The latter acts express my subjectivity 'here and now', while the former can be quite detached from this subjectivity – I may not be angry or aggressive at all at this point but merely taking part in the dance because I am paid to do so on behalf of someone else who *is* angry. In other words, the dance can be detached from the subjectivity of the dancer in a way in which the snarling *cannot* from the snarler. Both dancing and snarling are manifestations of bodily expressivity, but only the former has the character of an objectively available sign. Signs and sign systems are all characterized by 'detachability', but they can be differentiated in terms of the degree to which they may be detached from face-to-face situations. Thus a dance is evidently less detached than a material artifact signifying the same subjective meaning.

Language, which may be defined here as a system of vocal signs, is the most important sign system of human society. Its foundation is, of course, in the intrinsic capacity of the human organism for vocal expressivity, but we can begin to speak of language only when vocal expressions have become capable of detachment from the immediate 'here and now' of subjective states. It is not yet language if I snarl, grunt, howl or hiss, although these vocal expressions are capable of becoming linguistic in so far as they are integrated into an objectively available sign system. The common objectivations of everyday life are maintained primarily by linguistic signification. Everyday life is, above all, life with and by means of the language I share with my fellowmen. An understanding of language is thus essential for any understanding of the reality of everyday life.

Language has its origins in the face-to-face situation, but can be readily detached from it. This is not only because I can shout in the dark or across a distance, speak on the telephone or via the radio, or convey linguistic signification by means of writing (the latter constituting, as it were, a sign system of the second degree). The detachment of language lies much more basically in its capacity to communicate meanings that are not direct expressions of subjectivity 'here and now'. It shares this capacity with other sign systems, but its immense variety and complexity make it much more readily detachable from the face-to-face situation than any other (for example, a system of gesticulations). I can speak about innumerable matters that are not present at all in the face-to-face situation, including matters I never have and never will experience directly. In this way, language is capable of becoming the objective repository of vast accumulations of meaning and experience, which it can then preserve in time and transmit to following generations.

In the face-to-face situation language possesses an inherent quality of reciprocity that distinguishes it from any other sign system. The ongoing production of vocal signs in conversation can be sensitively synchronized with the ongoing subjective intentions of the conversants. I speak as I think; so does my partner in the conversation. Both of us hear what each says at virtually the same instant, which makes possible a continuous, synchronized, reciprocal access to our two subjectivities, an intersubjective closeness in the face-to-face situation that no other sign system can duplicate. What is more, I hear *myself* as I speak; my own subjective meanings are made objectively and continuously available to me and *ipso facto* become 'more real' to me. Another way of putting this is to recall the previous point about my 'better knowledge' of the other as against my knowledge of myself in the face-to-face situation. This apparently paradoxical fact has been previously explained by the massive, continuous and prereflective availability of the other's being in the face-to-face situation, as against the requirement of reflection for the availability of my own. Now, however, as I objectivate my own being by means of language, my own being becomes massively and continuously available to myself at the same time that it is so available to him, and I can spontaneously respond to it without the 'interruption' of deliberate reflection. It can, therefore, be said that language makes 'more real' my subjectivity not only to my conversation partner but also to myself. This capacity of language to crystallize and stabilize for me my own subjectivity is retained (albeit with modifications) as language is detached from the face-to-face situation. This very important characteristic of language is well caught in the saying that men must talk about themselves until they know themselves.

Language originates in and has its primary reference to everyday life; it refers above all to the reality I experience in wide-awake consciousness, which is dominated by the pragmatic motive (that is, the cluster of meanings directly pertaining to present or future actions) and which I share with others in a taken-for-granted manner. Although language can also be employed to refer to other realities, which will be discussed further in a moment, it even then retains its rootage in the common-sense reality of everyday life. As a sign system, language has the quality of objectivity. I encounter language as a facticity external to myself and it is coercive in its effect on me. Language forces me into its patterns. I cannot use the rules of German syntax when I speak English; I cannot use words invented by my three-year-old son if I want to communicate outside the family; I must take into account prevailing standards of proper speech for various occasions, even if I would prefer my private 'improper' ones. Language provides me with a ready-made possibility for the ongoing objectification of my unfolding experience. Put differently, language is pliantly expansive so as to allow me to objectify a great variety of experiences coming my way in the course of my life. Language also typifies experiences, allowing me to subsume them under broad categories in terms of which they have meaning not only to myself but also to my fellowmen. As it typifies, it also anonymizes experiences, for the typified experience can, in principle, be duplicated by anyone falling into the category in question. For instance, I have a quarrel with my mother-in-law. This concrete and subjectively unique experience is typified linguistically under the category of 'mother-in-law trouble'. In this typification it makes sense to myself, to others, and, presumably, to my mother-in-law. The same typification, however, entails anonymity. Not only I but *anyone* (more accurately, anyone in the category of son-in-law) can have 'mother-in-law troubles'. In this way, my biographical experiences are ongoingly subsumed under general orders of meaning that are both objectively and subjectively real.

Because of its capacity to transcend the 'here and now', language bridges different zones within the reality of everyday life and integrates them into a meaningful whole. The transcendences have spatial, temporal and social dimensions. Through language I can transcend the gap between my manipulatory zone and that of the other; I can synchronize my biographical time sequence with his; and I can converse with him about individuals and collectivities with whom we are not at present in face-to-face interaction. As a result of these transcendences language is capable of 'making present' a variety of objects that are spatially, temporally and socially absent from the 'here and now'. *Ipso facto* a vast accumulation of experiences and meanings can become objectified in the 'here and now'. Put simply, through language an entire world can be actualized at any moment. This transcending and integrating power of language is retained when I am not actually conversing with another. Through linguistic objectification, even when 'talking to myself' in solitary thought, an entire world can be appresented to me at any moment. As far as social relations are concerned, language 'makes present' for me not only fellowmen who are physically absent at the moment, but fellowmen in the remembered or reconstructed past, as well as fellowmen projected as imaginary figures into the future. All these 'presences' can be highly meaningful, of course, in the ongoing reality of everyday life.

Moreover, language is capable of transcending the reality of everyday life altogether. It can refer to experiences pertaining to finite provinces of meaning, and it can span discrete spheres of reality. For instance, I can interpret 'the meaning' of a dream by integrating it linguistically within the order of everyday life. Such integration transposes the discrete reality of the dream into the reality of everyday life by making it an enclave within the latter. The dream is now meaningful in terms of the reality of everyday life rather than of its own discrete reality. Enclaves produced by such transposition belong, in a sense, to both spheres of reality. They are 'located' in one reality, but 'refer' to another.

Any significative theme that thus spans spheres of reality may be defined as a symbol, and the linguistic mode by which such transcendence is achieved may be called symbolic language. On the level of symbolism, then, linguistic signification attains the maximum detachment from the 'here and now' of everyday life, and language soars into regions that are not only *de facto* but *a priori* unavailable to everyday experience. Language now constructs immense edifices of symbolic representations that appear to tower over the reality of everyday life like gigantic presences from another world. Religion, philosophy, art, and science are the historically most important symbol systems of this kind. To name these is already to say that, despite the maximal detachment from everyday experience that the construction of these systems requires, they can be of very great importance indeed for the reality of everyday life. Language is capable not only of constructing symbols that are highly abstracted from everyday experience, but also of 'bringing back' these symbols and appresenting them as objectively real elements in everyday life. In this manner, symbolism and symbolic language become essential constituents of the reality of everyday life and of the common-sense apprehension of this reality. I live in a world of signs *and* symbols every day.

Language builds up semantic fields or zones of meaning that are linguistically circumscribed. Vocabulary, grammar and syntax are geared to the organization of these semantic fields. Thus language builds up classification schemes to differentiate objects by 'gender' (a quite different matter from sex, of course) or by number; forms to make statements of action as against statements of being; modes of indicating degrees of social intimacy, and so on. For example, in languages that distinguish intimate and formal discourse by means of pronouns (such as *tu* and *vous* in French, or *du* and *Sie* in German) this distinction marks the coordinates of a semantic field that could be called the zone of intimacy. Here lies the world of *tutoiement* or of *Bruderschaft*, with a rich collection of meanings that are continually available to me for the ordering of my social experience. Such a semantic field, of course, also exists for the English speaker, though it is more circumscribed linguistically. Or, to take another example, the sum of linguistic objectifications pertaining to my occupation constitutes another semantic field, which meaningfully orders all the routine events I encounter in my daily work. Within the semantic fields thus built up it is possible for both biographical and historical experience to be objectified, retained and accumulated. The accumulation, of course, is selective, with the semantic fields determining what will be retained and what 'forgotten' of the total experience of both the individual and the society. By virtue of this accumulation a social stock of knowledge is constituted, which is transmitted from generation to generation and which is available to the individual in everyday life. I live in the common-sense world of everyday life equipped with specific bodies of knowledge. What is more, I know that others share at least part of this knowledge, and they know that I know this. My interaction with others in everyday life is, therefore, constantly affected by our common participation in the available social stock of knowledge.

The social stock of knowledge includes knowledge of my situation and its limits. For instance, I know that I am poor and that, therefore, I cannot expect to live in a fashionable suburb. This knowledge is, of course, shared both by those who are poor themselves and those who are in a more privileged situation. Participation in the social stock of knowledge thus permits the 'location' of individuals in society and the 'handling' of them in the appropriate manner. This is not possible for one who does not participate in this knowledge, such as a foreigner, who may not recognize me as poor at all, perhaps because the criteria of poverty are quite different in his society – how can I be poor, when I wear shoes and do not seem to be hungry?

Since everyday life is dominated by the pragmatic motive, recipe knowledge, that is, knowledge limited to pragmatic competence in routine performances, occupies a prominent place in the social stock of knowledge. For example, I use the telephone every day for specific pragmatic purposes of my own. I know how to do this. I also know what to do if my telephone fails to function – which does not mean that I know how to repair it, but that I know whom to call on for assistance. My knowledge of the telephone also includes broader information on the system of telephonic communication – for instance, I know that some people have unlisted numbers, that under special circumstances I can get a simultaneous hook-up with two long-distance parties, that I must figure on the time difference if I want to call up somebody in Hong Kong, and so forth. All of this telephonic lore is recipe knowledge since it does not concern anything except what I have to know for my present and possible future pragmatic purposes. I am not interested in *why* the telephone works this way, in the enormous body of scientific and engineering knowledge that makes it possible to construct telephones. Nor am I interested in uses of the telephone that lie outside my purposes, say in combination with short-wave radio for the purpose of marine communication. Similarly, I have recipe knowledge of the workings of human relationships. For example, I know what I must do to apply for a passport. All I am interested in is getting the passport at the end of a certain waiting period. I do not care, and do not know, how my application is processed in government offices, by whom and after what steps approval is given, who puts which stamp in the document. I am not making a study of government bureaucracy – I just want to go on a vacation abroad. My interest in the hidden workings of the passport-getting procedure will be aroused only if I fail to get my passport in the end. At that point, very much as I call on a telephone-repair expert after my telephone has broken down, I call on an expert in passport-getting – a lawyer, say, or my Congressman, or the American Civil Liberties Union. *Mutatis mutandis*, a large part of the social stock of knowledge consists of recipes for the mastery of routine problems. Typically, I have little interest in going beyond this pragmatically necessary knowledge as long as the problems can indeed be mastered thereby.

The social stock of knowledge differentiates reality by degrees of familiarity. It provides complex and detailed information concerning those sectors of everyday life with which I must frequently deal. It provides much more general and imprecise information on remoter sectors. Thus my knowledge of my own occupation and its world is very rich and specific, while I have only very sketchy knowledge of the occupational worlds of others. The social stock of knowledge further supplies me with the typificatory schemes required for the major routines of everyday life, not only the typifications of others that have been discussed before, but typifications of all sorts of events and experiences, both social and natural. Thus I live in a world of relatives, fellow-workers and recognizable public functionaries. In this world, consequently, I experience family gatherings, professional meetings and encounters with the traffic police. The natural 'backdrop' of these events is also typified within the stock of knowledge. My world is structured in terms of routines applying in good or bad weather, in the hay-fever season and in situations when a speck of dirt gets caught under my eyelid. 'I know what to do' with regard to all these others and all these events within my everyday life. By presenting itself to me as an integrated whole the social stock of knowledge also provides me with the means to integrate discrete elements of my own knowledge. In other words, 'what everybody knows' has its own logic, and the same logic can be applied to order various things that I know. For example, I know that my friend Henry is an Englishman, and I know that he is always very punctual in keeping appointments. Since 'everybody knows' that punctuality is an English trait, I can now integrate these two elements of my knowledge of Henry into a typification that is meaningful in terms of the social stock of knowledge.

The validity of my knowledge of everyday life is taken for granted by myself and by others until further notice, that is, until a problem arises that cannot be solved in terms of it. As long as my knowledge works satisfactorily, I am generally ready to suspend doubts about it. In certain attitudes detached from everyday reality – telling a joke, at the theatre or in church, or engaging in philosophical speculation – I may perhaps doubt elements of it. But these doubts are 'not to be taken seriously'. For instance, as a businessman I know that it pays to be inconsiderate of others. I may laugh at a joke in which this maxim leads to failure, I may be moved by an actor or a preacher extolling the virtues of consideration and I may concede in a philosophical mood that all social relations should be governed by the Golden Rule. Having laughed, having been moved and having philosophized, I return to the 'serious' world of business, once more recognize the logic of its maxims, and act accordingly. Only when my maxims fail 'to deliver the goods' in the world to which they are intended to apply are they likely to become problematic to me 'in earnest'.

Although the social stock of knowledge appresents the everyday world in an integrated manner, differentiated according to zones of familiarity and remoteness, it leaves the totality of that world opaque. Put differently, the reality of everyday life always appears as a zone of lucidity behind which there is a background of darkness. As some zones of reality are illuminated, others are adumbrated. I cannot know everything there is to know about this reality. Even if, for instance, I am a seemingly all-powerful despot in my family, and know this, I cannot know all the factors that go into the continuing success of my despotism. I know that my orders are always obeyed, but I cannot be sure of all the steps and all the motives that lie between the issuance and the execution of my orders. There are always things that go on 'behind my back'. This is true *a fortiori* when social relationships more complex than those of the family are involved – and explains, incidentally, why despots are endemically nervous. My knowledge of everyday life has the quality of an instrument that cuts a path through a forest and, as it does so, projects a narrow cone of light on what lies just ahead and immediately around; on all sides of the path there continues to be darkness. This image pertains even more, of course, to the multiple realities in which everyday life is continually transcended. This latter statement can be paraphrased, poetically if not exhaustively, by saying that the reality of everyday life is overcast by the penumbras of our dreams.

My knowledge of everyday life is structured in terms of relevances. Some of these are determined by immediate pragmatic interests of mine, others by my general situation in society. It is irrelevant to me how my wife goes about cooking my favourite goulash as long as it turns out the way I like it. It is irrelevant to me that the stock of a company is falling, if I do not own such stock; or that Catholics are modernizing their doctrine, if I am an atheist; or that it is now possible to fly non-stop to Africa, if I do not want to go there. However, my relevance structures intersect with the relevance structures of others at many points, as a result of which we have 'interesting' things to say to each other. An important element of my knowledge of everyday life is the knowledge of the relevance structures of others. Thus I 'know better' than to tell my doctor about my investment problems, my lawyer about my ulcer pains, or my accountant about my quest for religious truth. The basic relevance structures referring to everyday life are presented to me ready-made by the social stock of knowledge itself. I know that 'woman talk' is irrelevant to me as a man, that 'idle speculation' is irrelevant to me as a man of action, and so forth. Finally, the social stock of knowledge as a whole has its own relevance structure. Thus, in terms of the stock of knowledge objectivated in American society, it is irrelevant to study the movements of the stars to predict the stock market, but it is relevant to study an individual's slips of the tongue to find out about his sex life, and so on. Conversely, in other societies, astrology may be highly relevant for economics, speech analysis quite irrelevant for erotic curiosity, and so on.

One final point should be made here about the social distribution of knowledge. I encounter knowledge in everyday life as socially distributed, that is, as possessed differently by different individuals and types of individuals. I do not share my knowledge equally with all my fellowmen, and there may be some knowledge that I share with no one. I share my professional expertise with colleagues, but not with my family, and I may share with nobody my knowledge of how to cheat at cards. The social distribution of knowledge of certain elements of everyday reality can become highly complex and even confusing to the outsider. I not only do not possess the knowledge supposedly required to cure me of a physical ailment, I may even lack the knowledge of which one of a bewildering variety of medical specialists claims jurisdiction over what ails me. In such cases, I require not only the advice of experts, but the prior advice of experts on experts. The social distribution of knowledge thus begins with the simple fact that I do not know everything known to my fellowmen, and vice versa, and culminates in exceedingly complex and esoteric systems of expertise. Knowledge of *how* the socially available stock of knowledge is distributed, at least in outline, is an important element of that same stock of knowledge. In everyday life I know, at least roughly, what I can hide from whom, whom I can turn to for information on what I do not know, and generally which types of individuals may be expected to have which types of knowledge.

Part Two

Society as
Objective Reality

I. Institutionalization

Organism and Activity

Man occupies a peculiar position in the animal kingdom.[1] Unlike the other higher mammals, he has no species-specific environment,[2] no environment firmly structured by his own instinctual organization. There is no man-world in the sense that one may speak of a dog-world or a horse-world. Despite an area of individual learning and accumulation, the individual dog or the individual horse has a largely fixed relationship to its environment, which it shares with all other members of its respective species. One obvious implication of this is that dogs and horses, as compared with man, are much more restricted to a specific geographical distribution. The specificity of these animals' environment, however, is much more than a geographical delimitation. It refers to the biologically fixed character of their relationship to the environment, even if geographical variation is introduced. In this sense, all non-human animals, as species and as individuals, live in closed worlds whose structures are predetermined by the biological equipment of the several animal species.

By contrast, man's relationship to his environment is characterized by world-openness.[3] Not only has man succeeded in establishing himself over the greater part of the earth's surface, his relationship to the surrounding environment is everywhere very imperfectly structured by his own biological constitution. The latter, to be sure, permits man to engage in different activities. But the fact that he continued to live a nomadic existence in one place and turned to agriculture in another cannot be explained in terms of biological processes. This does not mean, of course, that there are no biologically determined limitations to man's relations with his environment; his species-specific sensory and motor equipment imposes obvious limitations on his range of possibilities. The peculiarity of man's biological constitution lies rather in its instinctual component.

Man's instinctual organization may be described as under-developed, compared with that of the other higher mammals. Man does have drives, of course. But these drives are highly unspecialized and undirected. This means that the human organism is capable of applying its constitutionally given equipment to a very wide and, in addition, constantly variable and varying range of activities. This peculiarity of the human organism is grounded in its ontogenetic development.[4] Indeed, if one looks at the matter in terms of organismic development, it is possible to say that the foetal period in the human being extends through about the first year after birth.[5] Important organismic developments, which in the animal are completed in the mother's body, take place in the human infant after its separation from the womb. At this time, however, the human infant is not only *in* the outside world, but interrelating with it in a number of complex ways.

The human organism is thus still developing biologically while already standing in a relationship to its environment. In other words, the process of becoming man takes place in an interrelationship with an environment. This statement gains significance if one reflects that this environment is both a natural and a human one. That is, the developing human being not only interrelates with a particular natural environment, but with a specific cultural and social order, which is mediated to him by the significant others who have charge of him.[6] Not only is the survival of the human infant dependent upon certain social arrangements, the direction of his organismic development is socially determined. From the moment of birth, man's organismic development, and indeed a large part of his biological being as such, are subjected to continuing socially determined interference.

Despite the obvious physiological limits to the range of possible and different ways of becoming man in this double environmental interrelationship, the human organism manifests an immense plasticity in its response to the environmental forces at work on it. This is particularly clear when one observes the flexibility of man's biological constitution as it is subjected to a variety of socio-cultural determinations. It is an ethnological commonplace that the ways of becoming and being human are as numerous as man's cultures. Humanness is socio-culturally variable. In other words, there is no human nature in the sense of a biologically fixed substratum determining the variability of socio-cultural formations. There is only human nature in the sense of anthropological constants (for example, world-openness and plasticity of instinctual structure) that delimit and permit man's socio-cultural formations. But the specific shape into which this humanness is moulded is determined by those socio-cultural formations and is relative to their numerous variations. While it is possible to say that man has a nature, it is more significant to say that man constructs his own nature, or more simply, that man produces himself.[7]

The plasticity of the human organism and its susceptibility to socially determined interference is best illustrated by the ethnological evidence concerning sexuality.[8] While man possesses sexual drives that are comparable to those of the other higher mammals, human sexuality is characterized by a very high degree of pliability. It is not only relatively independent of temporal rhythms, it is pliable both in the objects towards which it may be directed and in its modalities of expression. Ethnological evidence shows that, in sexual matters, man is capable of almost anything. One may stimulate one's sexual imagination to a pitch of feverish lust, but it is unlikely that one can conjure up any image that will not correspond to what in some other culture is an established norm, or at least an occurrence to be taken in stride. If the term 'normality' is to refer either to what is anthropologically fundamental or to what is culturally universal, then neither it nor its antonym can be meaningfully applied to the varying forms of human sexuality. At the same time, of course, human sexuality is directed, sometimes rigidly structured, in every particular culture. Every culture has a distinctive sexual configuration, with its own specialized patterns of sexual conduct and its own 'anthropological' assumptions in the sexual area. The empirical relativity of these configurations, their immense variety and luxurious inventiveness, indicate that they are the product of man's own socio-cultural formations rather than of a biologically fixed human nature.[9]

The period during which the human organism develops

towards its completion in interrelationship with its environment is also the period during which the human self is formed. The formation of the self, then, must also be understood in relation to both the ongoing organismic development and the social process in which the natural and the human environment are mediated through the significant others.[10] The genetic presuppositions for the self are, of course, given at birth. But the self, as it is experienced later as a subjectively and objectively recognizable identity, is not. The same social processes that determine the completion of the organism produce the self in its particular, culturally relative form. The character of the self as a social product is not limited to the particular configuration the individual identifies as himself (for instance, as 'a man', in the particular way in which this identity is defined and formed in the culture in question), but to the comprehensive psychological equipment that serves as an appendage to the particular configuration (for instance, 'manly' emotions, attitudes and even somatic reactions). It goes without saying, then, that the organism and, even more, the self cannot be adequately understood apart from the particular social context in which they were shaped.

The common development of the human organism and the human self in a socially determined environment is related to the peculiarly human relationship between organism and self. This relationship is an eccentric one.[11] On the one hand, man *is* a body, in the same way that this may be said of every other animal organism. On the other hand, man *has* a body. That is, man experiences himself as an entity that is not identical with his body, but that, on the contrary, has that body at its disposal. In other words, man's experience of himself always hovers in a balance between being and having a body, a balance that must be redressed again and again. This eccentricity of man's experience of his own body has certain consequences for the analysis of human activity as conduct in the material environment and as externalization of subjective meanings. An adequate understanding of any human phenomenon will have to take both these aspects into consideration, for reasons that are grounded in fundamental anthropological facts.

It should be clear from the foregoing that the statement that man produces himself in no way implies some sort of Promethean vision of the solitary individual.[12] Man's self-production is always, and of necessity, a social enterprise. Men *together* produce a human environment, with the totality of its sociocultural and psychological formations. None of these formations may be understood as products of man's biological constitution, which, as indicated, provides only the outer limits for human productive activity. Just as it is impossible for man to develop as man in isolation, so it is impossible for man in isolation to produce a human environment. Solitary human being is being on the animal level (which, of course, man shares with other animals). As soon as one observes phenomena that are specifically human, one enters the realm of the social. Man's specific humanity and his sociality are inextricably intertwined. *Homo sapiens* is always, and in the same measure, *homo socius*.[13]

The human organism lacks the necessary biological means to provide stability for human conduct. Human existence, if it were thrown back on its organismic resources by themselves, would be existence in some sort of chaos. Such chaos is, however, empirically unavailable, even though one may theoretically conceive of it. Empirically, human existence takes place in a context of order, direction, stability. The question then arises: From what does the empirically existing stability of human order derive? An answer may be given on two levels. One may first point to the obvious fact that a given social order precedes any individual organismic development. That is, world-openness, while intrinsic to man's biological make-up, is always pre-empted by social order. One may say that the biologically intrinsic world-openness of human existence is always, and indeed must be, transformed by social order into a relative world-closedness. While this reclosure can never approximate the closedness of animal existence, if only because of its humanly produced and thus 'artificial' character, it is nevertheless capable, most of the time, of providing direction and stability for the greater part of human conduct. The question may then be pushed to another level. One may ask in what manner social order itself arises.

The most general answer to this question is that social order is a human product, or, more precisely, an ongoing human production. It is produced by man in the course of his ongoing externalization. Social order is not biologically given or derived from any biological *data* in its empirical manifestations. Social order, needless to add, is also not given in man's natural environment, though particular features of this may be factors in determining certain features of a social order (for example, its economic or technological arrangements). Social order is not part of the 'nature of things', and it cannot be derived from the 'laws of nature'.[14] Social order exists *only* as a product of human activity. No other ontological status may be ascribed to it without hopelessly obfuscating its empirical manifestations. Both in its genesis (social order is the result of past human activity) and its existence in any instant of time (social order exists only and in so far as human activity continues to produce it) it is a human product.

While the social products of human externalization have a character *sui generis* as against both their organismic and their environmental context, it is important to stress that externalization as such is an anthropological necessity.[15] Human being is impossible in a closed sphere of quiescent interiority. Human being must ongoingly externalize itself in activity. This anthropological necessity is grounded in man's biological equipment.[16] The inherent instability of the human organism makes it imperative that man himself provide a stable environment for his conduct. Man himself must specialize and direct his drives. These biological facts serve as a necessary presupposition for the production of social order. In other words, although no existing social order can be derived from biological *data*, the necessity for social order as such stems from man's biological equipment.

To understand the causes, other than those posited by the biological constants, for the emergence, maintenance and transmission of a social order one must undertake an analysis that eventuates in a theory of institutionalization.

Origins of Institutionalization　　　　　　　　　　✳

All human activity is subject to habitualization. Any action that is repeated frequently becomes cast into a pattern, which can then be reproduced with an economy of effort and which, *ipso facto*, is apprehended by its performer *as* that pattern. Habitualization further implies that the action in question may be performed again in the future in the same manner and with the same economical effort. This is true of non-social as well as of social activity. Even the solitary individual on the proverbial desert island habitualizes his activity. When he wakes up in the morning and resumes his attempts to construct a canoe out of matchsticks, he may mumble to himself, 'There I go again', as he starts on step one of an operating procedure consisting of, say, ten steps. In other words, even solitary man has at least the company of his operating procedures.

Habitualized actions, of course, retain their meaningful character for the individual although the meanings involved become embedded as routines in his general stock of knowledge, taken for granted by him and at hand for his projects into the future.[17] Habitualization carries with it the important psychological gain that choices are narrowed. While in theory there may be a hundred ways to go about the project of building a canoe out of matchsticks, habitualization narrows these down to one. This frees the individual from the burden of 'all those decisions', providing a psychological relief that has its basis in man's undirected instinctual structure. Habitualization provides the direction and the specialization of activity that is lacking in man's biological equipment, thus relieving the accumulation of tensions that result from undirected drives.[18] And by providing a stable background in which human activity may proceed with a minimum of decision-making most of the time, it frees energy for such decisions as may be necessary on certain occasions. In other words, the background of habitualized activity opens up a foreground for deliberation and innovation.[19]

In terms of the meanings bestowed by man upon his activity, habitualization makes it unnecessary for each situation to be defined anew, step by step.[20] A large variety of situations may be subsumed under its predefinitions. The activity to be undertaken in these situations can then be anticipated. Even alternatives of conduct can be assigned standard weights.

These processes of habitualization precede any institutionalization, indeed can be made to apply to a hypothetical solitary individual detached from any social interaction. The fact that even such a solitary individual, assuming that he has been formed as a self (as we would have to assume in the case of our matchstick-canoe builder), will habitualize his activity in accordance with biographical experience of a world of social institutions preceding his solitude need not concern us at the moment. Empirically, the more important part of the habitualization of human activity is coextensive with the latter's institutionalization. The question then becomes how do institutions arise.

Institutionalization occurs whenever there is a reciprocal typification of habitualized actions by types of actors. Put differently, any such typification is an institution.[21] What must be stressed is the reciprocity of institutional typifications and the typicality of not only the actions but also the actors in institutions. The typifications of habitualized actions that constitute institutions are always shared ones. They are *available* to all members of the particular social group in question, and the institution itself typifies individual actors as well as individual actions. The institution posits that actions of type X will be performed by actors of type X. For example, the institution of the law posits that heads shall be chopped off in specific ways under specific circumstances, and that specific types of individuals shall do the chopping (executioners, say, or members of an impure caste, or virgins under a certain age, or those who have been designated by an oracle).

Institutions further imply historicity and control. Reciprocal typifications of actions are built up in the course of a shared history. They cannot be created instantaneously. Institutions always have a history, of which they are the products. It is impossible to understand an institution adequately without an understanding of the historical process in which it was produced. Institutions also, by the very fact of their existence, control human conduct by setting up predefined patterns of conduct, which channel it in one direction as against the many other directions that would theoretically be possible. It is important to stress that this controlling character is inherent in institutionalization as such, prior to or apart from any mechanisms of sanctions specifically set up to support an institution. These mechanisms (the sum of which constitute what is generally called a system of social control) do, of course, exist in many institutions and in all the agglomerations of institutions that we call societies. Their controlling efficacy, however, is of a secondary or supplementary kind. As we shall see again later, the primary social control is given in the existence of an institution as such. To say that a segment of human activity has been institutionalized is already to say that this segment of human activity has been subsumed under social control. Additional control mechanisms are required only in so far as the processes of institutionalization are less than completely successful. Thus, for instance, the law may provide that anyone who breaks the incest taboo will have his head chopped off. This provision may be necessary because there have been cases when individuals offended against the taboo. It is unlikely that this sanction will have to be invoked continuously (unless the institution delineated by the incest taboo is itself in the course of disintegration, a special case that we need not elaborate here). It makes little sense, therefore, to say that human sexuality is socially controlled by beheading certain individuals. Rather, human sexuality is socially controlled by its institutionalization in the course of the particular history in question. One may add, of course, that the incest taboo itself is nothing but the negative side of an assemblage of typifications, which define in the first place which sexual conduct is incestuous and which is not.

In actual experience institutions generally manifest themselves in collectivities containing considerable numbers of people. It is theoretically important, however, to emphasize that the institutionalizing process of reciprocal typification would occur even if two individuals began to interact *de novo*. Institutionalization is incipient in every social situation continuing in time. Let us assume that two persons from entirely different social worlds begin to interact. By saying 'persons' we presuppose that the two individuals have formed selves, something that could, of course, have occurred only in a social process. We are thus for the moment excluding the cases of Adam and Eve, or of two 'feral' children meeting in a clearing of a primeval jungle. But we are assuming that the two individuals arrive at their meeting place from social worlds that have been historically produced in segregation from each other, and

73

that the interaction therefore takes place in a situation that has not been institutionally defined for either of the participants. It may be possible to imagine a Man Friday joining our matchstick-canoe builder on his desert island, and to imagine the former as a Papuan and the latter as an American. In that case, however, it is likely that the American will have read or at least have heard about the story of Robinson Crusoe, which will introduce a measure of predefinition of the situation at least for him. Let us, then, simply call our two persons A and B.

As A and B interact, in whatever manner, typifications will be produced quite quickly. A watches B perform. He attributes motives to B's actions and, seeing the actions recur, typifies the motives as recurrent. As B goes on performing, A is soon able to say to himself, 'Aha, there he goes again.' At the same time, A may assume that B is doing the same thing with regard to him. From the beginning, both A and B assume this reciprocity of typification. In the course of their interaction these typifications will be expressed in specific patterns of conduct. That is, A and B will begin to play roles vis-à-vis each other. This will occur even if each continues to perform actions different from those of the other. The possibility of taking the role of the other will appear with regard to the same actions performed by both. That is, A will inwardly appropriate B's reiterated roles and make them the models for his own role-playing. For example, B's role in the activity of preparing food is not only typified as such by A, but enters as a constitutive element into A's own food-preparation role. Thus a collection of reciprocally typified actions will emerge, habitualized for each in roles, some of which will be performed separately and some in common.[22] While this reciprocal typification is not yet institutionalization (since, there only being two individuals, there is no possibility of a typology of actors), it is clear that institutionalization is already present in nucleo.

At this stage one may ask what gains accrue to the two individuals from this development. The most important gain is that each will be able to predict the other's actions. Concomitantly, the interaction of both becomes predictable. The 'There he goes again' becomes a 'There we go again'. This relieves both individuals of a considerable amount of tension.

They save time and effort, not only in whatever external tasks they might be engaged in separately or jointly, but in terms of their respective psychological economies. Their life together is now defined by a widening sphere of taken-for-granted routines. Many actions are possible on a low level of attention. Each action of one is no longer a source of astonishment and potential danger to the other. Instead, much of what goes on takes on the triviality of what, to both, will be everyday life. This means that the two individuals are constructing a background, in the sense discussed before, which will serve to stabilize both their separate actions and their interaction. The construction of this background of routine in turn makes possible a division of labour between them, opening the way for innovations, which demand a higher level of attention. The division of labour and the innovations will lead to new habitualizations, further widening the background common to both individuals. In other words, a social world will be in process of construction, containing within it the roots of an expanding institutional order.

Generally, all actions repeated once or more tend to be habitualized to some degree, just as all actions observed by another necessarily involve some typification on his part. However, for the kind of reciprocal typification just described to occur there must be a continuing social situation in which the habitualized actions of two or more individuals interlock. Which actions are likely to be reciprocally typified in this manner?

The general answer is, those actions that are relevant to both A and B within their common situation. The areas likely to be relevant in this way will, of course, vary in different situations. Some will be those facing A and B in terms of their previous biographies, others may be the result of the natural, pre-social circumstances of the situation. What will in all cases have to be habitualized is the communication process between A and B. Labour, sexuality and territoriality are other likely foci of typification and habitualization. In these various areas the situation of A and B is paradigmatic of the institutionalization occurring in larger societies.

Let us push our paradigm one step further and imagine that A and B have children. At this point the situation changes qualitatively. The appearance of a third party changes the character of the ongoing social interaction between A and B, and it will change even further as additional individuals continue to be added.[23] The institutional world, which existed *in statu nascendi* in the original situation of A and B, is now passed on to others. In this process institutionalization perfects itself. The habitualizations and typifications undertaken in the common life of A and B, formations that until this point still had the quality of *ad hoc* conceptions of two individuals, now become historical institutions. With the acquisition of historicity, these formations also acquire another crucial quality, or, more accurately, perfect a quality that was incipient as soon as A and B began the reciprocal typification of their conduct: this quality is objectivity. This means that the institutions that have now been crystallized (for instance, the institution of paternity as it is encountered by the children) are experienced as existing over and beyond the individuals who 'happen to' embody them at the moment. In other words, the institutions are now experienced as possessing a reality of their own, a reality that confronts the individual as an external and coercive fact.[24]

As long as the nascent institutions are constructed and maintained only in the interaction of A and B, their objectivity remains tenuous, easily changeable, almost playful, even while they attain a measure of objectivity by the mere fact of their formati‧n. To put this a little differently, the routinized background of A's and B's activity remains fairly accessible to deliberate intervention by A and B. Although the routines, once established, carry within them a tendency to persist, the possibility of changing them or even abolishing them remains at hand in consciousness. A and B alone are responsible for having constructed this world. A and B remain capable of changing or abolishing it. What is more, since they themselves have shaped this world in the course of a shared biography which they can remember, the world thus shaped appears fully transparent to them. They understand the world that they themselves have made. All this changes in the process of transmission to the new generation. The objectivity of the institutional world 'thickens' and 'hardens', not only for the children, but (by a mirror effect) for the parents as well. The

'There we go again' now becomes 'This is how these things are done'. A world so regarded attains a firmness in consciousness; it becomes real in an ever more massive way and it can no longer be changed so readily. For the children, especially in the early phase of their socialization into it, it becomes *the* world. For the parents, it loses its playful quality and becomes 'serious'. For the children, the parentally transmitted world is not fully transparent. Since they had no part in shaping it, it confronts them as a given reality that, like nature, is opaque in places at least.

Only at this point does it become possible to speak of a social world at all, in the sense of a comprehensive and given reality confronting the individual in a manner analogous to the reality of the natural world. Only in this way, *as* an objective world, can the social formations be transmitted to a new generation. In the early phases of socialization the child is quite incapable of distinguishing between the objectivity of natural phenomena and the objectivity of the social formations.[25] To take the most important item of socialization, language appears to the child as inherent in the nature of things, and he cannot grasp the notion of its conventionality. A thing *is* what it is called, and it could not be called anything else. All institutions appear in the same way, as given, unalterable and self-evident. Even in our empirically unlikely example of parents having constructed an institutional world *de novo*, the objectivity of this world would be increased for them by the socialization of their children, because the objectivity experienced by the children would reflect back upon their own experience of this world. Empirically, of course, the institutional world transmitted by most parents already has the character of historical and objective reality. The process of transmission simply strengthens the parents' sense of reality, if only because, to put it crudely, if one says, 'This is how these things are done', often enough one believes it oneself.[26]

An institutional world, then, is experienced as an objective reality. It has a history that antedates the individual's birth and is not accessible to his biographical recollection. It was there before he was born, and it will be there after his death. This history itself, as the tradition of the existing institutions, has the character of objectivity. The individual's biography is apprehended as an episode located within the objective history of the society. The institutions, as historical and objective facticities, confront the individual as undeniable facts. The institutions are *there*, external to him, persistent in their reality, whether he likes it or not. He cannot wish them away. They resist his attempts to change or evade them. They have coercive power over him, both in themselves, by the sheer force of their facticity, and through the control mechanisms that are usually attached to the most important of them. The objective reality of institutions is not diminished if the individual does not understand their purpose or their mode of operation. He may experience large sectors of the social world as incomprehensible, perhaps oppressive in their opaqueness, but real none the less. Since institutions exist as external reality, the individual cannot understand them by introspection. He must 'go out' and learn about them, just as he must to learn about nature. This remains true even though the social world, as a humanly produced reality, is potentially understandable in a way not possible in the case of the natural world.[27]

It is important to keep in mind that the objectivity of the institutional world, however massive it may appear to the individual, is a humanly produced, constructed objectivity. The process by which the externalized products of human activity attain the character of objectivity is objectivation.[28] The institutional world is objectivated human activity, and so is every single institution. In other words, despite the objectivity that marks the social world in human experience, it does not thereby acquire an ontological status apart from the human activity that produced it. The paradox that man is capable of producing a world that he then experiences as something other than a human product will concern us later on. At the moment, it is important to emphasize that the relationship between man, the producer, and the social world, his product, is and remains a dialectical one. That is, man (not, of course, in isolation but in his collectivities) and his social world interact with each other. The product acts back upon the producer. Externalization and objectivation are moments in a continuing dialectical process. The third moment in this process, which is internalization (by which the objectivated social world is retrojected into consciousness in the course of socialization), will occupy us in considerable detail later on. It is already possible, however, to see the fundamental relationship of these three dialectical moments in social reality. Each of them corresponds to an essential characterization of the social world. *Society is a human product. Society is an objective reality. Man is a social product.* It may also already be evident that an analysis of the social world that leaves out any one of these three moments will be distortive.[29] One may further add that only with the transmission of the social world to a new generation (that is, internalization as effectuated in socialization) does the fundamental social dialectic appear in its totality. To repeat, only with the appearance of a new generation can one properly speak of a social world.

At the same point, the institutional world requires legitimation, that is, ways by which it can be 'explained' and justified. This is not because it appears less real. As we have seen, the reality of the social world gains in massivity in the course of its transmission. This reality, however, is a historical one, which comes to the new generation as a tradition rather than as a biographical memory. In our paradigmatic example, *A* and *B*, the original creators of the social world, can always reconstruct the circumstances under which their world and any part of it was established. That is, they can arrive at the meaning of an institution by exercising their powers of recollection. *A*'s and *B*'s children are in an altogether different situation. Their knowledge of the institutional history is by way of 'hearsay'. The original meaning of the institutions is inaccessible to them in terms of memory. It, therefore, becomes necessary to interpret this meaning to them in various legitimating formulas. These will have to be consistent and comprehensive in terms of the institutional order, if they are to carry conviction to the new generation. The same story, so to speak, must be told to all the children. It follows that the expanding institutional order develops a corresponding canopy of legitimations, stretching over it a protective cover of both cognitive and normative interpretation. These legitimations are learned by the new generation during the same process that socializes them into the institutional order. This, again, will occupy us in greater detail further on.

The development of specific mechanisms of social controls

also becomes necessary with the historicization and objectivation of institutions. Deviance from the institutionally 'programmed' courses of action becomes likely once the institutions have become realities divorced from their original relevance in the concrete social processes from which they arose. To put this more simply, it is more likely that one will deviate from programmes set up for one by others than from programmes that one has helped establish oneself. The new generation posits a problem of compliance, and its socialization into the institutional order requires the establishment of sanctions. The institutions must and do claim authority over the individual, independently of the subjective meanings he may attach to any particular situation. The priority of the institutional definitions of situations must be consistently maintained over individual temptations at redefinition. The children must be 'taught to behave' and, once taught, must be 'kept in line'. So, of course, must the adults. The more conduct is institutionalized, the more predictable and thus the more controlled it becomes. If socialization into the institutions has been effective, outright coercive measures can be applied economically and selectively. Most of the time, conduct will occur 'spontaneously' within the institutionally set channels. The more, on the level of meaning, conduct is taken for granted, the more possible alternatives to the institutional 'programmes' will recede, and the more predictable and controlled conduct will be.

In principle, institutionalization may take place in any area of collectively relevant conduct. In actual fact, sets of institutionalization processes take place concurrently. There is no *a priori* reason for assuming that these processes will necessarily 'hang together' functionally, let alone as a logically consistent system. To return once more to our paradigmatic example, slightly changing the fictitious situation, let us assume this time, not a budding family of parents and children, but a piquant triangle of a male A, a bisexual female B, and a Lesbian C. We need not belabour the point that the sexual relevances of these three individuals will not coincide. Relevance $A–B$ is not shared by C. The habitualizations engendered as a result of relevance $A–B$ need bear no relationship to those engendered by relevances $B–C$ and $C–A$. There is, after all, no reason why two processes of erotic habitualization, one hetero-sexual and one Lesbian, cannot take place side by side without functionally integrating with each other or with a third habitu-alization based on a shared interest in, say, the growing of flowers (or whatever other enterprise might be jointly relevant to an active heterosexual male and an active Lesbian). In other words, three processes of habitualization or incipient institutionalization may occur without their being functionally or logically integrated as social phenomena. The same reason-ing holds if A, B and C are posited as collectivities rather than individuals, regardless of what content their relevances might have. Also, functional or logical integration cannot be assumed *a priori* when habitualization or institutionalization processes are limited to the same individuals or collectivities, rather than to the discrete ones assumed in our example.

Nevertheless, the empirical fact remains that institutions do tend to 'hang together'. If this phenomenon is not to be taken for granted, it must be explained. How can this be done? First, one may argue that *some* relevances will be common to all members of a collectivity. On the other hand, many areas of conduct will be relevant only to certain types. The latter in-volves an incipient differentiation, at least in the way in which these types are assigned some relatively stable meaning. This assignment may be based on pre-social differences, such as sex, or on differences brought about in the course of social inter-action, such as those engendered by the division of labour. For example, only women may be concerned with fertility magic and only hunters may engage in cave painting. Or, only the old men may perform the rain ceremonial and only weapon-makers may sleep with their maternal cousins. In terms of their external social functionality, these several areas of conduct need not be integrated into *one* cohesive system. They can continue to coexist on the basis of segregated per-formances. But while performances can be segregated, mean-ings tend towards at least minimal consistency. As the individual reflects about the successive moments of his experience, he tries to fit their meanings into a consistent biographical framework. This tendency increases as the in-dividual shares with others his meanings and their biographical integration. It is possible that this tendency to integrate meanings is based on a psychological need, which may in turn be physiologically grounded (that is, that there may be a built-in 'need' for cohesion in the psycho-physiological constitution of man). Our argument, however, does not rest on such anthropological assumptions, but rather on the analysis of meaningful reciprocity in processes of institutionalization.

It follows that great care is required in any statements one makes about the 'logic' of institutions. The logic does not reside in the institutions and their external functionalities, but in the way these are treated in reflection about them. Put differently, reflective consciousness superimposes the quality of logic on the institutional order.[30]

Language provides the fundamental superimposition of logic on the objectivated social world. The edifice of legitimations is built upon language and uses language as its principal instrumentality. The 'logic' thus attributed to the institutional order is part of the socially available stock of knowledge and taken for granted as such. Since the well-socialized individual 'knows' that his social world is a consistent whole, he will be constrained to explain both its functioning and malfunctioning in terms of this 'knowledge'. It is very easy, as a result, for the observer of any society to assume that its institutions do indeed function and integrate as they are 'supposed to'.[31]

De facto, then, institutions are integrated. But their integration is not a functional imperative for the social processes that produce them; it is rather brought about in a derivative fashion. Individuals perform discrete institutionalized actions within the context of their biography. This biography is a reflected-upon whole in which the discrete actions are thought of, not as isolated events, but as related parts in a subjectively meaningful universe whose meanings are not specific to the individual, but socially articulated and shared. Only by way of this detour of socially shared universes of meaning do we arrive at the need for institutional integration.

This has far-reaching implications for any analysis of social phenomena. If the integration of an institutional order can be understood only in terms of the 'knowledge' that its members have of it, it follows that the analysis of such 'knowledge' will be essential for an analysis of the institutional order in question. It is important to stress that this does not exclusively or even primarily involve a preoccupation with complex theoretical systems serving as legitimations for the institutional order. Theories also have to be taken into account, of course. But theoretical knowledge is only a small and by no means the most important part of what passes for knowledge in a society. Theoretically sophisticated legitimations appear at particular moments of an institutional history. The primary knowledge about the institutional order is knowledge on the pre-theoretical level. It is the sum total of 'what everybody knows' about a social world, an assemblage of maxims, morals, proverbial nuggets of wisdom, values and beliefs, myths, and so forth, the theoretical integration of which requires considerable intellectual fortitude in itself, as the long line of heroic integrators from Homer to the latest sociological system-builders testifies. On the pre-theoretical level, however, every institution has a body of transmitted recipe knowledge, that is, knowledge that supplies the institutionally appropriate rules of conduct.[32]

Such knowledge constitutes the motivating dynamics of institutionalized conduct. It defines the institutionalized areas of conduct and designates all situations falling within them. It defines and constructs the roles to be played in the context of the institutions in question. *Ipso facto*, it controls and predicts all such conduct. Since this knowledge is socially objectivated *as* knowledge, that is, as a body of generally valid truths about reality, any radical deviance from the institutional order appears as a departure from reality. Such deviance may be designated as moral depravity, mental disease, or just plain ignorance. While these fine distinctions will have obvious consequences for the treatment of the deviant, they all share an inferior cognitive status within the particular social world. In this way, the particular social world becomes the world *tout court*. What is taken for granted as knowledge in the society comes to be coextensive with the knowable, or at any rate provides the framework within which anything not yet known will come to be known in the future. This is the knowledge that is learned in the course of socialization and that mediates the internalization within individual consciousness of the objectivated structures of the social world. Knowledge, in this sense, is at the heart of the fundamental dialectic of society. It 'programmes' the channels in which externalization produces an objective world. It objectifies this world through language and the cognitive apparatus based on language, that is, it orders it into objects to be apprehended as reality.[33] It is internalized again as objectively valid truth in the course of socialization. Knowledge about society is thus a *realization* in the double sense of the word, in the sense of apprehending the objectivated social reality, and in the sense of ongoingly producing this reality.

For example, in the course of the division of labour a body of knowledge is developed that refers to the particular activities involved. In its linguistic basis, this knowledge is already indispensable to the institutional 'programming' of these economic activities. There will be, say, a vocabulary designating the various modes of hunting, the weapons to be employed, the animals that serve as prey, and so on. There will further be a collection of recipes that must be learned if one is to hunt correctly. This knowledge serves as a channelling, controlling force in itself, an indispensable ingredient of the institutionalization of this area of conduct. As the institution of hunting is crystallized and persists in time, the same body of knowledge serves as an objective (and, incidentally, empirically verifiable) description of it. A whole segment of the social world is objectified by this knowledge. There will be an objective 'science' of hunting, corresponding to the objective reality of the hunting economy. The point need not be belaboured that here 'empirical verification' and 'science' are not understood in the sense of modern scientific canons, but rather in the sense of knowledge that may be borne out in experience and that can subsequently become systematically organized as a body of knowledge.

Again, the same body of knowledge is transmitted to the next generation. It is learned as objective truth in the course of socialization and thus internalized as subjective reality. This reality in turn has power to shape the individual. It will produce a specific type of person, namely the hunter, whose identity and biography *as* a hunter have meaning only in a universe constituted by the aforementioned body of knowledge as a whole (say, in a hunters' society) or in part (say, in our own society, in which hunters come together in a sub-universe of their own). In other words, no part of the institutionalization of hunting can exist without the particular knowledge that has been socially produced and objectivated with reference to this activity. To hunt and to be a hunter imply existence in a social world defined and controlled by this body of knowledge. *Mutatis mutandis*, the same applies to any area of institutionalized conduct.

Sedimentation and Tradition

Only a small part of the totality of human experiences is retained in consciousness. The experiences that are so retained become sedimented, that is, they congeal in recollection as recognizable and memorable entities.[34] Unless such sedimentation took place the individual could not make sense of his biography. Intersubjective sedimentation also takes place when several individuals share a common biography, experiences of which become incorporated in a common stock of knowledge. Intersubjective sedimentation can be called truly social only when it has been objectivated in a sign system of one kind or another, that is, when the possibility of reiterated objectification of the shared experiences arises. Only then is it likely that these experiences will be transmitted from one generation to the next, and from one collectivity to another. Theoretically, common activity, without a sign system, could be the basis for transmission. Empirically, this is improbable. An objectively available sign system bestows a status of incipient anonymity on the sedimented experiences by detaching them from their original context of concrete individual biographies and making them generally available to all who share, or may share in the future, in the sign system in question. The experiences thus become readily transmittable.

In principle, any sign system would do. Normally, of course, the decisive sign system is linguistic. Language objectivates the shared experiences and makes them available to all within the linguistic community, thus becoming both the basis and the instrument of the collective stock of knowledge. Furthermore, language provides the means for objectifying new experiences, allowing their incorporation into the already existing stock of knowledge, and it is the most important means by which the objectivated and objectified sedimentations are transmitted in the tradition of the collectivity in question.

For example, only some members of a hunting society have the experience of losing their weapons and being forced to fight a wild animal with their bare hands. This frightening experience, with whatever lessons in bravery, cunning and skill it yields, is firmly sedimented in the consciousness of the individuals who went through it. If the experience is shared by several individuals, it will be sedimented intersubjectively, may perhaps even form a profound bond between these individuals. As this experience is designated and transmitted linguistically, however, it becomes accessible and, perhaps, strongly relevant to individuals who have never gone through it. The linguistic designation (which, in a hunting society, we may imagine to be very precise and elaborate indeed – say, 'lone big kill, with one hand, of male rhinoceros', 'lone big kill, with two hands, of female rhinoceros', and so forth) abstracts the experience from its individual biographical occurrences. It becomes an objective possibility for everyone, or at any rate for everyone within a certain type (say, fully initiated hunters); that is, it becomes anonymous in principle even if it is still associated with the feats of specific individuals. Even to those who do not anticipate the experience in their own future biography (say, women forbidden to hunt), it may be relevant in a derived manner (say, in terms of the desirability of a future husband); in any case it is part of the common stock of knowledge. The objectification of the experience in the language (that is, its transformation into a generally available object of knowledge) then allows its incorporation into a larger body of tradition by way of moral instruction, inspirational poetry, religious allegory and whatnot. Both the experience in the narrower sense and its appendage of wider significations can then be taught to every new generation, or even diffused to an altogether different collectivity (say, an agricultural society that may attach quite different meanings to the whole business).

Language becomes the depository of a large aggregate of collective sedimentations, which can be acquired monothetically, that is, as cohesive wholes and without reconstructing their original process of formation.[35] Since the actual origin of the sedimentations has become unimportant, the tradition might invent quite a different origin without thereby threatening what has been objectivated. In other words, legitimations can succeed each other, from time to time bestowing new meanings on the sedimented experiences of the collectivity in question. The past history of the society can be reinterpreted without necessarily upsetting the institutional order as a result. For instance, in the above example, the 'big kill' may come to be legitimated as a deed of divine figures and any human repetition of it as an imitation of the mythological prototype.

This process underlines all objectivated sedimentations, not only institutionalized actions. It may refer, for instance, to the transmission of typifications of others not directly relevant to specific institutions. For example, others are typified as 'tall' or 'short', 'fat' or 'thin', 'bright' or 'dull', without any particular institutional implications being attached to these typifications. The process, of course, also applies to the transmission of sedimented meanings that meet the previously given specification of institutions. The transmission of the meaning of an institution is based on the social recognition of that institution as a 'permanent' solution to a 'permanent' problem of the given collectivity. Therefore, potential actors of institutionalized actions must be *systematically* acquainted with these meanings. This necessitates some form of 'educational' process. The institutional meanings must be impressed powerfully and unforgettably upon the consciousness of the individual. Since human beings are frequently sluggish and forgetful, there must also be procedures by which these meanings can be reimpressed and rememorized, if necessary by coercive and generally unpleasant means. Furthermore, since human beings are frequently stupid, institutional meanings tend to become simplified in the process of transmission, so that the given collection of institutional 'formulae' can be readily learned and memorized by successive generations. The 'formula' character of institutional meanings ensures their memorability. We have here on the level of sedimented meanings the same processes of routinization and trivialization that we have already noted in the discussion of institutionalization. Again, the stylized form in which heroic feats enter a tradition is a useful illustration.

The objectivated meanings of institutional activity are conceived of as 'knowledge' and transmitted as such. Some of this 'knowledge' is deemed relevant to all, some only to certain types. All transmission requires some sort of social apparatus. That is, some types are designated as transmitters, other types as recipients of the traditional 'knowledge'. The specific character of this apparatus will, of course, vary from society to society. There will also be typified procedures for the passage of the tradition from the knowers to the non-knowers. For example, the technical, magical and moral lore of hunting may be transmitted by maternal uncles to nephews of a certain age, by means of specified procedures of initiation. The typology of knowers and non-knowers, like the 'knowledge' that is supposed to pass between them, is a matter of social definition; both 'knowing' and 'not knowing' refer to what is socially defined as reality, and not to some extra-social criteria of cognitive validity. To put this crudely, maternal uncles do not transmit this particular stock of knowledge because they know it, but they know it (that is, are defined as knowers) *because* they are maternal uncles. If an institutionally designated maternal uncle, for particular reasons, turns out to be incapable of transmitting the knowledge in question, he is no longer a maternal uncle in the full sense of the word, and, indeed, institutional recognition of this status may be withdrawn from him.

Depending on the social span of relevance of a certain type of 'knowledge' and its complexity and importance in a particular collectivity, the 'knowledge' may have to be reaffirmed through symbolic objects (such as fetishes and military emblems), and/or symbolic actions (such as religious or military ritual). In other words, physical objects and actions may be called upon as mnemotechnic aids. All transmission of institutional meanings obviously implies control and legitimation procedures. These are attached to the institutions themselves and administered by the transmitting personnel. It may be stressed again here that no *a priori* consistency, let alone functionality, may be presumed as existing between different institutions and the forms of the transmission of knowledge pertaining to them. The problem of logical coherence arises first on the level of legitimation (where there may be conflict or competition between different legitimations and their administrative personnel), and secondly on the level of socialization (where there may be practical difficulties in the internalization of successive or competing institutional meanings). To return to a previous example, there is no *a priori* reason why institutional meanings that originated in a hunting society should not be diffused to an agricultural society. What is more, these meanings may, to an outside observer, appear to have dubious 'functionality' in the first society at the time of diffusion and no 'functionality' at all in the second. The difficulties that may arise here are connected with the theoretical activities of the legitimators and the practical ones of the 'educators' in the new society. The theoreticians have to satisfy themselves that a hunting goddess is a plausible denizen in an agrarian pantheon and the pedagogues have a problem explaining her mythological activities to children who have never seen a hunt. Legitimating theoreticians tend to have logical aspirations and children tend to be recalcitrant. This, however, is not a problem of abstract logic or technical functionality, but rather of ingenuity on the one hand and credulity on the other – a rather different proposition.

Roles

As we have seen, the origins of any institutional order lie in the typification of one's own and others' performances. This implies that one shares with others specific goals and interlocking phases of performance, and, further, that not only specific actions but forms of action are typified. That is, there will be the recognition not only of a particular actor performing an action of type X, but of type-X action as being performable by *any* actor to whom the relevance structure in question can be plausibly imputed. For example, one may recognize one's brother-in-law engaged in thrashing one's insolent offspring and understand that this particular action is only one instance of a form of action appropriate to other pairs of uncles and nephews, indeed, is a generally available pattern in a matrilocal society. Only if the latter typification prevails will this incident follow a socially taken-for-granted course, with the father discreetly withdrawing from the scene so as not to disturb the legitimate exercise of avuncular authority.

The typification of forms of action requires that these have an objective sense, which in turn requires a linguistic objectification. That is, there will be a vocabulary referring to these forms of action (such as 'nephew-thrashing', which will belong to a much larger linguistic structuring of kinship and its various rights and obligations). In principle, then, an action and its sense can be apprehended apart from individual performances of it and the variable subjective processes associated with them. Both self and other can be apprehended as performers of objective, generally known actions, which are recurrent and repeatable by *any* actor of the appropriate type.

This has very important consequences for self-experience. In the course of action there is an identification of the self with the objective sense of the action; the action that is going on determines, for that moment, the self-apprehension of the actor, and does so in the objective sense that has been socially ascribed to the action. Although there continues to be a marginal awareness of the body and other aspects of the self not directly involved in the action, the actor, for that moment, apprehends himself essentially in identification with the socially objectivated action ('I am now thrashing my nephew' —a taken-for-granted episode in the routine of everyday life). After the action has taken place there is a further important consequence, as the actor reflects about his action. Now a *part* of the self is objectified *as* the performer of this action, with the whole self again becoming relatively disidentified from the performed action. That is, it becomes possible to conceive of the self as having been only partially involved in the action (after all, the man in our example is other things besides being a nephew-thrasher). It is not difficult to see that, as these objectifications accumulate ('nephew-thrasher', 'sister-supporter', 'initiate-warrior', 'rain-dance virtuoso', and so forth), an entire sector of self-consciousness is structured in terms of these objectifications. In other words, a segment of the self is objectified in terms of the socially available typifications. This segment is the truly 'social self', which is subjectively experienced as distinct from and even confronting the self in its totality.[36] This important phenomenon, which allows an internal 'conversation' between the different segments of the self, will be taken up again later when we look at the process by which the socially constructed world is internalized in individual consciousness. For the moment, what is important is the relationship of the phenomenon to the objectively available typifications of conduct.

In sum, the actor identifies with the socially objectivated typifications of conduct *in actu*, but re-establishes distance from them as he reflects about his conduct afterwards. This distance between the actor and his action can be retained in consciousness and projected to future repetitions of the actions. In this way both acting self and acting others are apprehended not as unique individuals, but as *types*. By definition, these types are interchangeable.

We can properly begin to speak of roles when this kind of typification occurs in the context of an objectified stock of knowledge common to a collectivity of actors. Roles are types of actors in such a context.[37] It can readily be seen that the construction of role typologies is a necessary correlate of the institutionalization of conduct. Institutions are embodied in individual experience by means of roles. The roles, objectified linguistically, are an essential ingredient of the objectively available world of any society. By playing roles, the individual participates in a social world. By internalizing these roles, the same world becomes subjectively real to him.

In the common stock of knowledge there are standards of role performance that are accessible to all members of a society, or at least to those who are potential performers of the roles in question. This general accessibility is itself part of the same stock of knowledge; not only are the standards of role X generally known, but it is known *that* these standards are known. Consequently every putative actor of role X can be held responsible for abiding by the standards, which can be taught as part of the institutional tradition and used to verify the credentials of all performers and, by the same token, serve as controls.

The origins of roles lie in the same fundamental process of habitualization and objectivation as the origins of institutions. Roles appear as soon as a common stock of knowledge containing reciprocal typifications of conduct is in process of formation, a process that, as we have seen, is endemic to social interaction and prior to institutionalization proper. The question as to which roles become institutionalized is identical with the question as to which areas of conduct are affected by institutionalization, and may be answered the same way. *All* institutionalized conduct involves roles. Thus roles share in the controlling character of institutionalization. As soon as actors are typified as role performers, their conduct is *ipso facto* susceptible to enforcement. Compliance and non-compliance with socially defined role standards cease to be optional, though, of course, the severity of sanctions may vary from case to case.

The roles *represent* the institutional order.[38] This representation takes place on two levels. First, performance of the role represents itself. For instance, to engage in judging is to represent the role of judge. The judging individual is not acting 'on his own', but *qua* judge. Second, the role represents an entire institutional nexus of conduct. The role of judge stands in relationship to other roles, the totality of which comprises the institution of law. The judge acts as the representative of this institution. Only through such representation in performed roles can the institution manifest itself in actual experience. The institution, with its assemblage of 'programmed' actions, is like the unwritten libretto of a drama. The realization of the drama depends upon the reiterated performances of its prescribed roles by living actors. The actors embody the roles and actualize the drama by representing it on the given stage. Neither drama nor institution exist empirically apart from this recurrent realization. To say, then, that roles represent institutions is to say that roles make it possible for institutions to exist, ever again, as a real presence in the experience of living individuals.

Institutions are also represented in other ways. Their linguistic objectifications, from their simple verbal designations to their incorporation in highly complex symbolizations of reality, also represent them (that is, make them present) in experience. And they may be symbolically represented by physical objects, both natural and artificial. All these representations, however, become 'dead' (that is, bereft of subjective reality) unless they are ongoingly 'brought to life' in actual human conduct. The representation of an institution in and by roles is thus the representation *par excellence*, on which all other representations are dependent. For example, the institution of law is, of course, also represented by legal language, codes of law, theories of jurisprudence and, finally, by the ultimate legitimations of the institution and its norms in ethical, religious or mythological systems of thought. Such man-made phenomena as the awesome paraphernalia that frequently accompany the administration of law, and such natural ones as the clap of thunder that may be taken as the divine verdict in a trial by ordeal and may eventually even become a symbol of ultimate justice, further represent the institution. All these representations, however, derive their continuing significance and even intelligibility from their utilization in human conduct, which here, of course, is conduct typified in the institutional roles of the law.

When individuals begin to reflect upon these matters they face the problem of binding the various representations together in a cohesive whole that will make sense.[39] Any concrete role performance refers to the objective sense of the institution, and thus to the other complementary role performances, and to the sense of the institution as a whole. While the problem of integrating the various representations so involved is solved primarily on the level of legitimation, it is also dealt with in terms of certain roles. *All* roles represent the institutional order in the aforementioned sense. *Some* roles, however, symbolically represent that order in its totality more than others. Such roles are of great strategic importance in a society, since they represent not only this or that institution, but the integration of all institutions in a meaningful world. *Ipso facto*, of course, these roles help in maintaining such integration in the consciousness and conduct of the members of the society, that is, they have a special relationship to the legitimating apparatus of the society. Some roles have no functions *other than* this symbolic representation of the institutional order as an integrated totality, others take on this function from time to time in addition to the less exalted functions they routinely perform. The judge, for instance, may, on occasion, in some particularly important case, represent the total integration of society in this way. The monarch does so all the time and, indeed, in a constitutional monarchy, may have no other function than as a 'living symbol' for all levels of the society, down to the man in the street. Historically, roles that symbolically represent the total institutional order have been most commonly located in political and religious institutions.[40]

More important for our immediate considerations is the character of roles as mediators of specific sectors of the common stock of knowledge. By virtue of the roles he plays the individual is inducted into specific areas of socially objectivated knowledge, not only in the narrower cognitive sense, but also in the sense of the 'knowledge' of norms, values and even emotions. To be a judge obviously involves a knowledge of the law and probably also knowledge of a much wider range of human affairs that are legally relevant. It also involves, however, 'knowledge' of the values and attitudes deemed appropriate for a judge, extending as far as those proverbially deemed appropriate for a judge's wife. The judge must also have appropriate 'knowledge' in the domain of the emotions: he will have to know, for example, when to restrain his feelings of compassion, to mention a not unimportant psychological prerequisite for this role. In this way, each role opens an entrance into a specific sector of the society's total stock of knowledge. To learn a role it is not enough to acquire the routines immediately necessary for its 'outward' performance. One must also be initiated into the various cognitive and even affective layers of the body of knowledge that is directly *and* indirectly appropriate to this role.

This implies a social distribution of knowledge.[41] A society's stock of knowledge is structured in terms of what is generally relevant and what is relevant only to specific roles. This is true of even very simple social situations, such as our previous example of a social situation produced by the ongoing interaction of a man, a bisexual woman and a Lesbian. Here some

94

knowledge is relevant to all three individuals (for instance, knowledge of the procedures necessary to keep this company economically afloat), while other knowledge is relevant only to two of the individuals (the *savoir-faire* of Lesbian or, in the other case, of heterosexual seduction). In other words, the social distribution of knowledge entails a dichotomization in terms of general and role-specific relevance.

Given the historical accumulation of knowledge in a society, we can assume that, because of the division of labour, role-specific knowledge will grow at a faster rate than generally relevant and accessible knowledge. The multiplication of specific tasks brought about by the division of labour requires standardized solutions that can be readily learned and transmitted. These in turn require specialized knowledge of certain situations, and of the means/ends relationships in terms of which the situations are socially defined. In other words, specialists will arise, each of whom will have to know whatever is deemed necessary for the fulfilment of his particular task.

To accumulate role-specific knowledge a society must be so organized that certain individuals can concentrate on their specialities. If in a hunting society certain individuals are to become specialists as swordsmiths, there will have to be provisions to excuse them from the hunting activities that are incumbent on all other adult males. Specialized knowledge of a more elusive kind, such as the knowledge of mystagogues and other intellectuals, requires similar social organization. In all these cases the specialists become administrators of the sectors of the stock of knowledge that have been socially assigned to them.

At the same time, an important part of generally relevant knowledge is the typology of specialists. While the specialists are defined as individuals who know their specialities, everyone must know who the specialists are in case their specialities are needed. The man in the street is not expected to know the intricacies of the magic of inducing fertility or casting evil spells. What he *must* know, however, is which magicians to call upon if the need for either of these services arises. A typology of experts (what contemporary social workers call a referral guide) is thus part of the generally relevant and accessible stock of knowledge, while the knowledge that constitutes expertise is not. The practical difficulties that may arise in certain societies (for instance, when there are competing coteries of experts, or when specialization has become so complicated that the layman gets confused) need not concern us at the moment.

It is thus possible to analyse the relationship between roles and knowledge from two vantage points. Looked at from the perspective of the institutional order, the roles appear as institutional representations and mediations of the institutionally objectivated aggregates of knowledge. Looked at from the perspective of the several roles, each role carries with it a socially defined appendage of knowledge. Both perspectives, of course, point to the same global phenomenon, which is the essential dialectic of society. The first perspective can be summed up in the proposition that society exists only as individuals are conscious of it, the second in the proposition that individual consciousness is socially determined. Narrowing this to the matter of roles, we can say that, on the one hand, the institutional order is real only in so far as it is *realized* in performed roles and that, on the other hand, roles are representative of an institutional order that defines their character (including their appendages of knowledge) and from which they derive their objective sense.

The analysis of roles is of particular importance to the sociology of knowledge because it reveals the mediations between the macroscopic universes of meaning objectivated in a society and the ways by which these universes are subjectively real to individuals. Thus it is possible, for example, to analyse the macroscopic social roots of a religious world view in certain collectivities (classes, say, or ethnic groups, or intellectual coteries), and also to analyse the manner in which this world view is manifested in the consciousness of an individual. The two analyses can be brought together only if one inquires into the ways in which the individual, in his total social activity, relates to the collectivity in question. Such an inquiry will, of necessity, be an exercise in role analysis.[42]

Scope and Modes of Institutionalization   ✳

So far we have discussed institutionalization in terms of essential features that may be taken as sociological constants. Obviously we cannot in this treatise give even an overview of the countless variations in the historical manifestations and combinations of these constants – a task that could be achieved only by writing a universal history from the point of view of sociological theory. There are, however, a number of historical variations in the character of institutions that are so important for concrete sociological analyses that they should be at least briefly discussed. Our focus will, of course, continue to be on the relationship between institutions and knowledge.

In investigating any concrete institutional order, one may ask the following question: What is the scope of institutionalization within the totality of social actions in a given collectivity?˙ In other words, how large is the sector of institutionalized activity as compared with the sector that is left uninstitutionalized?[43] Clearly there is historical variability in this matter, with different societies allowing more or less room for uninstitutionalized actions. An important general consideration is what factors determine a wider as against a narrower scope of institutionalization.

Very formally, the scope of institutionalization depends on the generality of the relevance structures. If many or most relevance structures in a society are generally shared, the scope of institutionalization will be wide. If only few relevance structures are generally shared, the scope of institutionalization will be narrow. In the latter case, there is the further possibility that the institutional order will be highly fragmented, as certain relevance structures are shared by groups within the society but not by the society as a whole.

It may be heuristically useful to think here in terms of ideal–typical extremes. It is possible to conceive of a society in which institutionalization is total. In such a society, *all* problems are common, *all* solutions to these problems are socially objectivated and *all* social actions are institutionalized. The institutional order embraces the totality of social life, which

97

resembles the continuous performance of a complex, highly stylized liturgy. There is no role-specific distribution of knowledge, or nearly none, since all roles are performed within situations of equal relevance to all the actors. This heuristic model of a totally institutionalized society (a fit topic for nightmares, it might be remarked in passing) can be slightly modified by conceiving that all social actions are institutionalized, *but* not only around common problems. While the style of life such a society would impose on its members would be equally rigid, there would be a greater degree of role-specific distribution of knowledge. A number of liturgies would be going on at the same time, so to speak. Needless to say, neither the model of institutional totality nor its modification can be found in history. Actual societies can, however, be considered in terms of their approximation to this extreme type. It is then possible to say that primitive societies approximate the type to a much higher degree than civilized ones.[44] It may even be said that in the development of archaic civilizations there is a progressive movement away from this type.[45]

The opposite extreme would be a society in which there is only *one* common problem, and institutionalization occurs *only* with respect to actions concerned with this problem. In such a society there would be almost no common stock of knowledge. Almost all knowledge would be role-specific. In terms of macroscopic societies, even approximations of this type are historically unavailable. But certain approximations can be found in smaller social formations – for example, in libertarian colonies where *common* concerns are limited to economic arrangements, or in military expeditions consisting of a number of tribal or ethnic units whose only *common* problem is the waging of the war.

Apart from stimulating sociological fantasies, such heuristic fictions are useful only in so far as they help to clarify the conditions that favour approximations to them. The most general condition is the degree of division of labour, with the concomitant differentiation of institutions.[46] Any society in which there is increasing division of labour is moving away from the first extreme type described above. Another general condition, closely related to the previous one, is availability of an economic surplus, which makes it possible for certain individuals or groups to engage in specialized activities not directly concerned with subsistence.[47] These specialized activities, as we have seen, lead to specialization and segmentation in the common stock of knowledge. And the latter makes possible knowledge subjectively detached from *any* social relevance, that is, 'pure theory'.[48] This means that certain individuals are (to return to a previous example) freed from hunting not only to forge weapons but also to fabricate myths. Thus we have the 'theoretical life', with its luxurious proliferation of specialized bodies of knowledge, administered by specialists whose social prestige may actually depend upon their inability to do anything except theorize – which leads to a number of analytic problems to which we shall return later.

Institutionalization is not, however, an irreversible process, despite the fact that institutions, once formed, have a tendency to persist.[49] For a variety of historical reasons, the scope of institutionalized actions may diminish; de-institutionalization may take place in certain areas of social life.[50] For example, the private sphere that has emerged in modern industrial society is considerably de-institutionalized as compared to the public sphere.[51]

A further question, with respect to which institutional orders will vary historically, is: What is the relationship of the various institutions to each other, on the levels of performance and meaning?[52] In the first extreme type discussed above, there is a unity of institutional performances and meanings in each subjective biography. The entire social stock of knowledge is actualized in every individual biography. Everybody *does* everything and *knows* everything. The problem of the integration of meanings (that is, of the meaningful relationship of the various institutions) is an exclusively subjective one. The objective sense of the institutional order presents itself to each individual as given and generally known, socially taken for granted as such. If there is any problem at all, it is because of subjective difficulties the individual may have internalizing the socially agreed-upon meanings.

With increasing deviance from this heuristic model (that is, of course, with all actual societies, though not to the same degree) there will be important modifications in the givenness of the institutional meanings. The first two of these we have already indicated: a segmentation of the institutional order, with only certain types of individuals performing certain actions, and, following that, a social distribution of knowledge, with role-specific knowledge coming to be reserved to certain types. With these developments, however, a new configuration appears on the level of meaning. There will now be an *objective* problem with respect to an encompassing integration of meanings within the entire society. This is an altogether different problem from the merely subjective one of harmonizing the sense one makes of one's biography with the sense ascribed to it by society. The difference is as great as that between producing propaganda that will convince others and producing memoirs that will convince oneself.

In our example of the man/woman/Lesbian triangle we went to some lengths to show that it cannot be assumed *a priori* that different processes of institutionalization will 'hang together'. The relevance structure that is shared by the man and the woman ($A-B$) does not have to be integrated with the one shared by the woman and the Lesbian ($B-C$), or with the one shared by the Lesbian and the man ($C-A$). Discrete institutional processes can continue to coexist without overall integration. We then argued that the empirical fact that institutions *do* hang together, despite the impossibility of assuming this *a priori*, can be accounted for only in reference to the reflective consciousness of individuals who impose a certain logic upon their experience of the several institutions. We can now push this argument one step further by assuming that one of our three individuals (let us assume that it is the man, A) becomes dissatisfied with the lack of symmetry in the situation. This does not imply that the relevances in which he shares ($A-B$ and $C-A$) have changed for him. It is rather the relevance in which he has not previously shared ($B-C$) that now bothers him. This may be because it interferes with his own interests (C spends too much time making love with B and neglects her flower-arranging activities with him), or it may be that he has theoretical ambitions. In any case, he wants to unite the three discrete relevances and their concomitant habitualization processes into a cohesive, meaningful whole – $A-B-C$. How can he do this?

Let us imagine him a religious genius. One day he presents

the other two with a new mythology. The world was created in two stages, the dry land by the creator god copulating with his sister, the sea in an act of mutual masturbation by the latter and a twin goddess. And when the world was thus made, the creator god joined the twin goddess in the great flower dance, and in this way there came to be flora and fauna on the face of the dry land. The existing triangulation of heterosexuality, Lesbianism and flower cultivation is thus nothing less than a human imitation of the archetypal actions of the gods. Not bad? The reader with some background in comparative mythology will have no difficulty finding historical parallels to this cosmogonic vignette. Our man may have more difficulty getting the others to accept his theory. He will have a problem of propaganda. If, however, we assume that B and C have also had practical difficulties in keeping their various projects going, or (less likely) that they are inspired by A's vision of the cosmos, there is a good chance that he will be able to put his scheme over. Once he has succeeded and all three individuals 'know' that their several actions work together for the great society (which is A–B–C), this 'knowledge' will influence what goes on in the situation. For instance, C may be more amenable to budgeting her time in an equitable way between her two major enterprises.

If this extension of our example seems far-fetched, we can bring it closer to home by imagining a secularization process in the consciousness of our religious genius. Mythology no longer seems plausible. The situation has to be explained by social science. This, of course, is very easy. It is evident (to our religious genius turned social scientist, that is) that the two sorts of sexual activity going on in the situation express deep-seated psychological needs of the participants. He 'knows' that to frustrate these needs will lead to 'disfunctional' tensions. On the other hand, it is a fact that our trio sell their flowers for coconuts on the other end of the island. That settles it. Behaviour patterns A–B and B–C are functional in terms of the 'personality system', while C–A is functional in terms of the economic sector of the 'social system'. A–B–C is nothing but the rational outcome of functional integration on the intersystemic level. Again, if A is successful in propagandizing his two girls with *this* theory, their 'knowledge' of the functional imperatives involved in their situation will have certain controlling consequences for their conduct.

Mutatis mutandis, the same argument will hold if we transpose it from the face-to-face idyll of our example to the macro-social level. The segmentation of the institutional order and the concomitant distribution of knowledge will lead to the problem of providing integrative meanings that will encompass the society and provide an overall context of objective sense for the individual's fragmented social experience and knowledge. Furthermore, there will be not only the problem of overall meaningful integration, but also a problem of legitimating the institutional activities of one type of actor *vis-à-vis* other types. We may assume that there is a universe of meaning that bestows objective sense on the activities of warriors, farmers, traders and exorcists. This does not mean that there will be no conflict of interests between these types of actors. Even within the common universe of meaning, the exorcists may have a problem of 'explaining' some of their activities to the warriors, and so forth. The methods of such legitimation again vary historically.[53]

Another consequence of institutional segmentation is the possibility of socially segregated sub-universes of meaning. These result from accentuations of role specialization to the point where role-specific knowledge becomes altogether esoteric as against the common stock of knowledge. Such sub-universes of meaning may or may not be submerged from the common view. In certain cases, not only are the cognitive contents of the sub-universe esoteric, but even the existence of the sub-universe and of the collectivity that sustains it may be a secret. Sub-universes of meaning may be socially structured by various criteria – sex, age, occupation, religious inclination, aesthetic taste, and so on. The chance of sub-universes appearing, of course, increases steadily with progressive division of labour and economic surplus. A society with a subsistence economy can have cognitive segregation between men and women, or between old and young warriors, as in the 'secret societies' common in Africa and among American Indians. It may still be able to afford the esoteric existence of a few priests and magicians. Full-blown sub-universes of meaning, such as characterized, say, Hindu castes, the Chinese literary bureaucracy or the priestly coteries of ancient Egypt, require much more developed solutions of the economic problem.

Like all social edifices of meaning, the sub-universes must be 'carried' by a particular collectivity,[54] that is, by the group that ongoingly produces the meanings in question and within which these meanings have objective reality. Conflict or competition may exist between such groups. On the simplest level, there may be conflict over the allocation of surplus resources to the specialists in question, for example, over exemption from productive labour. Who is to be officially exempt, *all* medicine men, or only those who perform services in the household of the chief? Or, who is to receive a fixed stipend from the authorities, those who cure the sick with herbs or those who do it by going into a trance? Such social conflicts are readily translated into conflicts between rival schools of thought, each seeking to establish itself and to discredit if not liquidate the competitive body of knowledge. In contemporary society, we continue to have such conflicts (socio-economic as well as cognitive) between orthodox medicine and such rivals as chiropractice, homeopathy or Christian Science. In advanced industrial societies, with their immense economic surplus allowing large numbers of individuals to devote themselves full-time to even the obscurest pursuits, pluralistic competition between sub-universes of meaning of every conceivable sort becomes the normal state of affairs.[55]

With the establishment of sub-universes of meaning a variety of perspectives on the total society emerges, each viewing the latter from the angle of one sub-universe. The chiropractor has a different angle on society than the medical school professor, the poet than the business man, the Jew than the Gentile, and so on. It goes without saying that this multiplication of perspectives greatly increases the problem of establishing a stable symbolic canopy for the *entire* society. Each perspective, with whatever appendages of theories or even *Weltanschauungen*, will be related to the concrete social interests of the group that holds it. This does *not* mean, however, that the various perspectives, let alone the theories or *Weltanschauungen*, are nothing but mechanical reflections of the social interests. Especially on the theoretical level it is quite possible for knowledge to attain a great deal of detachment from the biographical and social interests of the knower. Thus there may be tangible social reasons why Jews have become preoccupied with certain scientific enterprises, but it is impossible to predict scientific positions in terms of their being held by Jews or non-Jews. In other words, the scientific universe of meaning is capable of attaining a good deal of autonomy as against its own social base. Theoretically, though in practice there will be great variations, this holds with any body of knowledge, even with cognitive perspectives on society.

What is more, a body of knowledge, once it is raised to the level of a relatively autonomous sub-universe of meaning, has the capacity to act back upon the collectivity that has produced it. For instance, Jews may become social scientists because they have special problems in society *as* Jews. But once they have been initiated into the social-scientific universe of discourse, they may not only look upon society from an angle that is no longer distinctively Jewish, but even their social activities *as* Jews may change as a result of their newly acquired social-scientific perspectives. The extent of such detachment of knowledge from its existential origins depends upon a considerable number of historical variables (such as the urgency of the social interests involved, the degree of theoretical refinement of the knowledge in question, the social relevance or irrelevance of the latter, and others). The important principle for our general considerations is that the relationship between knowledge and its social base is a dialectical one, that is, knowledge is a social product *and* knowledge is a factor in social change.[56] This principle of the dialectic between social production and the objectivated world that is its product has already been explicated; it is especially important to keep it in mind in any analysis of concrete subuniverses of meaning.

The increasing number and complexity of sub-universes make them increasingly inaccessible to outsiders. They become esoteric enclaves, 'hermetically sealed' (in the sense classically associated with the Hermetic *corpus* of secret lore) to all but those who have been properly initiated into their mysteries. The increasing autonomy of sub-universes makes for special problems of legitimation *vis-à-vis* both outsiders and insiders. The outsiders have to be *kept out*, sometimes even kept ignorant of the existence of the sub-universe. If, however, they are not so ignorant, and if the sub-universe requires various special privileges and recognitions from the larger society, there is the problem of keeping out the outsiders and at the same time having them acknowledge the legitimacy of this procedure. This is done through various techniques of intimidation, rational and irrational propaganda (appealing to the outsiders' interests and to their emotions), mystification and, generally, the manipulation of prestige symbols. The insiders, on the other hand, have to be *kept in*. This requires the development of both practical and theoretical procedures by which the temptation to escape from the sub-universe can be checked. We shall look at some of the details of this double problem of legitimation later. An illustration may serve for the moment. It is not enough to set up an esoteric sub-universe of medicine. The lay public must be convinced that this is right and beneficial, and the medical fraternity must be held to the standards of the sub-universe. Thus the general population is intimidated by images of the physical doom that follows 'going against doctor's advice'; it is persuaded *not* to do so by the pragmatic benefits of compliance, and by its own horror of illness and death. To underline its authority the medical profession shrouds itself in the age-old symbols of power and mystery, from outlandish costume to incomprehensible language, all of which, of course, are legitimated to the public and to itself in pragmatic terms. Meanwhile the fully accredited inhabitants of the medical world are kept from 'quackery' (that is, from stepping outside the medical sub-universe in thought or action) not only by the powerful external controls available to the profession, but by a whole body of professional knowledge that offers them 'scientific proof' of the folly and even wickedness of such deviance. In other words, an entire legitimating machinery is at work so that laymen will *remain* laymen, and doctors doctors, and (if at all possible) that both will do so happily.

Special problems arise as a result of differential rates of change of institutions and sub-universes.[57] This makes more difficult both the overall legitimation of the institutional order and the specific legitimations of particular institutions or sub-universes. A feudal society with a modern army, a landed aristocracy having to exist under conditions of industrial capitalism, a traditional religion forced to cope with the popularization of a scientific world view, the coexistence in one society of the theory of relativity and astrology – our contemporary experience is so full of examples of this sort that it is unnecessary to belabour the point. Suffice it to say that, under such conditions, the work of the several legitimators becomes especially strenuous.

A final question of great theoretical interest arising from the historical variability of institutionalization has to do with the manner in which the institutional order is objectified: To what extent is an institutional order, or any part of it, apprehended as a non-human facticity? This is the question of the reification of social reality.[58]

Reification is the apprehension of human phenomena as if they were things, that is, in non-human or possibly suprahuman terms. Another way of saying this is that reification is the apprehension of the products of human activity *as if* they were something other than human products – such as facts of nature, results of cosmic laws, or manifestations of divine will. Reification implies that man is capable of forgetting his own authorship of the human world, and, further, that the dialectic between man, the producer, and his products is lost to consciousness. The reified world is, by definition, a dehumanized world. It is experienced by man as a strange facticity, an *opus alienum* over which he has no control rather than as the *opus proprium* of his own productive activity.

It will be clear from our previous discussion of objectivation that, as soon as an objective social world is established, the possibility of reification is never far away.[59] The objectivity of the social world means that it confronts man as something outside of himself. The decisive question is whether he still retains the awareness that, however objectivated, the social world was made by men – and, therefore, can be remade by them. In other words, reification can be described as an extreme step in the process of objectivation, whereby the objectivated world loses its comprehensibility as a human enterprise and becomes fixated as a non-human, non-humanizable, inert facticity.[60] Typically, the real relationship between man and his world is reversed in consciousness. Man, the producer of a world, is apprehended as its product, and human activity as an epiphenomenon of non-human processes. Human meanings are no longer understood as world-producing but as being, in their turn, products of the 'nature of things'. It must be emphasized that reification is a modality of consciousness, more precisely, a modality of man's objectification of the human world. Even while apprehending the world in reified terms, man continues to produce it. That is, man is capable paradoxically of producing a reality that denies him.[61]

Reification is possible on both the pre-theoretical and theoretical levels of consciousness. Complex theoretical systems can be described as reifications, though presumably they have their roots in pre-theoretical reifications established in this or that social situation. Thus it would be an error to limit the concept of reification to the mental constructions of intellectuals. Reification exists in the consciousness of the man in the street and, indeed, the latter presence is more practically significant. It would also be a mistake to look at reification as a perversion of an originally non-reified apprehension of the social world, a sort of cognitive fall from grace. On the contrary, the available ethnological and psychological evidence seems to indicate the opposite, namely, that the original apprehension of the social world is highly reified both phylogenetically and ontogenetically.[62] This implies that an apprehension of reification *as* a modality of consciousness is dependent upon an at least relative *de*-reification of consciousness, which is a comparatively late development in history and in any individual biography.

Both the institutional order as a whole and segments of it may be apprehended in reified terms. For example, the entire order of society may be conceived of as of a microcosm reflecting the macrocosm of the total universe as made by the gods. Whatever happens 'here below' is but a pale reflection of what takes place 'up above'.[63] Particular institutions may be apprehended in similar ways. The basic 'recipe' for the reification of institutions is to bestow on them an ontological status independent of human activity and signification. Specific reifications are variations on this general theme. Marriage, for instance, may be reified as an imitation of divine acts of creativity, as a universal mandate of natural laws, as the necessary consequence of biological or psychological forces, or, for that matter, as a functional imperative of the social system. What all these reifications have in common is their obfuscation of marriage as an ongoing human production. As can be readily seen in this example, the reification may occur both theoretically and pre-theoretically. Thus the mystagogue can concoct a highly sophisticated theory reaching out from the concrete human event to the farthest corners of the divine cosmos, but an illiterate peasant couple being married may apprehend the event with a similarly reifying shudder of metaphysical dread. Through reification, the world of institutions appears to merge with the world of nature. It becomes necessity and fate, and is lived through as such, happily *or* unhappily as the case may be.

Roles may be reified in the same manner as institutions. The sector of self-consciousness that has been objectified in the role is then also apprehended as an inevitable fate, for which the individual may disclaim responsibility. The paradigmatic formula for this kind of reification is the statement 'I have no choice in the matter, I have to act this way because of my position' – as husband, father, general, archbishop, chairman of the board, gangster or hangman, as the case may be. This means that the reification of roles narrows the subjective distance that the individual may establish between himself and his role-playing. The distance implied in all objectification remains, of course, but the distance brought about by disidentification shrinks to the vanishing point. Finally, identity itself (the total self, if one prefers) may be reified, both one's own and that of others. There is then a total identification of the individual with his socially assigned typifications. He is apprehended as *nothing but* that type. This apprehension may be positively or negatively accented in terms of values or emotions. The identification of 'Jew' may be equally reifying for the anti-Semite and the Jew himself, except that the latter will accent the identification positively and the former negatively. Both reifications bestow an ontological and total status on a typification that is humanly produced and that, even as it is internalized, objectifies but a segment of the self.[64] Once more, such reifications may range from the pre-theoretical level of 'what everybody knows about Jews' to the most complex theories of Jewishness as a manifestation of biology ('Jewish blood'), psychology ('the Jewish soul') or metaphysics ('the mystery of Israel').

The analysis of reification is important because it serves as a standing corrective to the reifying propensities of theoretical thought in general and sociological thought in particular. It is particularly important for the sociology of knowledge, because it prevents it from falling into an undialectical conception of the relationship between what men do and what they think. The historical and empirical application of the sociology of knowledge must take special note of the social circumstances that favour de-reification – such as the overall collapse of institutional orders, the contact between previously segregated societies, and the important phenomenon of social marginality.[65] These problems, however, exceed the framework of our present considerations.

2. Legitimation

Origins of Symbolic Universes

Legitimation as a process is best described as a 'second-order' objectivation of meaning. Legitimation produces new meanings that serve to integrate the meanings already attached to disparate institutional processes. The function of legitimation is to make objectively available and subjectively plausible the 'first-order' objectivations that have been institutionalized.[66] While we define legitimation by this function, regardless of the specific motives inspiring any particular legitimating process, it should be added that 'integration', in one form or another, is also the typical purpose motivating the legitimators.

Integration and, correspondingly, the question of subjective plausibility refer to two levels. First, the totality of the institutional order should make sense, concurrently, to the participants in different institutional processes. Here the question of plausibility refers to the subjective recognition of an overall sense 'behind' the situationally predominant but only partial institutionalized motives of one's own as well as of one's fellowmen – as in the relation of the chief and the priest, or the father and the military commander, or even, in the case of one and the same individual, of the father, who is also the military commander of his son, to himself. This, then, is a 'horizontal' level of integration and plausibility, relating the total institutional order to several individuals participating in it in several roles, or to several partial institutional processes in which a single individual may participate at any given time.

Second, the totality of the individual's life, the successive passing through various orders of the institutional order, must be made subjectively meaningful. In other words, the individual biography, in its several, successive, institutionally predefined phases, must be endowed with a meaning that makes the whole subjectively plausible. A 'vertical' level within the life span of single individuals must, therefore, be added to the 'horizontal' level of integration and subjective plausibility of the institutional order.

As we have argued before, legitimation is not necessary in the first phase of institutionalization, when the institution is simply a fact that requires no further support either inter-subjectively or biographically; it is self-evident to all concerned. The problem of legitimation inevitably arises when the objectivations of the (now historic) institutional order are to be transmitted to a new generation. At that point, as we have seen, the self-evident character of the institutions can no longer be maintained by means of the individual's own recollection and habitualization. The unity of history and biography is broken. In order to restore it, and thus to make intelligible both aspects of it, there must be 'explanations' and justifications of the salient elements of the institutional tradition. Legitimation is this process of 'explaining' and justifying.[67]

Legitimation 'explains' the institutional order by ascribing cognitive validity to its objectivated meanings. Legitimation justifies the institutional order by giving a normative dignity to its practical imperatives. It is important to understand that legitimation has a cognitive as well as a normative element. In other words, legitimation is not just a matter of 'values'. It always implies 'knowledge' as well. For example, a kinship structure is not legitimated merely by the ethics of its particular incest taboos. There must first be 'knowledge' of the roles that define *both* 'right' *and* 'wrong' actions within the structure. The individual, say, may not marry within his clan. But he must first 'know' himself *as* a member of this clan. This 'knowledge' comes to him through a tradition that 'explains' what clans are in general and what his clan is in particular. Such 'explanations' (which typically constitute a 'history' and a 'sociology' of the collectivity in question, and which in the case of incest taboos probably contain an 'anthropology' as well) are as much legitimating instruments as ethical elements of the tradition. Legitimation not only tells the individual why he *should* perform one action and not another; it also tells him why things *are* what they are. In other words, 'knowledge' precedes 'values' in the legitimation of institutions.

It is possible to distinguish analytically between different levels of legitimation (empirically, of course, these levels overlap). Incipient legitimation is present as soon as a system of linguistic objectifications of human experience is transmitted. For example, the transmission of a kinship vocabulary *ipso facto* legitimates the kinship structure. The fundamental legitimating 'explanations' are, so to speak, built into the vocabulary. Thus a child learns that another child *is* a 'cousin', a piece of information that immediately and inherently legitimates the conduct with regard to 'cousins' that is learned along with the designation. To this first level of incipient legitimation belong all the simple traditional affirmations to the effect that 'This is how things are done' – the earliest and generally effective responses to a child's questions of 'Why?' This level, of course, is pre-theoretical. But it is the foundation of self-evident 'knowledge' on which all subsequent theories must rest – and, conversely, which they must attain if they are to become incorporated in tradition.

The second level of legitimation contains theoretical propositions in a rudimentary form. Here may be found various explanatory schemes relating sets of objective meanings. These schemes are highly pragmatic, directly related to concrete actions. Proverbs, moral maxims and wise sayings are common on this level. Here, too, belong legends and folk tales, frequently transmitted in poetic forms. Thus the child learns such adages as 'He who steals from his cousin gets warts on his hands' or 'Go when your wife cries, but *run* when your cousin calls for you'. Or he may be inspired by the 'Song of the Loyal Cousins Who Went Hunting Together' and frightened out of his wits by the 'Dirge for Two Cousins Who Fornicated'.

The third level of legitimation contains explicit theories by which an institutional sector is legitimated in terms of a differentiated body of knowledge. Such legitimations provide fairly comprehensive frames of reference for the respective sectors of institutionalized conduct. Because of their complexity and differentiation, they are frequently entrusted to specialized personnel who transmit them through formalized initiation procedures. Thus there may be an elaborate economic theory of 'cousinhood', its rights, obligations and standard operating procedures. This lore is administered by the old men of the clan, perhaps assigned to them after their own economic usefulness is at an end. The old men initiate the adolescents into this higher economics in the course of the puberty rites and appear as experts whenever there are problems of application. If we assume that the old men have no other tasks assigned to them, it is likely that they will spin out the theories in question among themselves even if there are no problems of application, or, more accurately, they will invent such problems in the course of their theorizing. In other words, with the development of specialized legitimating theories and their administration by full-time legitimators, legitimation begins to go beyond pragmatic application and to become 'pure theory'. With this step, the sphere of legitimations begins to attain a measure of autonomy *vis-à-vis* the legitimated institutions and eventually may generate its own institutional processes.[68] In our example, the 'science of cousinhood' may begin to have a life of its own quite independent of the activities of merely 'lay' cousins, and the body of 'scientists' may set up its own institutional processes over against the institutions that the 'science' was originally meant to legitimate. We may imagine an ironic culmination of this development when the word 'cousin' no longer applies to a kinship role but to the holder of a degree in the hierarchy of 'cousinhood' specialists.

Symbolic universes constitute the fourth level of legitimation. These are bodies of theoretical tradition that integrate different provinces of meaning and encompass the institutional order in a symbolic totality,[69] using the term 'symbolic' in the way we have previously defined. To reiterate, symbolic processes are processes of signification that refer to realities other than those of everyday experience. It may be readily seen how the symbolic sphere relates to the most comprehensive level of legitimation. The sphere of pragmatic application is transcended once and for all. Legitimation now takes place by means of symbolic totalities that cannot be experienced in everyday life at all – except, of course, in so far as one might speak of 'theoretical experience' (strictly speaking, a misnomer, to be used heuristically if at all). This level of legitimation is further distinguished from the preceding one by its scope of meaningful integration. Already on the preceding level it is possible to find a high degree of integration of particular provinces of meaning and discrete processes of institutionalized conduct. Now, however, *all* the sectors of the institutional order are integrated in an all-embracing frame of reference, which now constitutes a universe in the literal sense of the word, because *all* human experience can now be conceived of as taking place *within* it.

The symbolic universe is conceived of as the matrix of *all* socially objectivated and subjectively real meanings; the entire historic society and the entire biography of the individual are seen as events taking place *within* this universe. What is particularly important, the marginal situations of the life of the individual (marginal, that is, in not being included in the reality of everyday existence in society) are also encompassed by the symbolic universe.[70] Such situations are experienced in dreams and fantasies as provinces of meaning detached from everyday life, and endowed with a peculiar reality of their own. Within the symbolic universe these detached realms of reality are integrated within a meaningful totality that 'explains', perhaps also justifies them (for instance, dreams may be 'explained' by a psychological theory, both 'explained' *and* justified by a theory of metempsychosis, and either theory will be grounded in a much more comprehensive universe – a 'scientific' one, say, as against a 'metaphysical' one). The symbolic universe is, of course, constructed by means of social objectivations. Yet its meaning-bestowing capacity far exceeds the domain of social life, so that the individual may 'locate' himself within it even in his most solitary experiences.

On this level of legitimation, the reflective integration of discrete institutional processes reaches its ultimate fulfilment. A whole world is created. All the lesser legitimating theories are viewed as special perspectives on phenomena that are aspects of this world. Institutional roles become modes of participation in a universe that transcends *and* includes the institutional order. In our previous example, the 'science of cousinhood' is only a part of a much wider body of theory, which, almost certainly, will contain a general theory of the cosmos and a general theory of man. The ultimate legitimation for 'correct' actions in the kinship structure will then be their 'location' within a cosmological and anthropological frame of reference. Incest, for instance, will attain its ultimate negative sanction as an offence against the divine order of the cosmos and against the divinely established nature of man. So may economic misbehaviour, or any other deviance from the institutional norms. The limits of such ultimate legitimation are, in principle, coextensive with the limits of theoretical ambition and ingenuity on the part of the legitimators, the officially accredited definers of reality. In practice, of course, there will be variations in the degree of precision with which particular segments of the institutional order are placed in a cosmic context. Again, these variations may be due to particular pragmatic problems on which the legitimators are consulted, or they may be the result of autonomous developments in the theoretical fancy of the cosmological experts.

The crystallization of symbolic universes follows the previously discussed processes of objectivation, sedimentation and accumulation of knowledge. That is, symbolic universes are social products with a history. If one is to understand their meaning, one has to understand the history of their production. This is all the more important because these products of human consciousness, by their very nature, present themselves as full-blown and inevitable totalities.

We may now inquire further about the manner in which symbolic universes operate to legitimate individual biography and the institutional order. The operation is essentially the same in both cases. It is nomic, or ordering, in character.[71]

The symbolic universe provides order for the subjective apprehension of biographical experience. Experiences belonging to different spheres of reality are integrated by incorporation in the same, overarching universe of meaning. For example, the symbolic universe determines the significance of dreams within the reality of everyday life, re-establishing in each instance the paramount status of the latter and mitigating the shock that accompanies the passage from one reality to another.[72] The provinces of meaning that would otherwise remain unintelligible enclaves within the reality of everyday life are thus ordered in terms of a hierarchy of realities, *ipso facto* becoming intelligible and less terrifying. This integration of the realities of marginal situations within the paramount reality of everyday life is of great importance, because these situations constitute the most acute threat to taken-for-granted, routinized existence in society. If one conceives of the latter as the 'daylight side' of human life, then the marginal situations constitute a 'night side' that keeps lurking ominously on the periphery of everyday consciousness. Just because the 'night side' has its own reality, often enough of a sinister kind, it is a constant threat to the taken-for-granted, matter-of-fact, 'sane' reality of life in society. The thought keeps suggesting itself (the 'insane' thought *par excellence*) that, perhaps, the bright reality of everyday life is but an illusion, to be swallowed up at any moment by the howling nightmares of the other, the night-side reality. Such thoughts of madness and terror are contained by ordering all conceivable realities within the same symbolic universe that encompasses the reality of everyday life – to wit, ordering them in such a way that the latter reality retains its paramount, definitive (if one wishes, its 'most real') quality.

This nomic function of the symbolic universe for individual experience may be described quite simply by saying that it 'puts everything in its right place'. What is more, whenever one strays from the consciousness of this order (that is, when one finds oneself in the marginal situations of experience), the symbolic universe allows one 'to return to reality' – namely, to the reality of everyday life. Since this is, of course, the sphere to which all forms of institutional conduct and roles belong, the symbolic universe provides the ultimate legitimation of the institutional order by bestowing upon it the primacy in the hierarchy of human experience.

Apart from this crucially important integration of marginal realities, the symbolic universe provides the highest level of integration for the discrepant meanings actualized *within* everyday life in society. We have seen how meaningful integration of discrete sectors of institutionalized conduct takes place by means of reflection, both pre-theoretically and theoretically. Such meaningful integration does not presuppose the positing of a symbolic universe *ab initio*. It can take place without recourse to symbolic processes, that is, without transcending the realities of everyday experience. However, once the symbolic universe is posited, discrepant sectors of everyday life can be integrated by direct reference to the symbolic universe. For example, discrepancies between the meaning of playing the role of cousin and playing the role of landowner *can* be integrated without reference to a general mythology. But if a general mythological *Weltanschauung* is operative, it can be directly applied to the discrepancy in everyday life. To throw a cousin off a plot of land may then be not only bad economics or bad morals (negative sanctions that need not be extended to cosmic dimensions); it may be understood as a violation of the divinely constituted order of the universe. In this way, the symbolic universe orders and thereby legitimates everyday roles, priorities, and operating procedures by placing them *sub specie universi*, that is, in the context of the most general frame of reference conceivable. Within the same context even the most trivial transactions of everyday life may come to be imbued with profound significance. It can be readily seen how this procedure provides powerful legitimation for the institutional order as a whole as well as for particular sectors of it.

The symbolic universe also makes possible the ordering of the different phases of biography. In primitive societies the rites of passage represent this nomic function in pristine form. The periodization of biography is symbolized at each stage with reference to the totality of human meanings. To be a child, to be an adolescent, to be an adult, and so forth – each of these biographical phases is legitimated as a mode of being in the symbolic universe (most often, as a particular mode of relating to the world of the gods). We need not belabour the obvious point that such symbolization is conducive to feelings of security and belonging. It would be a mistake, however, to think here only of primitive societies. A modern psychological theory of personality development can fulfil the same function. In both cases, the individual passing from one biographical phase to another can view himself as repeating a sequence that is given in the 'nature of things', or in his own 'nature'. That is, he can reassure himself that he is living 'correctly'. The 'correctness' of his life programme is thus legitimated on the highest level of generality. As the individual looks back upon his past life, his biography is intelligible to him in these terms. As he projects himself into the future, he may conceive of his biography as unfolding within a universe whose ultimate coordinates are known.

The same legitimating function pertains to the 'correctness' of the individual's subjective identity. By the very nature of socialization, subjective identity is a precarious entity.[73] It is dependent upon the individual's relations with significant others, who may change or disappear. The precariousness is further increased by self-experiences in the afore-mentioned marginal situations. The 'sane' apprehension of oneself as possessor of a definite, stable and socially recognized identity is continually threatened by the 'surrealistic' metamorphoses of dreams and fantasies, even if it remains relatively consistent in everyday social interaction. Identity is ultimately legitimated by placing it within the context of a symbolic universe. Mythologically speaking, the individual's 'real' name is the one given to him by his god. The individual may thus 'know who he is' by anchoring his identity in a cosmic reality protected from both the contingencies of socialization and the malevolent self-transformations of marginal experience. Even if his neighbours do not know who he is, and even if he himself may fo·get in the throes of nightmare, he can reassure himself that his 'true self' is an ultimately real entity in an ultimately real universe. The gods know – or psychiatric science – or the party. In other words, the *realissimum* of identity need not be legitimated by being known at all times by the individual; it is enough, for purposes of legitimation, that it is *knowable*. Since the identity that is known or knowable by the gods, by psychiatry, or by the party is at the same time the identity that is assigned the status of paramount reality, legitimation again integrates all conceivable transformations of identity with the identity whose reality is grounded in everyday life in society. Once more, the symbolic universe establishes a hierarchy, from the 'most real' to the most fugitive self-apprehensions of identity. This means that the individual can live in society with some assurance that he *really* is what he considers himself to be as he plays his routine social roles, in broad daylight and under the eyes of significant others.

A strategic legitimating function of symbolic universes for individual biography is the 'location' of death. The experience of the death of others and, subsequently, the anticipation of one's own death posit the marginal situation *par excellence* for the individual.[74] Needless to elaborate, death also posits the most terrifying threat to the taken-for-granted realities of everyday life. The integration of death within the paramount reality of social existence is, therefore, of the greatest importance for any institutional order. This legitimation of death is, consequently, one of the most important fruits of symbolic universes. Whether it is done with or without recourse to mythological, religious or metaphysical interpretations of reality is not the essential question here. The modern atheist, for instance, who bestows meaning upon death in terms of a *Weltanschauung* of progressive evolution or of revolutionary history also does so by integrating death with a reality-spanning symbolic universe. All legitimations of death must carry out the same essential task – they must enable the individual to go on living in society after the death of significant others and to anticipate his own death with, at the very least, terror sufficiently mitigated so as not to paralyse the continued performance of the routines of everyday life. It may readily be seen that such legitimation is difficult to achieve, short of integrating the phenomenon of death within a symbolic universe. Such legitimation, then, provides the individual with a recipe for a 'correct death'. Optimally, this recipe will retain its plausibility when his own death is imminent and will allow him, indeed, to 'die correctly'.

It is in the legitimation of death that the transcending potency of symbolic universes manifests itself most clearly, and the fundamental terror-assuaging character of the ultimate legitimations of the paramount reality of everyday life is revealed. The primacy of the social objectivations of everyday life can retain its subjective plausibility only if it is constantly protected against terror. On the level of meaning, the institutional order represents a shield against terror. To be anomic, therefore, means to be deprived of this shield and to be exposed, alone, to the onslaught of nightmare. While the horror of aloneness is probably already given in the constitutional sociality of man, it manifests itself on the level of meaning in man's incapacity to sustain a meaningful existence in isolation from the nomic constructions of society. The symbolic universe shelters the individual from ultimate terror by bestowing ultimate legitimation upon the protective structures of the institutional order.[75]

Very much the same may be said about the social (as against the just discussed individual) significance of symbolic universes. They are sheltering canopies over the institutional order as well as over individual biography. They also provide the delimitation of social reality; that is, they set the limits of what is relevant in terms of social interaction. One extreme possibility of this, sometimes approximated in primitive societies, is the definition of *everything* as social reality; even inorganic matter is dealt with in social terms. A narrower, and more common, delimitation includes only the organic or animal worlds. The symbolic universe assigns ranks to various phenomena in a hierarchy of being, defining the range of the social within this hierarchy.[76] Needless to say, such ranks are also assigned to different types of men, and it frequently happens that broad categories of such types (sometimes *everyone* outside the collectivity in question) are defined as other than or less than human. This is commonly expressed linguistically (in the extreme case, with the name of the collectivity being equivalent to the term 'human'). This is not too rare, even in civilized societies. For example, the symbolic universe of traditional India assigned a status to the outcastes that was closer to that of animals than to the human status of the upper castes (an operation ultimately legitimated in the theory of *karma-samsara*, which embraced *all* beings, human or otherwise), and as recently as the Spanish conquests in America it was possible for the Spaniards to conceive of the Indians as belonging to a different species (*this* operation being legitimated in a less comprehensive manner by a theory that 'proved' that the Indians could not be descended from Adam and Eve).

The symbolic universe also orders history. It locates all collective events in a cohesive unity that includes past, present and future. With regard to the past, it establishes a 'memory' that is shared by all the individuals socialized within the collectivity.[77] With regard to the future, it establishes a common frame of reference for the projection of individual actions. Thus the symbolic universe links men with their predecessors and their successors in a meaningful totality,[78] serving to transcend the finitude of individual existence and bestowing meaning upon the individual's death. All the members of a society can now conceive of themselves as *belonging* to a meaningful universe, which was there before they were born and will be there after they die. The empirical community is transposed on to a cosmic plane and made majestically independent of the vicissitudes of individual existence.[79]

As we have already observed, the symbolic universe provides a comprehensive integration of *all* discrete institutional processes. The entire society now makes sense. Particular institutions and roles are legitimated by locating them in a comprehensively meaningful world. For example, the political order is legitimated by reference to a cosmic order of power and justice, and political roles are legitimated as representations of these cosmic principles. The institution of divine kingship in archaic civilizations is an excellent illustration of the manner in which this kind of ultimate legitimation operates. It is important, however, to understand that the institutional order, like the order of individual biography, is continually threatened by the presence of realities that are meaningless in *its* terms. The legitimation of the institutional order is also faced with the ongoing necessity of keeping chaos at bay. *All* social reality is precarious. *All* societies are constructions in the face of chaos. The constant possibility of anomic terror is actualized whenever the legitimations that obscure the precariousness are threatened or collapse. The dread that accompanies the death of a king, especially if it occurs with sudden violence, expresses this terror. Over and beyond emotions of sympathy or pragmatic political concerns, the death of a king under such circumstances brings the terror of chaos to conscious proximity. The popular reaction to the assassination of President Kennedy is a potent illustration. It may readily be understood why such events have to be followed at once with the most solemn reaffirmations of the continuing reality of the sheltering symbols.

The origins of a symbolic universe have their roots in the constitution of man. If man in society is a world-constructor, this is made possible by his constitutionally given world-openness, which already implies the conflict between order and chaos. Human existence is, *ab initio*, an ongoing externalization. As man externalizes himself, he constructs the world *into* which he externalizes himself. In the process of externalization, he projects his own meanings into reality. Symbolic universes, which proclaim that *all* reality is humanly meaningful and call upon the *entire* cosmos to signify the validity of human existence, constitute the furthest reaches of this projection.[80]

Conceptual Machineries of Universe-Maintenance ❊

Considered as a cognitive construction, the symbolic universe is theoretical. It originates in processes of subjective reflection, which, upon social objectivation, lead to the establishment of explicit links between the significant themes that have their roots in the several institutions. In this sense, the theoretical character of symbolic universes is indubitable, no matter how unsystematic or illogical such a universe may seem to an 'unsympathetic' outsider. However, one may and typically does live naïvely within a symbolic universe. Whereas the establishment of a symbolic universe presupposes theoretical reflection on the part of somebody (to whom the world or, more specifically, the institutional order appeared problematic), everybody may 'inhabit' that universe in a taken-for-granted attitude. If the institutional order is to be taken for granted in its totality as a meaningful whole, it must be legitimated by 'placement' in a symbolic universe. But, other things being equal, this universe itself does not require further legitimation. To begin with, it was the institutional order, not the symbolic universe, that appeared problematic and to which, consequently, theorizing was addressed. For example, returning to the previous illustration of kinship legitimation, once the institution of cousinship is 'located' in a cosmos of mythological cousins, it is no longer a simple matter of social fact without any 'additional' significance. The mythology itself, however, may be held to naïvely without theoretical reflection about *it*.

Only after a symbolic universe is objectivated as a 'first'

product of theoretical thought does the possibility of systematic reflection about the nature of that universe arise. Whereas the symbolic universe legitimates the institutional order on the highest level of generality, theorizing about the symbolic universe may be described as, so to speak, legitimation to the second degree. All legitimations, from the simplest pre-theoretical legitimations of discrete institutionalized meanings to the cosmic establishments of symbolic universes, may, in turn, be described as machineries of universe-maintenance. These, it will readily be seen, require a good deal of conceptual sophistication from the beginning.

Obviously there are difficulties in drawing firm lines between 'naïve' and 'sophisticated' in concrete instances. The analytic distinction, however, is useful even in such instances, because it draws attention to the question of the extent to which a symbolic universe is taken for granted. In this respect, of course, the analytic problem is similar to the one we have already encountered in our discussion of legitimation. There are various levels of the legitimation of symbolic universes just as there are of the legitimation of institutions, except that the former cannot be said to descend to the pre-theoretical level, for the obvious reason that a symbolic universe is itself a theoretical phenomenon and remains so even if naïvely held to.

As in the case of institutions, the question arises as to the circumstances under which it becomes necessary to legitimate symbolic universes by means of specific conceptual machineries of universe-maintenance. And again the answer is similar to the one given in the case of institutions. Specific procedures of universe-maintenance become necessary when the symbolic universe has become *a problem*. As long as this is not the case, the symbolic universe is self-maintaining, that is, self-legitimating by the sheer facticity of its objective existence in the society in question. One may conceive of a society in which this would be possible. Such a society would be a harmonious, self-enclosed, perfectly functioning 'system'. Actually, no such society exists. Because of the inevitable tensions of the processes of institutionalization, and by the very fact that all social phenomena are *constructions* produced historically through human activity, no society is totally taken for granted and so, *a fortiori*, is no symbolic universe. Every symbolic universe is incipiently problematic. The question, then, is the *degree* to which it has become problematic.

An intrinsic problem, similar to the one we discussed in connexion with tradition in general, presents itself with the process of transmission of the symbolic universe from one generation to another. Socialization is never completely successful. Some individuals 'inhabit' the transmitted universe more definitely than others. Even among the more or less accredited 'inhabitants', there will always be idiosyncratic variations in the way they conceive of the universe. Precisely because the symbolic universe cannot be experienced as such in everyday life, but transcends the latter by its very nature, it is not possible to 'teach' its meaning in the straightforward manner in which one can teach the meanings of everyday life. Children's questions about the symbolic universe have to be answered in a more complicated way than their questions about the institutional realities of everyday life. The questions of idiosyncratic adults require further conceptual elaboration. In the previous example, the meaning of cousinhood is continually represented by flesh-and-blood cousins playing cousin roles in the experienced routines of everyday life. Human cousins are empirically available. Divine cousins, alas, are not. This constitutes an intrinsic problem for the pedagogues of divine cousinhood. *Mutatis mutandis*, the same is true of the transmission of other symbolic universes.

This intrinsic problem becomes accentuated if deviant versions of the symbolic universe come to be shared by groups of 'inhabitants'. In that case, for reasons evident in the nature of objectivation, the deviant version congeals into a reality in its own right, which, by its existence within the society, challenges the reality status of the symbolic universe as originally constituted. The group that has objectivated this deviant reality becomes the carrier of an alternative definition of reality.[81] It is hardly necessary to belabour the point that such heretical groups posit not only a theoretical threat to the symbolic universe, but a practical one to the institutional order legitimated by the symbolic universe in question. The repressive procedures customarily employed against such groups by the custodians of the 'official' definitions of reality need not concern us in this context. What is important for our considerations is the need for such repression to be legitimated, which, of course, implies the setting in motion of various conceptual machineries designed to maintain the 'official' universe against the heretical challenge.

Historically, the problem of heresy has often been the first impetus for the systematic theoretical conceptualization of symbolic universes. The development of Christian theological thought as a result of a series of heretical challenges to the 'official' tradition provides excellent historical illustrations for this process. As in all theorizing, new theoretical implications within the tradition itself appear in the course of this process, and the tradition itself is pushed beyond its original form in new conceptualizations. For instance, the precise Christological formulations of the early church councils were necessitated not by the tradition itself but by the heretical challenges to it. As these formulations were elaborated, the tradition was maintained and expanded at the same time. Thus there emerged, among other innovations, a theoretical conception of the Trinity that was not only unnecessary but actually non-existent in the early Christian community. In other words, the symbolic universe is not only legitimated but also modified by the conceptual machineries constructed to ward off the challenge of heretical groups within a society.

A major occasion for the development of universe-maintaining conceptualization arises when a society is confronted with another society having a greatly different history.[82] The problem posed by such a confrontation is typically sharper than that posed by intra-societal heresies because here there is an alternative symbolic universe with an 'official' tradition whose taken-for-granted objectivity is equal to one's own. It is much less shocking to the reality status of one's own universe to have to deal with minority groups of deviants, whose contrariness is *ipso facto* defined as folly or wickedness, than to confront another society that views *one's own* definitions of reality as ignorant, mad or downright evil.[83] It is one thing to have some individuals around, even if they band together as a minority group, who cannot or will not abide by the institutional rules of cousinhood. It is quite another thing to meet an entire society that has never heard of these rules, perhaps does not even have a word for 'cousin', and that nevertheless seems to get along very well as a going concern. The alternative universe presented by the other society must be met with the best possible reasons for the superiority of one's own. This necessity requires a conceptual machinery of considerable sophistication.

The appearance of an alternative symbolic universe poses a threat because its very existence demonstrates empirically that one's own universe is less than inevitable. As anyone can see now, it is possible to live in this world without the institution of cousinhood after all. And it is possible to deny or even mock the gods of cousinhood without at once causing the downfall of the heavens. This shocking fact must be accounted for theoretically, if nothing more. Of course it may also happen that the alternative universe has a missionary appeal. Individuals or groups within one's own society might be tempted to 'emigrate' from the traditional universe or, even more serious a danger, to change the old order in the image of the new. It is easy to imagine, for example, how the advent of the patriarchal Greeks must have upset the universe of the matriarchal societies then existing along the eastern Mediterranean. The Greek universe must have had considerable appeal for the henpecked *males* of these societies, and we know that the Great Mother made quite an impression on the Greeks themselves. Greek mythology is full of the conceptual elaborations that proved necessary to take care of this problem.

It is important to stress that the conceptual machineries of universe-maintenance are themselves products of social activity, as are all forms of legitimation, and can only rarely be understood apart from the other activities of the collectivity in question. Specifically, the success of particular conceptual machineries is related to the power possessed by those who operate them.[84] The confrontation of alternative symbolic universes implies a problem of power – which of the conflicting definitions of reality will be 'made to stick' in the society. Two societies confronting each other with conflicting universes will both develop conceptual machineries designed to maintain their respective universes. From the point of view of intrinsic plausibility the two forms of conceptualization may seem to the outside observer to offer little choice. Which of the two will win, however, will depend more on the power than on the theoretical ingenuity of the respective legitimators. It is possible to imagine that equally sophisticated Olympian and Chthonic mystagogues met together in ecumenical consultations, discussing the merits of their respective universes *sine ira et studio*, but it is more likely that the issue was decided on the less rarefied level of military might. The historical outcome of each clash of gods was determined by those who wielded the better weapons rather than those who had the better arguments. The same, of course, may be said of intrasocietal conflicts of this kind. He who has the bigger stick has the better chance of imposing his definitions of reality. This is a safe assumption to make with regard to any larger collectivity, although there is always the possibility of politically disinterested theoreticians convincing each other without recourse to the cruder means of persuasion.

The conceptual machineries that maintain symbolic universes always entail the systematization of cognitive and normative legitimations, which were already present in the society in a more naïve mode, and which crystallized in the symbolic universe in question. In other words, the material out of which universe-maintaining legitimations are constructed is mostly a further elaboration, on a higher level of theoretical integration, of the legitimations of the several institutions. Thus there is usually a continuity between the explanatory and exhortatory schemes, which serve as legitimations on the lowest theoretical level, and the imposing intellectual constructions that expound the cosmos. The relationship between cognitive and normative conceptualizations, here as elsewhere, is empirically fluid; normative conceptualizations always imply certain cognitive presuppositions. The analytic distinction is useful, however, especially because it draws attention to varying degrees of differentiation between these two conceptual spheres.

It would be obviously absurd to attempt here a detailed discussion of the different conceptual machineries of universe-maintenance that are historically available to us.[85] But a few remarks about some conspicuous types of conceptual machineries are in order – mythology, theology, philosophy and science. Without proposing an evolutionary scheme for such types, it is safe to say that mythology represents the most archaic form of universe-maintenance, as indeed it represents the most archaic form of legitimation generally.[86] Very likely mythology is a necessary phase in the development of human thought as such.[87] In any case, the oldest universe-maintaining conceptualizations available to us are mythological in form. For our purposes, it is sufficient to define mythology as a conception of reality that posits the ongoing penetration of the world of everyday experience by sacred forces.[88] Such a conception naturally entails a high degree of continuity between social and cosmic order, and between all their respective legitimations;[89] all reality appears as made of one cloth.

Mythology as a conceptual machinery is closest to the naïve level of the symbolic universe – the level on which there is the least necessity for theoretical universe-maintenance beyond the actual positing of the universe in question as an objective reality. This explains the historically recurrent phenomenon of inconsistent mythological traditions continuing to exist side by side without theoretical integration. Typically, the inconsistency is felt only *after* the traditions have become problematic and some sort of integration has already taken place. The 'discovery' of such inconsistency (or, if one prefers, its *ex post facto* assumption) is usually made by the specialists in the tradition, who are also the most common integrators of the discrete traditional themes. Once the need for integration is felt, the consequent mythological reconstructions may have considerable theoretical sophistication. The example of Homer may suffice to make this point.

Mythology is also close to the naïve level in that, although there are specialists in the mythological tradition, their knowledge is not far removed from what is generally known. Initiation into the tradition administered by these specialists may be difficult in extrinsic ways. It may be limited to select candidates, to special occasions or times, and it may involve arduous ritual preparation. It is, however, rarely difficult in terms of the intrinsic qualities of the body of knowledge itself, which is not difficult to acquire. To safeguard the specialists' monopolistic claim the non-accessibility of their lore must be institutionally established. That is, a 'secret' is posited, and an intrinsically exoteric body of knowledge is institutionally defined in esoteric terms. A brief look at the 'public relations' of contemporary coteries of theoreticians will reveal that this ancient legerdemain is far from dead today. All the same, there are important sociological differences between societies in which all universe-maintaining conceptualizations are mythological and societies in which they are not.

More elaborate mythological systems strive to eliminate inconsistencies and maintain the mythological universe in theoretically integrated terms. Such 'canonical' mythologies, as it were, go over into theological conceptualization proper. For our present purposes, theological thought may be distinguished from its mythological predecessor simply in terms of its greater degree of theoretical systematization. Theological concepts are further removed from the naïve level. The cosmos may still be conceived of in terms of the sacred forces or beings of the old mythology, but these sacred entities have been removed to a greater distance. Mythological thought operates within the continuity between the human world and the world of the gods. Theological thought serves to mediate between these two worlds, precisely because their original continuity now appears broken. With the transition from mythology to theology, everyday life appears less ongoingly penetrated by sacred forces. The body of theological knowledge is, consequently, further removed from the general stock of knowledge of the society and thus becomes *intrinsically* more difficult to acquire. Even where it is not deliberately institutionalized as esoteric, it remains 'secret' by virtue of its unintelligibility to the general populace. This has the further consequence that the populace may remain relatively unaffected by the sophisticated universe-maintaining theories concocted by the theological specialists. The coexistence of naïve mythology among the masses and a sophisticated theology among an élite of theoreticians, *both* serving to maintain the same symbolic universe, is a frequent historical phenomenon. Only with this phenomenon in mind, for example, is it possible to call traditional societies of the Far East 'Buddhist', or, for that matter, to call medieval society 'Christian'.

Theology is paradigmatic for the later philosophical and scientific conceptualizations of the cosmos. While theology may be closer to mythology in the religious contents of its definitions of reality, it is closer to the later secularized conceptualizations in its social location. Unlike mythology, the other three historically dominant forms of conceptual machinery became the property of specialist élites, whose bodies of knowledge were increasingly removed from the common knowledge of the society at large. Modern science is an extreme step in this development, and in the secularization and sophistication of universe-maintenance. Science not only completes the removal of the sacred from the world of everyday life, but removes universe-maintaining knowledge as such from that world. Everyday life becomes bereft of both sacred legitimation and the sort of theoretical intelligibility that would link it with the symbolic universe in its intended totality. Put more simply, the 'lay' member of society no longer knows how his universe is to be conceptually maintained, although, of course, he still knows who the specialists of universe-maintenance are presumed to be. The interesting problems posed by this situation belong to an empirical sociology of knowledge of contemporary society and cannot be further pursued in this context.

It goes without saying that the types of conceptual machinery appear historically in innumerable modifications and combinations, and that the types we have discussed are not necessarily exhaustive. But two applications of universe-maintaining conceptual machinery still remain to be discussed in the context of general theory: therapy and nihilation.

Therapy entails the application of conceptual machinery to ensure that actual or potential deviants stay within the institutionalized definitions of reality, or, in other words, to prevent the 'inhabitants' of a given universe from 'emigrating'. It does this by applying the legitimating apparatus to individual 'cases'. Since, as we have seen, every society faces the danger of individual deviance, we may assume that therapy in one form or another is a global social phenomenon. Its specific institutional arrangements, from exorcism to psycho-analysis, from pastoral care to personnel counselling programmes, belong, of course, under the category of social control. What interests us here, however, is the *conceptual* aspect of therapy. Since therapy must concern itself with deviations from the 'official' definitions of reality, it must develop a conceptual machinery to account for such deviations and to maintain the realities thus challenged. This requires a body of knowledge that include a theory of deviance, a diagnostic apparatus, and a conceptual system for the 'cure of souls'.

For example, in a collectivity that has institutionalized military homosexuality the stubbornly heterosexual individual is a sure candidate for therapy, not only because his sexual interests constitute an obvious threat to the combat efficiency of his unit of warrior-lovers, but also because his deviance is psychologically subversive to the others' spontaneous virility. After all, some of them, perhaps 'subconsciously', might be tempted to follow his example. On a more fundamental level, the deviant's conduct challenges the societal reality as such, putting in question its taken-for-granted cognitive ('virile men by nature love one another') and normative ('virile men *should* love one another') operating procedures. Indeed, the deviant probably stands as a living insult to the gods, who love one another in the heavens as their devotees do on earth. Such radical deviance requires therapeutic practice soundly grounded in therapeutic theory. There must be a theory of deviance (a 'pathology', that is) that accounts for this shocking condition (say, by positing demonic possession). There must be a body of diagnostic concepts (say, a symptomatology, with appropriate skills for applying it in trials by ordeal), which optimally not only permits precise specification of acute conditions, but also detection of 'latent hetero-sexuality' and the prompt adoption of preventive measures. Finally, there must be conceptualization of the curative process itself (say, a catalogue of exorcizing techniques, each with an adequate theoretical foundation).

Such a conceptual machinery permits its therapeutic application by the appropriate specialists, and may also be internalized by the individual afflicted with the deviant condition. Internalization in itself will have therapeutic efficacy. In our example, the conceptual machinery may be so designed as to arouse guilt in the individual (say, a 'heterosexual panic'), a not too difficult feat if his primary socialization has been even minimally successful. Under the pressure of this guilt, the individual will come to accept subjectively the conceptualization of his condition with which the therapeutic practitioners confront him; he develops 'insight', and the diagnosis becomes subjectively real to him. The conceptual machinery may be further developed to allow conceptualization (and thus conceptual liquidation) of any doubts regarding the therapy felt by either therapist or 'patient'. For instance, there may be a theory of 'resistance' to account for the doubts of the latter and a theory of 'counter-transference' to account for those of the former. Successful therapy establishes a symmetry between the conceptual machinery and its subjective appropriation in the individual's consciousness; it re-socializes the deviant into the objective reality of the symbolic universe of the society. There is, of course, considerable subjective satisfaction in such a return to 'normalcy'. The individual may now return to the amorous embrace of his platoon commander in the happy knowledge that he has 'found himself', and that he is right once more in the eyes of the gods.

Therapy uses a conceptual machinery to keep everyone within the universe in question. Nihilation, in its turn, uses a similar machinery to liquidate conceptually everything *outside* the same universe. This procedure may also be described as a kind of negative legitimation. Legitimation maintains the reality of the socially constructed universe; nihilation *denies* the reality of whatever phenomena or interpretations of phenomena do not fit into that universe. This may be done in two ways. First, deviant phenomena may be given a negative ontological status, with or without a therapeutic intent. The nihilating application of the conceptual machinery is most often used with individuals or groups foreign to the society in question and thus ineligible for therapy. The conceptual operation here is rather simple. The threat to the social definitions of reality is neutralized by assigning an inferior ontological status, and thereby a not-to-be-taken-seriously cognitive status, to all definitions existing outside the symbolic universe. Thus, the threat of neighbouring anti-homosexual groups can be conceptually liquidated for our homosexual society by looking upon these neighbours as less than human, congenitally befuddled about the right order of things, dwellers in a hopeless cognitive darkness. The fundamental syllogism goes as follows: The neighbours are a tribe of barbarians. The neighbours are anti-homosexual. Therefore, their anti-homosexuality is barbaric nonsense, not to be taken seriously by reasonable men. The same conceptual procedure may, of course, also be applied to deviants within the society. Whether one then proceeds from nihilation to therapy, or rather goes on to liquidate physically what one has liquidated conceptually, is a practical question of policy. The material power of the conceptually liquidated group will be a not insignificant factor in most cases. Sometimes, alas, circumstances force one to remain on friendly terms with barbarians.

Second, nihilation involves the more ambitious attempt to account for all deviant definitions of reality *in terms of* concepts belonging to one's own universe. In a theological frame of reference, this entails the transition from heresiology to apologetics. The deviant conceptions are not merely assigned a negative status, they are grappled with theoretically in detail. The final goal of this procedure is to *incorporate* the deviant conceptions within one's own universe, and thereby to liquidate them ultimately. The deviant conceptions must, therefore, be *translated* into concepts derived from one's own universe. In this manner, the negation of one's universe is subtly changed into an affirmation of it. The presupposition is always that the negator does not really know what he is saying. His statements become meaningful only as they are translated into more 'correct' terms, that is, terms deriving from the universe he negates. For example, our homosexual theoreticians may argue that all men are by nature homosexual. Those who deny this, by virtue of being possessed by demons or simply because they are barbarians, are denying their own nature. Deep down within themselves, they know that this is so. One need, therefore, only search their statements carefully to discover the defensiveness and bad faith of their position. Whatever they say in this matter can thus be translated into an affirmation of the homosexual universe, which they ostensibly negate. In a theological frame of reference the same procedure demonstrates that the devil unwittingly glorifies God, that all unbelief is but unconscious dishonesty, even that the atheist is *really* a believer.

The therapeutic and nihilating applications of conceptual machineries are inherent in the symbolic universe as such. If the symbolic universe is to comprehend all reality, nothing can be allowed to remain outside its conceptual scope. In principle, at any rate, its definitions of reality must encompass the totality of being. The conceptual machineries by which this totalization is attempted vary historically in their degree of sophistication. *In nuce* they appear as soon as a symbolic universe has been crystallized.

Social Organization for Universe-Maintenance ✳

Because they are historical products of human activity, all socially constructed universes change, and the change is brought about by the concrete actions of human beings. If one gets absorbed in the intricacies of the conceptual machineries by which any specific universe is maintained, one may forget this fundamental sociological fact. Reality is socially defined. But the definitions are always *embodied*, that is, concrete individuals and groups of individuals serve as definers of reality. To understand the state of the socially constructed universe at any given time, or its change over time, one must understand the social organization that permits the definers to do their defining. Put a little crudely, it is essential to keep pushing questions about the historically available conceptualizations of reality from the abstract 'What?' to the sociologically concrete 'Says who?'[90]

As we have seen, the specialization of knowledge and the concomitant organization of personnel for the administration of the specialized bodies of knowledge develop as a result of the division of labour. It is possible to conceive of an early stage of this development in which there is no competition between the different experts. Each area of expertise is defined by the pragmatic facts of the division of labour. The hunting expert will not claim fishing expertise and will thus have no ground for competing with the one who does.

As more complex forms of knowledge emerge and an economic surplus is built up, experts devote themselves full-time to the subjects of their expertise, which, with the development of conceptual machineries, may become increasingly removed from the pragmatic necessities of everyday life. Experts in these rarefied bodies of knowledge lay claim to a novel status. They are not only experts in this or that sector of the societal stock of knowledge, they claim ultimate jurisdiction over that stock of knowledge in its totality. They are, literally, universal experts. This does *not* mean that they claim to know everything, but rather that they claim to know the ultimate significance of what everybody knows and does. Other men may continue to stake out particular sectors of reality, but they claim expertise in the ultimate definitions of reality as such.

This stage in the development of knowledge has a number of consequences. The first, which we have already discussed, is the emergence of pure theory. Because the universal experts operate on a level of considerable abstraction from the vicissitudes of everyday life, both others and they themselves may conclude that their theories have no relation whatever to the ongoing life of the society, but exist in a sort of Platonic heaven of ahistorical and asocial ideation. This is, of course, an illusion, but it can have great socio-historical potency, by virtue of the relationship between the reality-defining and reality-producing process.

A second consequence is a strengthening of traditionalism in the institutionalized actions thus legitimated, that is, a strengthening of the inherent tendency of institutionalization towards inertia.[91] Habitualization and institutionalization in themselves limit the flexibility of human actions. Institutions tend to persist unless they become 'problematic'. Ultimate legitimations inevitably strengthen this tendency. The more abstract the legitimations are, the less likely they are to be modified in accordance with changing pragmatic exigencies. If there is a tendency to go on as before anyway, the tendency is obviously strengthened by having excellent reasons for doing so. This means that institutions may persist even when, to an outside observer, they have lost their original functionality or practicality. One does certain things not because they *work*, but because they *are right* – right, that is, in terms of the ultimate definitions of reality promulgated by the universal experts.[92]

The emergence of full-time personnel for universe-maintaining legitimation also brings with it occasions for social

conflict. Some of this conflict is between experts and practitioners. The latter, for reasons that need not be belaboured,
may come to resent the experts' grandiose pretensions and the
concrete social privileges that accompany them. What is likely
to be particularly galling is the experts' claim to know the
ultimate significance of the practitioners' activity better than
the practitioners themselves. Such rebellions on the part of
'laymen' may lead to the emergence of rival definitions of
reality and, eventually, to the appearance of new experts in
charge of the new definitions. Ancient India provides us with
some of the best historical illustrations of this. The Brahmans,
qua experts in ultimate reality, succeeded to an astounding
degree in impressing their definitions of reality upon society
at large. Whatever may have been its origins, it was as a Brahman construction that the caste system expanded over a period
of centuries until it covered most of the Indian subcontinent.
Indeed, the Brahmans were invited by one ruling prince after
another to serve as 'social engineers' for the setting up of the
system in new territories (partly because the system was seen
as identical with higher civilization, partly also, no doubt, because the princes understood its immense capacity for social
control). The Code of Manu gives us an excellent idea of both
the Brahman design for society and the very mundane advan-
tages that accrued to the Brahmans in consequence of being
accepted as the cosmically ordained designers. It was inevitable, however, that conflict would ensue between the theoreticians and the practitioners of power in such a situation.
The latter were represented by the Kshatriyas, the military
and princely caste. The epic literature of ancient India, the
Mahabharata and the Ramayana, give eloquent witness to this
conflict. Not accidentally the two great theoretical rebellions
against the Brahman universe, Jainism and Buddhism, had
their social locations in the Kshatriya caste. Needless to say,
both the Jain and the Buddhist re-definitions of reality produced their own expert personnel, as was probably also the
case with the epic poets who challenged the Brahman universe
in a less comprehensive and less sophisticated manner.[93]

This brings us to another, equally important, possibility of
conflict – that between rival coteries of experts. As long as
theories continue to have immediate pragmatic applications,

what rivalry may exist is fairly amenable to settlement by means of pragmatic testing. There may be competing theories of boar-hunting in which rival coteries of hunting experts develop vested interests. The question can be decided with relative ease by seeing which theory is most conducive to killing the most boars. No such possibility exists for deciding between, say, a polytheistic and a henotheistic theory of the universe. The respective theoreticians are forced to substitute abstract argumentation for pragmatic testing. By its very nature such argumentation does not carry the inherent conviction of pragmatic success. What is convincing to one man may not be to another. We cannot really blame such theoreticians if they resort to various sturdier supports for the frail power of mere argument – such as, say, getting the authorities to employ armed might to enforce one argument against its competitors. In other words, definitions of reality may be enforced by the police. This, incidentally, need not mean that such definitions will remain less convincing than those accepted 'voluntarily' – power in society includes the power to determine decisive socialization processes and, therefore, the power to *produce* reality. In any case, highly abstract symbolizations (that is, theories greatly removed from the concrete experience of everyday life) are validated by social rather than empirical support.[94] It is possible to say that in this manner a pseudo-pragmatism is reintroduced. The theories may again be said to be convincing because they *work* – work, that is, in the sense of having become standard, taken-for-granted knowledge in the society in question.

These considerations imply that there will always be a social-structural base for competition between rival definitions of reality and that the outcome of the rivalry will be affected, if not always determined outright, by the development of this base. It is quite possible for abstruse theoretical formulations to be concocted in near-total isolation from the broad movements in the social structure, and in such cases competition between rival experts may occur in a sort of societal vacuum. For instance, two coteries of eremetical dervishes may go on disputing about the ultimate nature of the universe in the midst of the desert, with nobody on the outside being in the least interested in the dispute. As soon, however, as one or the other of these viewpoints gets a hearing in the surrounding society, it will be largely extra-theoretical interests that will decide the outcome of the rivalry. Different social groups will have different affinities with the competing theories and will, subsequently, become 'carriers' of the latter.[95] Thus dervish theory *A* may appeal to the upper stratum and dervish theory B to the middle stratum of the society in question, for reasons far removed from the passions that animated the original inventors of these theories. The competing coteries of experts will then come to attach themselves to the 'carrier' groups, and their subsequent fate will depend on the outcome of whatever conflict led these groups to adopt the respective theories. Rival definitions of reality are thus decided upon in the sphere of rival social interests whose rivalry is in turn 'translated' into theoretical terms. Whether the rival experts and their respective supporters are 'sincere' in their subjective relationship to the theories in question is of only secondary interest for a sociological understanding of these processes.

When not only theoretical but practical competition arises between groups of experts dedicated to different ultimate definitions of reality, the de-pragmatization of theory is reversed and the pragmatic potency of the theories in question becomes an extrinsic one; that is, a theory is 'demonstrated' to be pragmatically superior not by virtue of its intrinsic qualities, but by its applicability to the social interests of the group that has become its 'carrier'. There is considerable historical variability in the social organization of theoretical experts resulting from this. While it is obviously impossible to give an exhaustive typology here, it will be useful to look at some of the more general types.

There is first of all, perhaps paradigmatically, the possibility of the universal experts holding an effective monopoly over all ultimate definitions of reality in a society. Such a situation may be regarded as paradigmatic because there is good reason for thinking that it is typical of the earlier phases of human history. Such a monopoly means that a single symbolic tradition maintains the universe in question. To be in the society then implies acceptance of this tradition. The experts in the tradition are recognized as such by virtually all members of the society and have no effective competitors to deal with. All primitive societies empirically open to our inspection seem to fall under this type, and, with some modifications, most archaic civilizations do too.[96] This does not imply that such societies have no sceptics, that everyone has without exception fully internalized the tradition, but rather that what scepticism there is has not been socially organized to offer a challenge to the upholders of the 'official' tradition.[97]

In such a situation the monopolistic tradition and its expert administrators are sustained by a unified power structure. Those who occupy the decisive power positions are ready to use their power to impose the traditional definitions of reality on the population under their authority. Potentially competitive conceptualizations of the universe are liquidated as soon as they appear – either physically destroyed ('whoever does not worship the gods must die') or integrated within the tradition itself (the universal experts argue that the competing pantheon Y is 'really' nothing but another aspect or nomenclature for the traditional pantheon X). In the latter case, if the experts succeed with their argument and the competition is liquidated by 'merger', as it were, the tradition becomes enriched and differentiated. The competition may also be segregated within the society and thus made innocuous as far as the traditional monopoly is concerned – for example, no member of the conquering or ruling group may worship gods of type Y, but the subjugated or lower strata may do so. The same protective segregation may be applied to foreigners or 'guest peoples'.[98]

Medieval Christendom (certainly not to be called primitive or archaic, but still a society with an effective symbolic monopoly) provides excellent illustrations of all three liquidating procedures. Open heresy had to be physically destroyed, whether it was embodied in an individual (say, a witch) or a collectivity (say, the Albigensian community). At the same time, the Church, as the monopolistic guardian of the Christian tradition, was quite flexible in incorporating within that tradition a variety of folk beliefs and practices so long as these did not congeal into articulate, heretical challenges to the Christian universe as such. It did not matter if the peasants took one of their old gods, 'baptized' him as a Christian saint, and continued to tell the old stories and to celebrate the old feasts associated with him. And certain competing definitions of reality at least could be segregated within Christendom without being viewed as a threat to it. The most important case of this, of course, is that of the Jews, although similar situations also arose where Christians and Muslims were forced to live close to one another in times of peace. This sort of segregation, incidentally, also protected the Jewish and Muslim universes from Christian 'contamination'. As long as competing definitions of reality can be conceptually and socially segregated as appropriate to strangers, and *ipso facto* as irrelevant to oneself, it is possible to have fairly friendly relations with these strangers. The trouble begins whenever the 'strangeness' is broken through and the deviant universe appears as a possible habitat for one's own people. At that point, the traditional experts are likely to call for the fire and the sword – or, alternatively, particularly if fire and sword turn out to be unavailable, to enter into ecumenical negotiations with the competitors.

Monopolistic situations of this kind presuppose a high degree of social-structural stability, and are themselves structurally stabilizing. Traditional definitions of reality inhibit social change. Conversely, breakdown in the taken-for-granted acceptance of the monopoly accelerates social change. It should not surprise us, then, that a profound affinity exists between those with an interest in maintaining established power positions and the personnel administering monopolistic traditions of universe-maintenance. In other words, conservative political forces tend to support the monopolistic claims of the universal experts, whose monopolistic organizations in turn tend to be politically conservative. Historically, of course, most of these monopolies have been religious. It is thus possible to say that Churches, understood as monopolistic combinations of full-time experts in a religious definition of reality, are inherently conservative once they have succeeded in establishing their monopoly in a given society. Conversely, ruling groups with a stake in the maintenance of the political *status quo* are inherently churchly in their religious orientation and, by the same token, suspicious of all innovations in the religious tradition.[99]

Monopolistic situations may fail to be established or maintained for a variety of historical reasons, both 'international' and 'domestic'. It is then possible for a struggle between competing traditions and their administrative personnel to continue for a long time. When a particular definition of reality comes to be attached to a concrete power interest, it may be called an ideology.[100] It should be stressed that this term has little utility if it is applied to the sort of monopolistic situation discussed above. It makes little sense, for example, to speak of Christianity as an ideology in the Middle Ages – even though it had obvious political uses for the ruling groups – for the simple reason that the Christian universe was 'inhabited' by everyone in medieval society, by the serfs just as much as by their lords. In the period following the Industrial Revolution, however, there is a certain justification in calling Christianity a bourgeois ideology, because the bourgeoisie used the Christian tradition and its personnel in its struggle against the new industrial working class, which in most European countries could no longer be regarded as 'inhabiting' the Christian universe.[101] It also makes little sense to use the term if two different definitions of reality confront each other in inter-societal contact – for example, if one spoke of the 'Christian ideology' of the Crusaders and the 'Muslim ideology' of the Saracens. The distinctiveness of ideology is rather that the *same* overall universe is interpreted in different ways, depending upon concrete vested interests within the society in question.

Frequently an ideology is taken on by a group because of specific theoretical elements that are conducive to its interests. For example, when an impoverished peasant group struggles against an urban merchant group that has financially enslaved it, it may rally around a religious doctrine that upholds the virtues of agrarian life, condemns the money economy and its credit system as immoral, and generally decries the luxuries of urban living. The ideological 'gain' of such a doctrine for the peasants is obvious. Good illustrations of this may be found in the history of ancient Israel. It would be erroneous, however, to imagine that the relationship between an interest group and its ideology is always so logical. Every group engaged in social conflict requires solidarity. Ideologies generate solidarity. The choice of a particular ideology is not necessarily based on its intrinsic theoretical elements, but may stem from a chance encounter. It is far from clear, for example, that it was intrinsic elements in Christianity that made the latter politically 'interesting' to certain groups in the age of Constantine. It seems rather that Christianity (originally a lower-middle-class ideology if anything) was harnessed by powerful interests for political purposes with little relationship to its religious contents. Something else might have served equally well – Christianity just happened to be around at some crucial moments of decision. Of course, once the ideology is adopted by the group in question (more accurately, once the particular doctrine *becomes* the ideology of the group in question) it is modified in accordance with the interests it must now legitimate. This entails a process of selection and addition in regard to the original body of theoretical propositions. But there is no reason to assume that these modifications have to affect the totality of the adopted doctrine. There may be large elements in an ideology that bear no particular relationship to the legitimated interests, but that are vigorously affirmed by the 'carrier' group simply because it has committed itself to the ideology. In practice this may lead power holders to support their ideological experts in theoretical squabbles that are quite irrelevant to their interests. Constantine's involvement in the Christological controversies of the time is a good case in point.

It is important to bear in mind that most modern societies are pluralistic. This means that they have a shared core universe taken for granted as such, and different partial universes coexisting in a state of mutual accommodation. The latter probably have some ideological functions, but outright conflict between ideologies has been replaced by varying degrees of tolerance or even cooperation. Such a situation, brought about by a constellation of non-theoretical factors, presents the traditional experts with severe theoretical problems. Administering a tradition with age-old monopolistic pretensions they have to find ways of theoretically legitimating the de-monopolization that has taken place. Sometimes they take the option of continuing to voice the old totalitarian claims as if nothing had happened, but very few people are likely to take these claims seriously. Whatever the experts do, the pluralistic situation changes not only the social position of the traditional definitions of reality, but also the way in which these are held in the consciousness of individuals.[102]

The pluralistic situation presupposes an urban society with a highly developed division of labour, a concomitant high differentiation in the social structure and high economic surplus. These conditions, which obviously prevail in modern industrial society, existed in at least certain sectors of earlier societies. The cities of the later Graeco-Roman period may serve as an example here. The pluralistic situation goes with conditions of rapid social change, indeed pluralism itself is an accelerating factor precisely because it helps to undermine the change-resistant efficacy of the traditional definitions of reality. Pluralism encourages both scepticism and innovation and is thus inherently subversive of the taken-for-granted reality of the traditional *status quo*. One can readily sympathize with the experts in the traditional definitions of reality when they think back nostalgically to the times when these definitions had a monopoly in the field.

One historically important type of expert, possible in principle in any of the situations just discussed, is the intellectual, whom we may define as an expert whose expertise is not wanted by the society at large.[103] This implies a redefinition of knowledge *vis-à-vis* the 'official' lore, that is, it implies more than just a somewhat deviant interpretation of the latter. The intellectual is thus, by definition, a marginal type. Whether he was first marginal and then became an intellectual (as, for example, in the case of many Jewish intellectuals in the modern West), or whether his marginality was the direct result of his intellectual aberrations (the case of the ostracized heretic), need not concern us here.[104] In either case, his social marginality expresses his lack of theoretical integration within the universe of his society. He appears as the counter-expert in the business of defining reality. Like the 'official' expert, he has a design for society at large. But while the former's design is in tune with the institutional programmes, serving as their theoretical legitimation, the intellectual's exists in an institutional vacuum, socially objectivated at best in a sub-society of fellow-intellectuals. The extent to which such a sub-society is capable of surviving obviously depends on structural configurations in the larger society. It is safe to say that a certain degree of pluralism is a necessary condition.

The intellectual has a number of historically interesting options open to him in his situation. He may withdraw into an intellectual sub-society, which may then serve as an emotional refuge and (more importantly) as the social base for the objectivation of his deviant definitions of reality. In other words, the intellectual may feel 'at home' in the sub-society as he does not in the larger society, and at the same time be able subjectively to maintain his deviant conceptions, which the larger society nihilates, because in the sub-society there are others who regard these as reality. He will then develop various procedures to protect the precarious reality of the sub-society from the nihilating threats from the outside. On the theoretical level, these procedures will include the therapeutic defences we have discussed previously. Practically, the most important procedure will be the limitation of all significant relationships to fellow-members of the sub-society. The outsider is avoided because he always embodies the threat of nihilation. The religious sect may be taken as the prototype for sub-societies of this kind.[105] Within the sheltering community of the sect even the most wildly deviant conceptions take on the character of objective reality. Conversely, sectarian withdrawal is typical of situations in which previously objectivated definitions of reality disintegrate, that is, become de-objectivated in the larger society. The details of these processes belong to a historical sociology of religion, though it must be added that various secularized forms of sectarianism are a key characteristic of intellectuals in modern pluralistic society.

A historically very important option, of course, is revolution. Here the intellectual sets out to realize his design for society *in* society. It is impossible to discuss here the various forms this option has taken historically,[106] but one important theoretical point must be made. Just as the withdrawing intellectual needs others to assist him in maintaining his deviant definitions of reality *as* reality, so the revolutionary intellectual needs others to confirm *his* deviant conceptions. This requirement is much more basic than the obvious fact that no conspiracy can succeed without organization. The revolutionary intellectual must have others who maintain for him the *reality* (that is, the subjective plausibility in his own consciousness) of the revolutionary ideology. All socially meaningful definitions of reality must be objectivated by social processes. Consequently, subuniverses require sub-societies as their objectivating base, and counter-definitions of reality require counter-societies. Needless to add, any practical success of the revolutionary ideology will fortify the reality it possesses within the sub-society and within the consciousness of the sub-society's members. Its reality takes on massive proportions when entire social strata become its 'carriers'. The history of modern revolutionary movements affords many illustrations of the transformation of revolutionary intellectuals into 'official' legitimators following the victory of such movements.[107] This suggests not only that there is considerable historical variability in the social career of revolutionary intellectuals, but that different options and combinations may occur within the biography of individuals as well.

In the foregoing discussion we have emphasized the structural aspects in the social existence of universe-maintaining personnel. No genuine sociological discussion could do otherwise. Institutions and symbolic universes are legitimated by living individuals, who have concrete social locations and concrete social interests. The history of legitimating theories is always part of the history of the society as a whole. No 'history of ideas' takes place in isolation from the blood and sweat of general history. But we must once again stress that this does not mean that these theories are nothing but reflections of 'underlying' institutional processes; the relationship between 'ideas' and their sustaining social processes is always a dialectical one. It is correct to say that theories are concocted in order to legitimate already existing social institutions. But it also happens that social institutions are changed in order to bring them into conformity with already existing theories, that is, to make them more 'legitimate'. The experts in legitimation may operate as theoretical justifiers of the *status quo*; they may also appear as revolutionary ideologists. Definitions of reality have self-fulfilling potency. Theories can be *realized* in history, even theories that were highly abstruse when they were first conceived by their inventors. Karl Marx brooding in the British Museum Reading Room has become a proverbial example of this historical possibility. Consequently, social change must always be understood as standing in a dialectical relationship to the 'history of ideas'. Both 'idealistic' and 'materialistic' understandings of the relationship overlook this dialectic, and thus distort history. The same dialectic prevails in the overall transformations of symbolic universes that we have had occasion to look at. What remains sociologically essential is the recognition that all symbolic universes and all legitimations are human products; their existence has its base in the lives of concrete individuals, and has no empirical status apart from these lives.

Part Three

Society as
Subjective Reality

1. Internalization of Reality

Primary Socialization

Since society exists as both objective and subjective reality, any adequate theoretical understanding of it must comprehend both these aspects. As we have already argued, these aspects receive their proper recognition if society is understood in terms of an ongoing dialectical process composed of the three moments of externalization, objectivation and internalization. As far as the societal phenomenon is concerned, these moments are *not* to be thought of as occurring in a temporal sequence. Rather society and each part of it are simultaneously characterized by these three moments, so that any analysis in terms of only one or two of them falls short. The same is true of the individual member of society, who simultaneously externalizes his own being into the social world and internalizes it as an objective reality. In other words, to be in society is to participate in its dialectic.

The individual, however, is not born a member of society. He is born with a predisposition towards sociality, and he becomes a member of society. In the life of every individual, therefore, there *is* a temporal sequence, in the course of which he is inducted into participation in the societal dialectic. The beginning point of this process is internalization: the immediate apprehension or interpretation of an objective event as expressing meaning, that is, as a manifestation of another's subjective processes which thereby becomes subjectively meaningful to myself. This does not mean that I understand the other adequately. I may indeed misunderstand him: he is laughing in a fit of hysteria, but I understand his laughter as expressing mirth. But his subjectivity is nevertheless objectively available to me and becomes meaningful to me, whether or not there is congruence between his and my subjective process. Full congruence between the two subjective meanings, and reciprocal knowledge of the congruence, presupposes signification, as previously discussed. However, internalization in the general sense used here underlies both signification and its own more complex forms. More precisely, internalization in this general sense is the basis, first, for an understanding of one's fellowmen and, second, for the apprehension of the world as a meaningful and social reality.[1]

This apprehension does not result from autonomous creations of meaning by isolated individuals, but begins with the individual 'taking over' the world in which others already live. To be sure, the 'taking over' is in itself, in a sense, an original process for every human organism, and the world, once 'taken over', *may* be creatively modified or (less likely) even recreated. In any case, in the complex form of internalization, I not only 'understand' the other's momentary subjective processes, I 'understand' the world in which he lives, and that world becomes my own. This presupposes that he and I share time in a more than ephemeral way and a comprehensive perspective, which links sequences of situations together intersubjectively. We now not only understand each other's definitions of shared situations, we define them reciprocally. A nexus of motivations is established between us and extends into the future. Most importantly, there is now an ongoing mutual identification between us. We not only live in the same world, we participate in each other's being.

Only when he has achieved this degree of internalization is an individual a member of society. The ontogenetic process by which this is brought about is socialization, which may thus be defined as the comprehensive and consistent induction of an individual into the objective world of a society or a sector of it. Primary socialization is the first socialization an individual undergoes in childhood, through which he becomes a member of society. Secondary socialization is any subsequent process that inducts an already socialized individual into new sectors of the objective world of his society. We may leave aside here the special question of the acquisition of knowledge about the objective world of societies other than the one of which we first became a member, and the process of internalizing such a world as reality – a process that exhibits, at least superficially, certain similarities with both primary and secondary socialization, yet is structurally identical with neither.[2]

It is at once evident that primary socialization is usually the most important one for an individual, and that the basic structure of all secondary socialization has to resemble that of primary socialization. Every individual is born into an objective social structure within which he encounters the significant others who are in charge of his socialization.[3] These significant others are imposed upon him. Their definitions of his situation are posited for him as objective reality. He is thus born into not only an objective social structure but also an objective social world. The significant others who mediate this world to him modify it in the course of mediating it. They select aspects of it in accordance with their own location in the social structure, and also by virtue of their individual, biographically rooted idiosyncrasies. The social world is 'filtered' to the individual through this double selectivity. Thus the lower-class child not only absorbs a lower-class perspective on the social world, he absorbs it in the idiosyncratic coloration given it by his parents (or whatever other individuals are in charge of his primary socialization). The same lower-class perspective may induce a mood of contentment, resignation, bitter resentment, or seething rebelliousness. Consequently, the lower-class child will not only come to inhabit a world greatly different from that of an upper-class child, but may do so in a manner quite different from the lower-class child next door.[4]

It should hardly be necessary to add that primary socialization involves more than purely cognitive learning. It takes place under circumstances that are highly charged emotionally. Indeed, there is good reason to believe that without such emotional attachment to the significant others the learning process would be difficult if not impossible.[5] The child identifies with the significant others in a variety of emotional ways. Whatever they may be, internalization occurs only as identification occurs. The child takes on the significant others' roles and attitudes, that is, internalizes them and makes them his own. And by this identification with significant others the child becomes capable of identifying himself, of acquiring a subjectively coherent and plausible identity. In other words, the self is a reflected entity, reflecting the attitudes first taken by significant others towards it;[6] the individual becomes what he is addressed as by his significant others. This is not a one-sided, mechanistic process. It entails a dialectic between identification by others and self-identification, between objectively assigned and subjectively appropriated identity. The dialectic, which is present each moment the individual *identifies with* his significant others, is, as it were, the particularization in individual life of the general dialectic of society that has already been discussed.

Although the details of this dialectic are, of course, of great importance for social psychology, it would exceed our present purpose if we were to follow up its implications for social-psychological theory.[7] What is most important for our considerations here is the fact that the individual not only takes on the roles and attitudes of others, but in the same process takes on their world. Indeed, identity is objectively defined as location in a certain world and can be subjectively appropriated only *along with* that world. Put differently, all identifications take place within horizons that imply a specific social world. The child learns that he *is* what he is called. Every name implies a nomenclature, which in turn implies a designated social location.[8] To be given an identity involves being assigned a specific place in the world. As this identity is subjectively appropriated by the child ('I *am* John Smith'), so is the world to which this identity points. Subjective appropriation of identity and subjective appropriation of the social world are merely different aspects of the *same* process of internalization, mediated by the *same* significant others.

Primary socialization creates in the child's consciousness a progressive abstraction from the roles and attitude of specific others to roles and attitudes *in general*. For example, in the internalization of norms there is a progression from, 'Mummy is angry with me *now*' to, 'Mummy is angry with me *whenever* I spill the soup'. As additional significant others (father, grandmother, older sister, and so on) support the mother's negative attitude towards soup-spilling, the generality of the norm is subjectively extended. The decisive step comes when the child recognizes that *everybody* is against soup-spilling, and the norm is generalized to, '*One* does not spill soup' – 'one' being himself as part of a generality that includes, in principle, *all* of society in so far as it is significant to the child. This abstraction from the roles and attitudes of concrete significant others is called the generalized other.[9] Its formation within consciousness means that the individual now identifies not only with concrete others but with a generality of others, that is, with a society. Only by virtue of this generalized identification does his own self-identification attain stability and continuity. He now has not only an identity *vis-à-vis* this or that significant other, but an identity *in general*, which is subjectively apprehended as remaining the same no matter what others, significant or not, are encountered. This newly coherent identity incorporates within itself all the various internalized roles and attitudes – including, among many other things, the self-identification as a non-spiller of soups.

The formation within consciousness of the generalized other marks a decisive phase in socialization. It implies the internalization of society as such and of the objective reality established therein, and, at the same time, the subjective establishment of a coherent and continuous identity. Society, identity *and* reality are subjectively crystallized in the same process of internalization. This crystallization is concurrent with the internalization of language. Indeed, for reasons evident from the foregoing observations on language, language constitutes both the most important content and the most important instrument of socialization.

When the generalized other has been crystallized in consciousness, a symmetrical relationship is established between objective and subjective reality. What is real 'outside' corresponds to what is real 'within'. Objective reality can readily be 'translated' into subjective reality, and vice versa. Language, of course, is the principal vehicle of this ongoing translating process in both directions. It should, however, be stressed that the symmetry between objective and subjective reality cannot be complete. The two realities correspond to each other, but they are not coextensive. There is always more objective reality 'available' than is actually internalized in any individual consciousness, simply because the contents of socialization are determined by the social distribution of knowledge. No individual internalizes the totality of what is objectivated as reality in his society, not even if the society and its world are relatively simple ones. On the other hand, there are always elements of subjective reality that have not originated in socialization, such as the awareness of one's own body prior to and apart from any socially learned apprehension of it. Subjective biography is not fully social. The individual apprehends himself as a being both inside *and* outside society.[10] This implies that the symmetry between objective and subjective reality is never a static, once-for-all state of affairs. It must always be produced and reproduced *in actu*. In other words, the relationship between the individual and the objective social world is like an ongoing balancing act. The anthropological roots of this are, of course, the same as those we discussed in connexion with the peculiar position of man in the animal kingdom.

In primary socialization there is no *problem* of identification. There is no choice of significant others. Society presents the candidate for socialization with a predefined set of significant others, whom he must accept as such with no possibility of opting for another arrangement. *Hic Rhodus, hic salta.* One must make do with the parents that fate has regaled one with. This unfair disadvantage inherent in the situation of being a child has the obvious consequence that, although the child is not simply passive in the process of his socialization, it is the adults who set the rules of the game. The child can play the game with enthusiasm or with sullen resistance. But, alas, there is no other game around. This has an important corollary. Since the child has no choice in the selection of his significant others, his identification with them is quasi-automatic. For the same reason, his internalization of their particular reality is quasi-inevitable. The child does not internalize the world of his significant others as one of many possible worlds. He internalizes it as *the* world, the only existent and only conceivable world, the world *tout court*. It is for this reason that the world internalized in primary socialization is so much more firmly entrenched in consciousness than worlds internalized in secondary socializations. However much the original sense of inevitability may be weakened in subsequent disenchantments, the recollection of a never-to-be-repeated certainty – the certainty of the first dawn of reality – still adheres to the first world of childhood. Primary socialization thus accomplishes what (in hindsight, of course) may be seen as the most important confidence trick that society plays on the individual – to make appear as necessity what is in fact a bundle of contingencies, and thus to make meaningful the accident of his birth.

The specific contents that are internalized in primary socialization vary, of course, from society to society. Some are found everywhere. It is language that must be internalized above all. With language, and by means of it, various motivational and interpretative schemes are internalized as institutionally defined – wanting to act like a brave little boy, for instance, and assuming little boys to be naturally divided into the brave and the cowardly. These schemes provide the child with institutionalized programmes for everyday life, some immediately applicable to him, others anticipating conduct socially defined for later biographical stages – the bravery that will allow him to get through a day beset with tests of will from one's peers and from all sorts of others, and also the bravery that will be required of one later – when one is initiated as a warrior, say, or when one might be called by the god. These programmes, both the immediately applicable and the anticipatory, differentiate one's identity from that of others – such as girls, slave boys, or boys from another clan. Finally, there is internalization of at least the rudiments of the legitimating apparatus; the child learns 'why' the programmes are what they are. One must be brave because one wants to become a real man; one must perform the rituals because otherwise the gods will be angry; one must be loyal to the chief because only if one does will the gods support one in times of danger; and so on.

In primary socialization, then, the individual's first world is constructed. Its peculiar quality of firmness is to be accounted for, at least in part, by the inevitability of the individual's relationship to his very first significant others. The world of childhood, in its luminous reality, is thus conducive to confidence not only in the persons of the significant others but in their definitions of the situation. The world of childhood is massively and indubitably real.[11] Probably this could not be otherwise at this stage in the development of consciousness. Only later can the individual afford the luxury of at least a modicum of doubt. And probably this necessity of a proto-realism in the apprehension of the world pertains phylo-genetically as well as ontogenetically.[12] In any case, the world of childhood is so constituted as to instil in the individual a nomic structure in which he may have confidence that 'every-thing is all right' – to repeat what is possibly the most frequent sentence mothers say to their crying offspring. The later dis-covery that some things are far from 'all right' may be more or less shocking, depending on biographical circumstances, but in either case the world of childhood is likely to retain its peculiar reality in retrospection. It remains the 'home world', however far one may travel from it in later life into regions where one does not feel at home at all.

Primary socialization involves learning sequences that are socially defined. At age A the child should learn X, at age B he should learn Y, and so on. Every such programme entails some social recognition of biological growth and differentia-tion. Thus every programme, in any society, must recognize that a one-year-old child cannot be expected to learn what a three-year-old can. Also, most programmes are likely to define the matter differently for boys and girls. Such minimal recog-nition is, of course, imposed on society by biological facts. Beyond this, however, there is great socio-historical variability in the definition of the stages in the learning sequence. What is still defined as childhood in one society may be defined as well into adulthood in another. And the social implications of childhood may vary greatly from one society to another – for instance, in terms of emotional qualities, moral accountability, or intellectual capacities. Contemporary Western civilization (at least prior to the Freudian movement) tended to regard children as naturally 'innocent' and 'sweet'; other societies considered them 'by nature sinful and unclean', different from adults only in terms of their strength and understanding. There have been similar variations in terms of children's availability, for sexual activity, criminal responsibility, divine inspiration, and so on. Such variations in the social definition of childhood and its stages will obviously affect the learning programme.[13]

The character of primary socialization is also affected by the requirements of the stock of knowledge to be transmitted. Certain legitimations may require a higher degree of linguistic complexity for their understanding than others. We might guess, for instance, that a child would need less words to understand that he must not masturbate because that makes his guardian angel angry than to understand the argument that masturbation will interfere with his later sexual adjustment. The requirements of the overall institutional order will further affect primary socialization. Different skills are required at different ages in one society as against another, or indeed in varying sectors of the same society. The age at which, in one society, it may be deemed proper for a child to be able to drive an automobile may, in another, be the age at which he is expected to have killed his first enemy. An upper-class child may learn the 'facts of life' at an age when a lower-class child has mastered the rudiments of abortion technique. Or, an upper-class child may experience his first stirrings of patriotic emotion about the time that his lower-class contemporary first experiences hatred of the police and everything they stand for.

Primary socialization ends when the concept of the generalized other (and all that goes with it) has been established in the consciousness of the individual. At this point he is an effective member of society and in subjective possession of a self and a world. But this internalization of society, identity and reality is not a matter of once and for all. Socialization is never total and never finished. This presents us with two further problems: First, how the reality internalized in primary socialization is maintained in consciousness, and second, how further internalizations – or secondary socializations – in the later biography of the individual take place. We will take up these problems in reverse order.

Secondary Socialization

It is possible to conceive of a society in which no further socialization takes place after primary socialization. Such a society would, of course, be one with a very simple stock of knowledge. All knowledge would be generally relevant, with different individuals varying only in their perspectives on it. This conception is useful in positing a limiting case, but there is no society known to us that does not have *some* division of labour and, concomitantly, *some* social distribution of knowledge; and as soon as this is the case, secondary socialization becomes necessary.

Secondary socialization is the internalization of institutional or institution-based 'sub-worlds'. Its extent and character are therefore determined by the complexity of the division of labour and the concomitant social distribution of knowledge. Of course, generally relevant knowledge, too, may be socially distributed – for example, in the form of class-based 'versions' – but what we have in mind here is the social distribution of 'special knowledge' – knowledge that arises as a result of the division of labour and whose 'carriers' are institutionally defined. Forgetting for a moment its other dimensions, we may say that secondary socialization is the acquisition of role-specific knowledge, the roles being directly or indirectly rooted in the division of labour. There is some justification for such a narrow definition, but this is by no means the whole story. Secondary socialization requires the acquisition of role-specific vocabularies, which means, for one thing, the internalization of semantic fields structuring routine interpretations and conduct within an institutional area. At the same time 'tacit understandings', evaluations and affective colorations of these semantic fields are also acquired. The 'sub-worlds' internalized in secondary socialization are generally partial realities in contrast to the 'base-world' acquired in primary socialization. Yet they, too, are more or less cohesive realities, characterized by normative and affective as well as cognitive components.

Furthermore, they, too, require at least the rudiments of a legitimating apparatus, often accompanied by ritual or material symbols. For example, a differentiation may arise between foot soldiers and cavalry. The latter will have to have special training, which will probably involve more than learning the purely physical skills necessary to handle military horses. The language of the cavalry will become quite different from that of the infantry. A terminology will be built up referring to horses, their qualities and uses, and to situations arising as a result of cavalry life, which will be quite irrelevant to the foot soldier. The cavalry will also use a different language in more than an instrumental sense. An angry infantryman swears by making reference to his aching feet, while the cavalryman may mention his horse's backside. In other words, a body of images and allegories is built up on the instrumental basis of cavalry language. This role-specific language is internalized *in toto* by the individual as he is trained for mounted combat. He becomes a cavalryman not only by acquiring the requisite skills but by becoming capable of understanding and using this language. He can then communicate with his fellow-horsemen in allusions rich in meaning to them but quite obtuse to men in the infantry. It goes without saying that this process of internalization entails subjective identification with the role and its appropriate norms – 'I am a horseman', 'A horseman never lets the enemy see the tail of his mount', 'Never let a woman forget the feel of the spurs', 'A fast rider in war, a fast rider in gambling', and so forth. As the need arises, this body of meanings will be sustained by legitimations, ranging from simple maxims like the foregoing to elaborate mythological constructions. Finally, there may be a variety of representative ceremonies and physical objects – say, the annual celebration of the feast of the horse-god at which all meals are taken on horseback and the newly initiated horsemen receive the horse-tail fetishes they will henceforth carry around their necks.

The character of such secondary socialization depends upon the status of the body of knowledge concerned within the symbolic universe as a whole. Training is necessary to learn to make a horse pull a manure cart or to fight on it in battle. But a society that limits its use of horses to the pulling of manure carts is unlikely to embellish this activity with elaborate rituals or fetishism, and the personnel to whom this task has been assigned is unlikely to identify with the role in any profound manner; the legitimations, such as they are, are likely to be of a compensatory kind. Thus there is a great deal of socio-historical variability in the representations involved in secondary socialization. In most societies, however, some rituals accompany the transition from primary to secondary socialization.[14]

The formal processes of secondary socialization are determined by its fundamental problem: it always presupposes a preceding process of primary socialization; that is, that it must deal with an already formed self and an already internalized world. It cannot construct subjective reality *ex nihilo*. This presents a problem because the already internalized reality has a tendency to persist. Whatever new contents are now to be internalized must somehow be superimposed upon this already present reality. There is, therefore, a problem of consistency between the original and the new internalizations. The problem may be more or less difficult of solution in different cases. Having learned that cleanliness is a virtue in one's own person, it is not difficult to transfer the same virtue to one's horse. But having learned that certain obscenities are reprehensible as a pedestrian child, it may need some explanation that they are now *de rigueur* as a member of the cavalry. To establish and maintain consistency, secondary socialization presupposes conceptual procedures to integrate different bodies of knowledge.

In secondary socialization, biological limitations become decreasingly important to the learning sequences, which now come to be established in terms of intrinsic properties of the knowledge to be acquired; that is, in terms of the foundational structure of that knowledge. For example, in order to learn certain hunting techniques one must first learn mountain-climbing; or in order to learn calculus one must first learn algebra. The learning sequences can also be manipulated in terms of the vested interests of the personnel administering the body of knowledge. For example, it can be established that one must learn divination from animal entrails before one can learn divination from the flight of birds, or that one must have a high-school diploma before one can enrol in an embalming school, or that one must pass an examination in Gaelic before being eligible for a position in the Irish civil service. Such stipulations are extrinsic to the knowledge pragmatically required for the performance of the roles of diviner, embalmer or Irish civil servant. They are established institutionally to enhance the prestige of the roles in question or to meet other ideological interests. A grade-school education may be perfectly sufficient to grasp the curriculum of an embalming school, and Irish civil servants carry on their normal business in the English language. It may even happen that the learning sequences thus manipulated are pragmatically disfunctional. For instance, it may be stipulated that a college background in 'general culture' should precede the professional training of research sociologists, while their actual activities might in fact be more efficiently carried on if they were unburdened with 'culture' of this sort.

While primary socialization cannot take place without an emotionally charged identification of the child with his significant others, most secondary socialization can dispense with this kind of identification and proceed effectively with only the amount of mutual identification that enters into any communication between human beings. Put crudely, it is necessary to love one's mother, but not one's teacher. Socialization in later life typically begins to take on an affectivity reminiscent of childhood when it seeks radically to transform the subjective reality of the individual. This posits special problems that we shall analyse a little further on.

In primary socialization the child does not apprehend his significant others as institutional functionaries, but as mediators of reality *tout court*; the child internalizes the world of his parents as *the* world, and not as the world appertaining to a specific institutional context. Some of the crises that occur after primary socialization are indeed caused by the recognition that the world of one's parents is *not* the only world there is, but has a very specific social location, perhaps even one with a pejorative connotation. For example, the older child comes to recognize that the world represented by his parents, the same world that he had previously taken for granted as inevitable reality, is actually the world of uneducated, lower-class, rural Southerners. In secondary socialization, the institutional context is usually apprehended. Needless to say, this need not involve a sophisticated understanding of all the implications of the institutional context. Yet the Southern child, to stay within the same example, does apprehend his school teacher as an institutional functionary in a way he never did his parents, and he understands the teacher's role as representing institutionally specific meanings – such as those of the nation as against the region, of the national middle-class world as against the lower-class ambience of his home, of the city as against the countryside. Hence the social interaction between teachers and learners can be formalized. The teachers need not be significant others in any sense of the word. They are institutional functionaries with the formal assignment of transmitting specific knowledge. The roles of secondary socialization carry a high degree of anonymity; that is, they are readily detached from their individual performers. The same knowledge taught by one teacher could also be taught by another. Any functionary of this type could teach this type of knowledge. The individual functionaries may, of course, be subjectively differentiated in various ways (as more or less congenial, better or worse teachers of arithmetic, and so on), but they are in principle interchangeable.

This formality and anonymity are, of course, linked with the affective character of social relations in secondary socialization. Their most important consequence, however, is to bestow on the contents of what is learned in secondary socialization much less subjective inevitability than the contents of primary socialization possess. Therefore, the reality accent of knowledge internalized in secondary socialization is more easily bracketed (that is, the subjective sense that these internalizations are real is more fugitive). It takes severe biographical shocks to disintegrate the massive reality internalized in early childhood; much less to destroy the realities internalized later. Beyond this, it is relatively easy to set aside the reality of the secondary internalizations. The child lives willy-nilly in the world as defined by his parents, but he can cheerfully leave the world of arithmetic behind him as soon as he leaves the classroom.

This makes it possible to detach a part of the self and its concomitant reality as relevant only to the role-specific situation in question. The individual then establishes distance between his total self and its reality on the one hand, and the role-specific partial self and its reality on the other.[15] This important feat is possible only after primary socialization has taken place. Put crudely once more, it is easier for the child 'to hide' from his teacher than from his mother. Conversely, it is possible to say that the development of this capacity 'to hide' is an important aspect of the process of growing into adulthood.

The reality accent of knowledge internalized in primary socialization is given quasi-automatically. In secondary socialization it must be reinforced by specific pedagogic techniques, 'brought home' to the individual. The phrase is suggestive. The original reality of childhood is 'home'. It posits itself as such, inevitably and, as it were, 'naturally'. By comparison with it, all later realities are 'artificial'. Thus the school teacher tries to 'bring home' the contents he is imparting by making them vivid (that is, making them seem as alive as the 'home world' of the child), relevant (that is, linking them to the relevance structures already present in the 'home world') and interesting (that is, inducing the attentiveness of the child to detach itself from its 'natural' objects to these more 'artificial' ones). These manoeuvres are necessary because an internalized reality is already there, persistently 'in the way' of new internalizations. The degree and precise character of these pedagogic techniques will vary with the motivations the individual has for the acquisition of the new knowledge.

The more these techniques make subjectively plausible a continuity between the original and the new elements of knowledge, the more readily they acquire the accent of reality. One learns a second language by building on the taken-for-granted reality of one's 'mother tongue'. For a long time, one continually retranslates into the original language whatever elements of the new language one is acquiring. Only in this way can the new language begin to have any reality. As this reality comes to be established in its own right, it slowly becomes possible to forego retranslation. One becomes capable of 'thinking in' the new language. Nevertheless, it is rare that a language learned in later life attains the inevitable, self-evident reality of the first language learned in childhood. Hence derives, of course, the affective quality of the 'mother tongue'. *Mutatis mutandis*, the same characteristics of building from the 'home' reality, linking up with it as learning proceeds and only slowly breaking this linkage, appertain to other learning sequences in secondary socialization.

The facts that the processes of secondary socialization do not presuppose a high degree of identification and its contents do not possess the quality of inevitability can be pragmatically useful because they permit learning sequences that are rational and emotionally controlled. But because the contents of this type of internalization have a brittle and unreliable subjective reality compared to the internalizations of primary socialization, in some cases special techniques must be developed to produce whatever identification and inevitability are deemed necessary. The need for such techniques may be intrinsic in terms of learning and applying the contents of internalization, or it may be posited for the sake of the vested interests of the personnel administering the socialization process in question. For example, an individual who wants to become an accomplished musician must immerse himself in his subject to a degree quite unnecessary for an individual learning to be an engineer. Engineering education can take place effectively through formal, highly rational, emotionally neutral processes. Musical education, on the other hand, typically involves much higher identification with a maestro and a much more profound immersion in musical reality. This difference comes from the intrinsic differences between engineering and musical knowledge, and between the ways of life in which these two bodies of knowledge are practically applied. A professional revolutionary, too, needs an immeasurably higher degree of identification and inevitability than an engineer. But here the necessity comes not from intrinsic properties of the knowledge itself, which may be quite simple and sparse in content, but from the personal commitment required of a revolutionary in terms of the vested interests of the revolutionary movement. Sometimes the necessity for the intensifying techniques may come from both intrinsic and extrinsic factors. The socialization of religious personnel is one example.

The techniques applied in such cases are designed to intensify the affective charge of the socialization process. Typically, they involve the institutionalization of an elaborate initiation process, a novitiate, in the course of which the individual comes to commit himself fully to the reality that is being internalized. When the process requires an actual transformation of the individual's 'home' reality, it comes to replicate as closely as possible the character of primary socialization, as we shall see a little later. But even short of such transformation, secondary socialization becomes affectively charged to the degree to which immersion in and commitment to the new reality are institutionally defined as necessary. The relation-ship of the individual to the socializing personnel becomes correspondingly charged with 'significance', that is, the socializing personnel take on the character of significant others *vis-à-vis* the individual being socialized. The individual then commits himself in a comprehensive way to the new reality. He 'gives himself' to music, to the revolution, to the faith, not just partially but with what is subjectively the whole of his life. The readiness to sacrifice oneself is, of course, the final consequence of this type of socialization.

An important circumstance that may posit a need for such intensification is competition between the reality-defining personnel of various institutions. In the case of revolutionary training the intrinsic problem is the socialization of the indivi-dual in a counter-definition of reality – counter, that is, to the definitions of the 'official' legitimators of the society. But there will also have to be intensification in the socialization of the musician in a society that offers sharp competition to the aesthetic values of the musical community. For example, it may be assumed that a musician in the making in contem-porary America must commit himself to music with an emo-tional intensity that was unnecessary in nineteenth-century Vienna, precisely because in the American situation there is powerful competition from what will subjectively appear as the 'materialistic' and 'mass culture' world of the 'rat race'. Similarly, religious training in a pluralistic situation posits the need for 'artificial' techniques of reality-accentuation that are unnecessary in a situation dominated by a religious monopoly. It is still 'natural' to become a Catholic priest in Rome in a way that it is not in America. Consequently, American theo-logical seminaries must cope with the problem of 'reality-slipping' and devise techniques for 'making stick' the same reality. Not surprisingly, they have hit upon the obvious ex-pedient of sending their most promising students to Rome for a while.

Similar variations may exist within the same institutional context, depending upon the tasks assigned to different cate-gories of personnel. Thus the degree of commitment to the military required of career officers is quite different from that required of draftees, a fact clearly reflected in the respective training processes. Similarly, different commitments to the institutional reality are demanded from an executive and from lower-echelon white-collar personnel, from a psycho-analyst and from a psychiatric social worker, and so forth. An executive must be 'politically sound' in a way not incumbent on the supervisor of the typing pool, and a 'didactic analysis' is imposed upon the psycho-analyst but only suggested to the social worker, and so on. There are, then, highly differentiated systems of secondary socialization in complex institutions, sometimes geared very sensitively to the differential requirements of the various categories of institutional personnel.[16]

The institutionalized distribution of tasks between primary and secondary socialization varies with the complexity of the social distribution of knowledge. As long as it is relatively uncomplicated, the same institutional agency can proceed from primary to secondary socialization and carry on the latter to a considerable extent. In cases of very high complexity, specialized agencies for secondary socialization may have to be developed, with full-time personnel specially trained for the educational tasks in question. Short of this degree of specialization, there may be a sequence of socializing agencies combining this task with others. In the latter case, for example, it may be established that at a certain age a boy is transferred from his mother's hut to the warriors' barracks, where he will be trained to become a horseman. This need not entail full-time educational personnel. The older horsemen may teach the younger ones. The development of modern education is, of course, the best illustration of secondary socialization taking place under the auspices of specialized agencies. The resultant decline in the position of the family with regard to secondary socialization is too well known to require further elaboration here.[17]

Maintenance and Transformation of Subjective Reality   ✳

Since socialization is never complete and the contents it internalizes face continuing threats to their subjective reality, every viable society must develop procedures of reality-maintenance to safeguard a measure of symmetry between objective and subjective reality. We have already discussed this problem in connexion with legitimation. Our focus here is on the defence of subjective rather than objective reality; reality as apprehended in individual consciousness rather than on reality as institutionally defined.

Primary socialization internalizes a reality apprehended as inevitable. This internalization may be deemed successful if the sense of inevitability is present most of the time, at least while the individual is active in the world of everyday life. But even when the world of everyday life retains its massive and taken-for-granted reality *in actu*, it is threatened by the marginal situations of human experience that cannot be completely bracketed in everyday activity. There is always the haunting presence of metamorphoses, those actually remembered and those only sensed as sinister possibilities. There are also the more directly threatening competing definitions of reality that may be encountered socially. It is one thing for a well-behaved man to dream of unspeakable orgies in nocturnal solitude. It is quite another to see these dreams empirically enacted by a libertarian colony next door. Dreams can more easily be quarantined within consciousness as 'nonsense' to be shrugged aside or as mental aberrations to be silently repented; they retain the character of phantasms *vis-à-vis* the reality of everyday life. An actual acting-out forces itself upon consciousness much more clamorously. It may have to be destroyed in fact before it can be coped with in the mind. In any case, it cannot be denied as one can at least try to deny the metamorphoses of marginal situations.

The more 'artificial' character of secondary socialization makes the subjective reality of its internalizations even more vulnerable to challenging definitions of reality, not because they are not taken for granted or are apprehended as less than real in everyday life, but because their reality is less deeply rooted in consciousness and thus more susceptible to displacement. For example, both the prohibition on nudity, which is related to one's sense of shame and internalized in primary socialization, and the canons of proper dress for different social occasions, which are acquired as secondary internalizations, are taken for granted in everyday life. As long as they are not socially challenged, neither constitutes a problem for the individual. However, the challenge would have to be much stronger in the former case than in the latter to crystallize as a threat to the taken-for-granted reality of the routines in question. A relatively minor shift in the subjective definition of reality would suffice for an individual to take for granted that one may go to the office without a tie. A much more drastic shift would be necessary to have him go, as a matter of course, without any clothes at all. The former shift could be socially mediated by nothing more than a change of job – say, from a rural to a metropolitan college campus. The latter would entail a social revolution in the individual's milieu; it would be subjectively apprehended as a profound conversion, probably after an initially intense resistance.

The reality of secondary internalizations is less threatened by marginal situations, because it is usually irrelevant to them. What may happen is that such reality is apprehended as trivial precisely because its irrelevance to the marginal situation is revealed. Thus it may be said that the imminence of death profoundly threatens the reality of one's previous self-identifications as a· man, a moral being, or a Christian. One's self-identification as an assistant manager in the ladies' hosiery department is not so much threatened as trivialized in the same situation. Conversely, it may be said that the maintenance of primary internalizations in the face of marginal situations is a fair measure of their subjective reality. The same test would be quite irrelevant when applied to most secondary socializations. It makes sense to die as a man, hardly to die as an assistant manager in the ladies' hosiery department. Again, where secondary internalizations are socially expected to have this degree of reality-persistence in the face of marginal situations, the concomitant socialization procedures will have to be intensified and reinforced in the manner discussed before. Religious and military processes of secondary socialization could again be cited in illustration.

It is convenient to distinguish between two general types of reality-maintenance – routine maintenance and crisis maintenance. The former is designed to maintain the internalized reality in everyday life, the latter in situations of crises. Both entail fundamentally the same social processes, though some differences must be noted.

As we have seen, the reality of everyday life maintains itself by being embodied in routines, which is the essence of institutionalization. Beyond this, however, the reality of everyday life is ongoingly reaffirmed in the individual's interaction with others. Just as reality is originally internalized by a social process, so it is maintained in consciousness by social processes. These latter processes are not drastically different from those of the earlier internalization. They also reflect the basic fact that subjective reality must stand in a relationship with an objective reality that is socially defined.

In the social process of reality-maintenance it is possible to distinguish between significant others and less important others.[18] In an important way all, or at least most, of the others encountered by the individual in everyday life serve to reaffirm his subjective reality. This occurs even in a situation as 'non-significant' as riding on a commuter train. The individual may not know anyone on the train and may speak to no one. All the same, the crowd of fellow-commuters reaffirms the basic structure of everyday life. By their overall conduct the fellow-commuters extract the individual from the tenuous reality of early-morning grogginess and proclaim to him in no uncertain terms that the world consists of earnest men going to work, of responsibility and schedules, of the New Haven Railroad and the *New York Times*. The last, of course, reaffirms the widest coordinates of the individual's reality. From the weather report to the help-wanted ads it assures him that he is, indeed, in the most real world possible. Concomitantly, it affirms the less-than-real status of the sinister ecstasies experienced before breakfast – the alien shape of allegedly familiar objects upon waking from a disturbing dream, the shock of non-recognition of one's own face in the bathroom mirror, the unspeakable suspicion a little later that one's wife and children are mysterious strangers. Most individuals susceptible to such metaphysical terrors manage to exorcize them to a degree in the course of their rigidly performed morning rituals, so that the reality of everyday life is at least gingerly established by the time they step out of their front door. But the reality begins to be fairly reliable only in the anonymous community of the commuter train. It attains massivity as the train pulls into Grand Central Station. *Ergo sum*, the individual can now murmur to himself, and proceed to the office wide-awake and self-assured.

It would, therefore, be a mistake to assume that only significant others serve to maintain subjective reality. But significant others occupy a central position in the economy of reality-maintenance. They are particularly important for the ongoing confirmation of that crucial element of reality we call identity. To retain confidence that he is indeed who he thinks he is, the individual requires not only the implicit confirmation of this identity that even casual everyday contacts will supply, but the explicit and emotionally charged confirmation that his significant others bestow on him. In the previous illustration, our suburbanite is likely to look to his family and other private associates within the family ambience (neighbourhood, church, club, and the like) for such confirmation, though close business associates may also fulfil this function. If he moreover sleeps with his secretary, his identity is both confirmed and amplified. This assumes that the individual likes the identity being confirmed. The same process pertains to the confirmation of identities that the individual may not like. Even casual acquaintances may confirm his self-identification as a hopeless failure, but wife, children and secretary ratify this with undeniable finality. The process from objective reality-definition to subjective reality-maintenance is the same in both cases.

The significant others in the individual's life are the principal agents for the maintenance of his subjective reality. Less significant others function as a sort of chorus. Wife, children and secretary solemnly reaffirm each day that one is a man of importance, or a hopeless failure; maiden aunts, cooks and elevator operators lend varying degrees of support to this. It is, of course, quite possible that there is some disagreement between these people. The individual then faces a problem of consistency, which he can, typically, solve either by modifying his reality or his reality-maintaining relationships. He may have the alternative of accepting his identity as a failure on the one hand, or of firing his secretary or divorcing his wife on the other. He also has the option of downgrading some of these people from their status of significant others and turning instead to others for his significant reality-confirmations – his psycho-analyst, say, or his old cronies at the club. There are many possible complexities in this organization of reality-maintaining relationships, especially in a highly mobile and role-differentiated society.[19]

The relation between the significant others and the 'chorus' in reality-maintenance is a dialectical one; that is, they interact with each other as well as with the subjective reality they serve to confirm. A solidly negative identification on the part of the wider milieu may eventually affect the identification offered by the significant others – when even the elevator operator fails to say 'sir', the wife may give up her identification of her husband as a man of importance. Conversely, the significant others may eventually have an effect on the wider milieu – a 'loyal' wife can be an asset in several ways as the individual seeks to get across a certain identity to his business associates. Reality-maintenance and reality-confirmation thus involve the totality of the individual's social situation, though the significant others occupy a privileged position in these processes.

The relative importance of the significant others and the 'chorus' can be seen most easily if one looks at instances of *dis*-confirmation of subjective reality. A reality-disconfirming act by the wife, taken by itself, has far greater potency than a similar act by a casual acquaintance. Acts by the latter have to acquire a certain density to equal the potency of the former. The reiterated opinion of one's best friend that the newspapers are not reporting substantial developments going on beneath the surface may carry more weight than the same opinion expressed by one's barber. However, the same opinion expressed in succession by ten casual acquaintances may begin to outweigh a contrary opinion of one's best friend. The crystallization subjectively arrived at as a result of these various definitions of reality will then determine how one is likely to react to the appearance of a solid phalanx of grim, silent, briefcase-carrying Chinese on the commuter train one morning; that is, will determine the weight one gives the phenomenon in one's own definition of reality. To take another illustration, if one is a believing Catholic the reality of one's faith need not be threatened by non-believing business associates. It is very likely to be threatened, however, by a non-believing wife. In a pluralistic society, therefore, it is logical for the Catholic Church to tolerate a broad variety of inter-faith associations in economic and political life, but to continue to frown on inter-faith marriage. Generally speaking, in situations where there is competition between different reality-defining agencies, all sorts of secondary-group relationships with the competitors may be tolerated, as long as there are firmly established primary-group relationships within which *one* reality is on-goingly reaffirmed against the competitors.[20] The manner in which the Catholic Church has adapted itself to the pluralistic situation in America is an excellent illustration.

The most important vehicle of reality-maintenance is con-versation. One may view the individual's everyday life in terms of the working away of a conversational apparatus that ongoingly maintains, modifies and reconstructs his subjective reality.[21] Conversation means mainly, of course, that people speak with one another. This does not deny the rich aura of non-verbal communication that surrounds speech. Neverthe-less speech retains a privileged position in the total conversa-tional apparatus. It is important to stress, however, that the greater part of reality-maintenance in conversation is implicit, not explicit. Most conversation does not in so many words define the nature of the world. Rather, it takes place against the background of a world that is silently taken for granted. Thus an exchange such as, 'Well, it's time for me to get to the station', and 'Fine, darling, have a good day at the office', implies an entire world *within which* these apparently simple propositions make sense. By virtue of this implication the exchange confirms the subjective reality of this world.

If this is understood, one will readily see that the great part, if not all, of everyday conversation maintains subjective reality. Indeed, its massivity is achieved by the accumulation and consistency of casual conversation – conversation that can *afford to be casual* precisely because it refers to the routines of a taken-for-granted world. The loss of casualness signals a break in the routines and, at least potentially, a threat to the taken-for-granted reality. Thus one may imagine the effect on casualness of an exchange like this: 'Well, it's time for me to get to the station', 'Fine, darling, don't forget to take along your gun.'

At the same time that the conversational apparatus ongoingly maintains reality, it ongoingly modifies it. Items are dropped and added, weakening some sectors of what is still being taken for granted and reinforcing others. Thus the subjective reality of something that is never talked about comes to be shaky. It is one thing to engage in an embarrassing sexual act. It is quite another to talk about it beforehand or afterwards. Conversely, conversation gives firm contours to items previously apprehended in a fleeting and unclear manner. One may have doubts about one's religion; these doubts become real in a quite different way as one discusses them. One then 'talks oneself into' these doubts; they are objectified as reality within one's own consciousness. Generally speaking, the conversational apparatus maintains reality by 'talking through' various elements of experience and allocating them a definite place in the real world.

This reality-generating potency of conversation is already given in the fact of linguistic objectification. We have seen how language objectifies the world, transforming the *panta rhei* of experience into a cohesive order. In the establishment of this order language *realizes* a world, in the double sense of apprehending and producing it. Conversation is the actualizing of this realizing efficacy of language in the face-to-face situations of individual existence. In conversation the objectifications of language become objects of individual consciousness. Thus the fundamental reality-maintaining fact is the continuing use of the same language to objectify unfolding biographical experience. In the widest sense, all who employ this same language are reality-maintaining others. The significance of this can be further differentiated in terms of what is meant by a 'common language' – from the group-idiosyncratic language of primary groups to regional or class dialects to the national community that defines itself in terms of language. There are corresponding 'returns to reality' for the individual who goes back to the few individuals who understand his in-group allusions, to the section to which his accent belongs, or to the large collectivity that has identified itself with a particular linguistic tradition – in reverse order, say, a return to the

United States, to Brooklyn, and to the people who went to the same public school.

In order to maintain subjective reality effectively, the conversational apparatus must be continual and consistent. Disruptions of continuity or consistency *ipso facto* posit a threat to the subjective reality in question. We have already discussed the expedients that the individual may adopt to meet the threat of inconsistency. Various techniques to cope with the threat of discontinuity are also available. The use of correspondence to continue significant conversation despite physical separation may serve as an illustration.[22] Different conversations can be compared in terms of the density of the reality they produce or maintain. On the whole, frequency of conversation enhances its reality-generating potency, but lack of frequency can sometimes be compensated for by the intensity of the conversation when it does take place. One may see one's lover only once a month, but the conversation then engaged in is of sufficient intensity to make up for its relative infrequency. Certain conversations may also be explicitly defined and legitimated as having a privileged status – such as conversations with one's confessor, one's psycho-analyst, or a similar 'authority' figure. The 'authority' here lies in the cognitively and normatively superior status that is assigned to these conversations.

Subjective reality is thus always dependent upon specific plausibility structures, that is, the specific social base and social processes required for its maintenance. One can maintain one's self-identification as a man of importance only in a milieu that confirms this identity; one can maintain one's Catholic faith only if one retains one's significant relationship with the Catholic community; and so forth. Disruption of significant conversation with the mediators of the respective plausibility structures threatens the subjective realities in question. As the example of correspondence indicates, the individual may resort to various techniques of reality-maintenance even in the absence of actual conversation, but the reality-generating potency of these techniques is greatly inferior to the face-to-face conversations they are designed to replicate. The longer these techniques are isolated from face-to-face confirmations, the less likely they will be to retain the accent of reality. The individual living for many years among people of a different faith and cut off from the community of those sharing his own may continue to identify himself as, say, a Catholic. Through prayer, religious exercises, and similar techniques his old Catholic reality may continue to be subjectively relevant to him. At the very least the techniques may sustain his continued self-identification as a Catholic. They will, however, become subjectively empty of 'living' reality unless they are 'revitalized' by social contact with other Catholics. To be sure, an individual usually remembers the realities of his past. But the way to 'refresh' these memories is to converse with those who share their relevance.[23]

The plausibility structure is also the social base for the particular suspension of doubt without which the definition of reality in question cannot be maintained in consciousness. Here specific social sanctions against such reality-disintegrating doubts have been internalized and are ongoingly reaffirmed. Ridicule is one such sanction. As long as he remains within the plausibility structure, the individual feels himself to be ridiculous whenever doubts about the reality concerned arise subjectively. He knows that others would smile at him if he voiced them. He can silently smile at himself, mentally shrug his shoulders – and continue to exist within the world thus sanctioned. Needless to say, this procedure of autotherapy will be much more difficult if the plausibility structure is no longer available as its social matrix. The smile will become forced, and eventually is likely to be replaced by a pensive frown.

In crisis situations the procedures are essentially the same as in routine maintenance, except that the reality-confirmations have to be explicit and intensive. Frequently, ritual techniques are brought into play. While the individual may improvise reality-maintaining procedures in the face of crisis, the society itself sets up specific procedures for situations recognized as involving the risk of a breakdown in reality. Included in these predefined situations are certain marginal situations, of which death is by far the most important. Crises in reality, however, may occur in a considerably wider number of cases than are posited by marginal situations. They may be either collective or individual, depending upon the character of the challenge to the socially defined reality. For example, collective rituals of reality-maintenance may be institutionalized for times of natural catastrophe, individual ones for times of personal misfortune. Or, to take another example, specific reality-maintaining procedures may be established to cope with foreigners and their potential threat to the 'official' reality. The individual may have to go through an elaborate ritual purification after contact with a foreigner. The ablution is internalized as a subjective nihilation of the alternative reality represented by the foreigner. Taboos, exorcisms and curses against foreigners, heretics or madmen similarly serve the purpose of individual 'mental hygiene'. The violence of these defensive procedures will be proportional to the seriousness with which the threat is viewed. If contacts with the alternative reality and its representatives become frequent, the defensive procedures may, of course, lose their crisis character and become routinized. Every time one meets a foreigner, say, one must spit three times – without giving much further thought to the matter.

Everything that has been said so far on socialization implies the possibility that subjective reality can be transformed. To be in society already entails an ongoing process of modification of subjective reality. To talk about transformation, then, involves a discussion of different degrees of modification. We will concentrate here on the extreme case, in which there is a near-total transformation; that is, in which the individual 'switches worlds'. If the processes involved in the extreme case are clarified, those of less extreme cases will be understood more easily.

Typically, the transformation is subjectively apprehended as total. This, of course, is something of a misapprehension. Since subjective reality is never totally socialized, it cannot be totally transformed by social processes. At the very least the transformed individual will have the same body and live in the same physical universe. Nevertheless, there are instances of transformation that appear total if compared with lesser modifications. Such transformations we will call alternations.[24]

Alternation requires processes of re-socialization. These processes resemble primary socialization, because they have radically to re-assign reality accents and, consequently, must replicate to a considerable degree the strongly affective identification with the socializing personnel that was characteristic of childhood. They are different from primary socialization because they do not start *ex nihilo*, and as a result must cope with a problem of dismantling, disintegrating the preceding nomic structure of subjective reality. How can this be done?

A 'recipe' for successful alternation has to include both social and conceptual conditions, the social, of course, serving as the matrix of the conceptual. The most important social condition is the availability of an effective plausibility structure, that is, a social base serving as the 'laboratory' of transformation. This plausibility structure will be mediated to the individual by means of significant others, with whom he must establish strongly affective identification. No radical transformation of subjective reality (including, of course, identity) is possible without such identification, which inevitably replicates childhood experiences of emotional dependency on significant others.[25] These significant others are the guides into the new reality. They represent the plausibility structure in the roles they play *vis-à-vis* the individual (roles that are typically defined explicitly in terms of their re-socializing function), and they mediate the new world to the individual. The individual's world now finds its cognitive and affective focus in the plausibility structure in question. Socially, this means an intense concentration of all significant interaction within the group that embodies the plausibility structure and particularly upon the personnel assigned the task of re-socialization.

The historical prototype of alternation is religious conversion. The above considerations can be applied to this by saying, *extra ecclesiam nulla salus*. By *salus* we mean here (with due apologies to the theologians who had other things in mind when they coined the phrase) the empirically successful accomplishment of conversion. It is only within the religious community, the *ecclesia*, that the conversion can be effectively maintained as plausible. This is not to deny that conversion may antedate affiliation with the community – Saul of Tarsus sought out the Christian community *after* his 'Damascus experience'. But this is not the point. To have a conversion experience is nothing much. The real thing is to be able to keep on taking it seriously; to retain a sense of its plausibility.

This is where the religious community comes in. It provides the indispensable plausibility structure for the new reality. In other words, Saul may have become Paul in the aloneness of religious ecstasy, but he could *remain* Paul only in the context of the Christian community that recognized him as such and confirmed the 'new being' in which he now located this identity. This relationship of conversion and community is not a peculiarly Christian phenomenon (despite the historically peculiar features of the Christian *ecclesia*). One cannot remain a Muslim outside the *'umma* of Islam, a Buddhist outside the *sangha*, and probably not a Hindu anywhere outside India. Religion requires a religious community, and to live in a religious world requires affiliation with that community.[26] The plausibility structures of religious conversion have been imitated by secular agencies of alternation. The best examples are in the areas of political indoctrination and psychotherapy.[27]

The plausibility structure must become the individual's world, displacing all other worlds, especially the world the individual 'inhabited' before his alternation. This requires segregation of the individual from the 'inhabitants' of other worlds, especially his 'cohabitants' in the world he has left behind. Ideally this will be physical segregation. If that is not possible for whatever reasons, the segregation is posited by definition; that is, by a definition of those others that nihilates them. The alternating individual disaffiliates himself from his previous world and the plausibility structure that sustained it, bodily if possible, mentally if not. In either case he is no longer 'yoked together with unbelievers', and thus is protected from their potential reality-disrupting influence. Such segregation is particularly important in the early stages of alternation (the 'novitiate' phase). Once the new reality has congealed, circumspect relations with outsiders may again be entered into, although those outsiders who used to be biographically significant are still dangerous. They are the ones who will say, 'Come off it, Saul', and there may be times when the old reality they invoke takes the form of temptation.

Alternation thus involves a reorganization of the conversational apparatus. The partners in significant conversation change. And in conversation with the new significant others subjective reality is transformed. It is maintained by continuing conversation with them, or within the community they represent. Put simply, this means that one must now be very careful with whom one talks. People and ideas that are discrepant with the new definitions of reality are systematically avoided.[28] Since this can rarely be done with total success, if only because of the memory of past reality, the new plausibility structure will typically provide various therapeutic procedures to take care of 'backsliding' tendencies. These procedures follow the general pattern of therapy, as discussed earlier.

The most important conceptual requirement for alternation is the availability of a legitimating apparatus for the whole sequence of transformation. What must be legitimated is not only the new reality, but the stages by which it is appropriated and maintained, and the abandonment or repudiation of all alternative realities. The nihilating side of the conceptual machinery is particularly important in view of the dismantling problem that must be solved. The old reality, as well as the collectivities and significant others that previously mediated it to the individual, must be reinterpreted *within* the legitimating apparatus of the new reality. This reinterpretation brings about a rupture in the subjective biography of the individual in terms of 'B.C.' and 'A.D.', 'pre-Damascus' and 'post-Damascus'. Everything preceding the alternation is now apprehended as leading towards it (as an 'Old Testament', so to speak, or as *praeparatio evangelii*), everything following it as flowing from its new reality. This involves a reinterpretation of past biography *in toto*, following the formula, 'Then I *thought* . . . now I *know*'. Frequently this includes the retrojection into the past of present interpretative schemas (the formula for this being, 'I already knew then, though in an unclear manner . . .') and motives that were not subjectively present in the past but that are now necessary for the reinterpretation of what took place then (the formula being, 'I *really* did this because . . .'). Pre-alternation biography is typically nihilated *in toto* by subsuming it under a negative category occupying a strategic position in the new legitimating apparatus: 'When I was still living a life of sin', 'When I was still caught in bourgeois consciousness', 'When I was still motivated by these unconscious neurotic needs'. The biographical rupture is thus identified with a cognitive separation of darkness and light.

In addition to this reinterpretation *in toto* there must be particular reinterpretations of past events and persons with past significance. The alternating individual would, of course, be best off if he could completely forget some of these. But to forget completely is notoriously difficult. What is necessary, then, is a radical reinterpretation of the meaning of these past events or persons in one's biography. Since it is relatively easier to invent things that never happened than to forget those that actually did, the individual may fabricate and insert events wherever they are needed to harmonize the remembered with the reinterpreted past. Since it is the new reality rather than the old that now appears dominatingly plausible to him, he may be perfectly 'sincere' in such a procedure – subjectively, he is not telling lies about the past but bringing it in line with *the* truth that, necessarily, embraces both present and past. This point, incidentally, is very important if one wishes to understand adequately the motives behind the historically recurrent falsifications and forgeries of religious documents. Persons, too, particularly significant others, are reinterpreted in this fashion. The latter now become unwilling actors in a drama whose meaning is necessarily opaque to them; and, not surprisingly, they typically reject such an assignment. This is the reason prophets typically fare badly in their home towns, and it is in this context that one may understand Jesus's statement that his followers must leave behind them their fathers and mothers.

It is not difficult now to propose a specific 'prescription' for alternation into any conceivable reality, however implausible from the standpoint of the outsider. It is possible to prescribe specific procedures for, say, convincing individuals that they can communicate with beings from outer space provided that and as long as they stay on a steady diet of raw fish. We can leave it to the imagination of the reader, if he is so inclined, to work out the details of such a sect of Ichthyosophists. The 'prescription' would entail the construction of an Ichthyosophist plausibility structure, properly segregated from the outside world and equipped with the necessary socializing and therapeutic personnel; the elaboration of an Ichthyosophist body of knowledge, sufficiently sophisticated to explain why the self-evident nexus between raw fish and galactic telepathy had not been discovered before; and the necessary legitimations and nihilations to make sense of the individual's journey towards this great truth. If these procedures are followed carefully, there will be a high probability of success once an individual has been lured or kidnapped into the Ichthyosophist brainwashing institute.

There are in practice, of course, many intermediate types between re-socialization as just discussed and secondary socialization that continues to build on the primary internalizations. In these there are partial transformations of subjective reality or of designated sectors of it. Such partial transformations are common in contemporary society in connexion with the individual's social mobility and occupational training.[29] Here the transformation of subjective reality can be considerable, as the individual is made into an acceptable upper-middle-class type or an acceptable physician, and as he internalizes the appropriate reality-appendages. But these transformations typically fall far short of re-socialization. They build on the basis of primary internalizations and generally avoid abrupt discontinuities within the subjective biography of the individual. As a result, they face the problem of maintaining consistency between the earlier and later elements of subjective reality. This problem, not present in this form in re-socialization, which ruptures the subjective biography and reinterprets the past rather than correlating the present with it, becomes more acute the closer secondary socialization gets to re-socialization without actually becoming it. Re-socialization is a cutting of the Gordian knot of the consistency problem – by giving up the quest for consistency and reconstructing reality *de novo*.

The procedures for maintaining consistency also involve a tinkering with the past, but in a less radical manner – an approach dictated by the fact that in such cases there is usually a continuing association with persons and groups who were significant before. They continue to be around, are likely to protest too fanciful reinterpretations, and must themselves be convinced that such transformations as have taken place are plausible. For example, in the case of transformations occurring in conjunction with social mobility, there are ready-made interpretative schemes that explain what has happened to all concerned *without* positing a total metamorphosis of the individual concerned. Thus the parents of such an upwardly mobile individual will accept certain changes in the latter's demeanour and attitudes as a necessary, possibly even desirable, accompaniment of his new station in life. 'Of course', they will agree, Irving has had to de-emphasize his Jewishness now that he has become a successful doctor in suburbia; 'of course' he dresses and speaks differently; 'of course' he now votes Republican; 'of course' he married a Vassar girl – and perhaps it will also become a matter of course that he only rarely comes to visit his parents. Such interpretative schemes, which are ready-made in a society with high upward mobility and already internalized by the individual before he himself is actually mobile, guarantee biographical continuity and smooth inconsistencies as they arise.[30]

Similar procedures take place in situations where transformations are fairly radical but defined as temporary in duration – for example, in training for short-term military service or in cases of short-term hospitalization.[31] Here the difference from full re-socialization is particularly easy to see – by comparing what happens with training for career military service or with the socialization of chronic patients. In the former instances, consistency with the previous reality and identity (existence as a civilian or as a healthy person) is already posited by the assumption that one will eventually return to these.

Broadly speaking, one may say that the procedures involved are of opposite character. In re-socialization the past is re-interpreted to conform to the present reality, with the tendency to retroject into the past various elements that were subjectively unavailable at the time. In secondary socialization the present is interpreted so as to stand in a continuous relationship with the past, with the tendency to minimize such transformations as have actually taken place. Put differently, the reality-base for re-socialization is the present, for secondary socialization the past.

2. Internalization and Social Structure

Socialization always takes place in the context of a specific social structure. Not only its contents but also its measure of 'success' have social-structural conditions and social-structural consequences. In other words, the micro-sociological or social-psychological analysis of phenomena of internalization must always have as its background a macro-sociological understanding of their structural aspects.[32]

On the level of theoretical analysis attempted here we cannot enter into a detailed discussion of the different empirical relationships between the contents of socialization and social-structural configurations.[33] Some general observations may, however, be made on the social-structural aspects of the 'success' of socialization. By 'successful socialization' we mean the establishment of a high degree of symmetry between objective and subjective reality (as well as identity, of course). Conversely, 'unsuccessful socialization' is to be understood in terms of asymmetry between objective and subjective reality. As we have seen, totally successful socialization is anthropologically impossible. Totally unsuccessful socialization is, at the very least, extremely rare, limited to cases of individuals with whom even minimal socialization fails because of extreme organic pathology. Our analysis must, therefore, be concerned with gradations on a continuum whose extreme poles are empirically unavailable. Such analysis is useful because it permits some general statements about the conditions and consequences of successful socialization.

Maximal success in socialization is likely to occur in societies with very simple division of labour and minimal distribution of knowledge. Socialization under such conditions produces identities that are socially predefined and profiled to a high degree. Since every individual is confronted with essentially the same institutional programme for his life in the society, the total force of the institutional order is brought to bear with more or less equal weight on each individual, producing a compelling massivity for the objective reality to be internalized. Identity then is highly profiled in the sense of representing fully the objective reality within which it is located. Put simply, everyone pretty much *is* what he is supposed to be. In such a society identities are easily recognizable, objectively and subjectively. Everybody knows who everybody else is and who he is himself. A knight *is* a knight and a peasant *is* a peasant, to others as well as to themselves. There is, therefore, no *problem* of identity. The question, 'Who am I?' is unlikely to arise in consciousness, since the socially predefined answer is massively real subjectively and consistently confirmed in all significant social interaction. This by no means implies that the individual is happy with his identity. It was probably never very agreeable to be a peasant, for instance. To be a peasant entailed problems of all sorts, subjectively real, pressing and far from happiness-producing. It did *not* entail the problem of identity. One was a miserable, perhaps even a rebellious peasant. But one *was* a peasant. Persons formed under such conditions are unlikely to conceive of themselves in terms of 'hidden depths', in a psychological sense. 'Surface' and 'under-the-surface' selves are differentiated only in terms of the range of subjective reality present to consciousness in any given moment, not in terms of a permanent differentiation of 'layers' of the self. For example, the peasant apprehends himself in one role as he is beating his wife and in another as he cringes before his lord. In each case, the other role is 'under the surface', that is, not attended to in the peasant's consciousness. But neither role is posited as a 'deeper' or 'more real' self. In other words, the individual in such a society not only is what he is supposed to be, but he is that in a unified, 'unstratified' way.[34]

Under such conditions unsuccessful socialization occurs only as a result of biographical accidents, either biological or social. For example, a child's primary socialization may be impaired because of a physical deformity that is socially stigmatized or because of a stigma based on social definitions.[35] The cripple and the bastard are prototypes of these two cases.

There is also the possibility of socialization being intrinsically prevented by biological handicaps, as in the case of extreme mental deficiency. All these cases have the character of individual misfortune. They do not provide the ground for the institutionalization of counter-identities and counter-reality. Indeed, this fact provides the measure of misfortune present in such biographies. In a society of this kind, the individual cripple or bastard has virtually no subjective defence against the stigmatic identity assigned to him. He *is* what he is supposed to be, to himself as to his significant others and to the community as a whole. To be sure, he may react to this fate with resentment or rage, but it is *qua* inferior being that he is resentful or enraged. His resentment and rage may even serve as decisive ratifications of his socially defined identity as an inferior being, since his betters, by definition, are above these brutish emotions. He is imprisoned in the objective reality of his society, although that reality is subjectively present to him in an alien and truncated manner. Such an individual will be unsuccessfully socialized, that is, there will be a high degree of asymmetry between the socially defined reality in which he is *de facto* caught, as in an alien world, and his own subjective reality, which reflects that world only very poorly. The asymmetry will, however, have no cumulative structural consequences because it lacks a social base within which it could crystallize into a counter-world, with its own institutionalized cluster of counter-identities. The unsuccessfully socialized individual himself is socially predefined as a profiled type – the cripple, the bastard, the idiot, and so on. Consequently, whatever contrary self-identifications may at times arise in his own consciousness lack any plausibility structure that would transform them into something more than ephemeral fantasies.

Incipient counter-definitions of reality and identity are present as soon as any such individuals congregate in socially durable groups. This triggers a process of change that will introduce a more complex distribution of knowledge. A counter-reality may now begin to be objectivated in the marginal group of the unsuccessfully socialized. At this point, of course, the group will initiate its own socialization processes. For example, lepers and the offspring of lepers may be stigmatized in a society. Such stigmatization may be limited to those physically afflicted with the disease, or it may include others by social definition – say, anyone born in an earthquake. Thus individuals may be defined as lepers from birth, and this definition may severely affect their primary socialization – say, under the auspices of a crazy old woman, who keeps them physically alive beyond the confines of the community and transmits to them a bare minimum of the community's institutional traditions. As long as such individuals, even if they number more than a handful, do, not form a counter-community of their own, both their objective and subjective identities will be predefined in accordance with the community's institutional programme for them. They will *be* lepers, and nothing else.

The situation begins to change when there is a leper colony sufficiently large and durable to serve as a plausibility structure for counter-definitions of reality – and of the fate of being a leper. To be a leper, be it in terms of biological or social assignment, may now be known as the special mark of divine election. The individuals prevented from fully internalizing the reality of the community may now be socialized into the counter-reality of the lepers' colony; that is, unsuccessful socialization into one social world may be accompanied by successful socialization into another. At any early stage of such a process of change the crystallization of counter-reality and counter-identity may be hidden from the knowledge of the larger community, which still predefines and ongoingly identifies these individuals as lepers, and nothing else. It does not know that, 'really', they are the special sons of the gods. At this point an individual assigned to the leper category may discover 'hidden depths' within himself. The question 'Who am I?' becomes possible simply because two conflicting answers are socially available – the crazy old woman's ('You are a leper') and that of the colony's own socializing personnel ('You are a son of god'). As the individual accords a privileged status within his consciousness to the colony's definitions of reality and of himself, a rupture occurs between his 'visible' conduct in the larger community and his 'invisible' self-identification as someone quite different. In other words, a cleavage appears between 'appearance' and 'reality' in the individual's self-apprehension. He no longer is what he is supposed to be. He *acts* the leper – he *is* a son of god. If we are to push the example one step further, to the point when this cleavage becomes known to the non-leprous community, it is not difficult to see that the community's reality, too, will be affected by this change. Minimally, it will no longer be so easy to recognize the identity of those defined as lepers – one will no longer be sure whether an individual so defined identifies himself in the same way or not. Maximally, it will no longer be an easy matter to recognize anybody's identity – for if lepers can refuse to be what they are supposed to be, so can others; perhaps, so can oneself. If this process appears fanciful at first, it is beautifully illustrated by Gandhi's designation of *harijans*, that is, 'children of God', for the outcastes of Hinduism.

Once there is a more complex distribution of knowledge in a society, unsuccessful socialization may be the result of different significant others mediating different objective realities to the individual. Put differently, unsuccessful socialization may be the result of heterogeneity in the socializing personnel. This may occur in a number of ways. There may be situations in which all the significant others of primary socialization mediate a common reality, but from considerably different perspectives. To a degree, of course, every significant other has a different perspective on the common reality simply by virtue of being a specific individual with a specific biography. But the consequences we have in mind here occur only when the differences between the significant others pertain to their social types rather than their individual idiosyncrasies. For example, men and women may 'inhabit' considerably different social worlds in a society. If both men and women function as significant others in primary socialization, they mediate these discrepant realities to the child. This by itself does not raise the threat of unsuccessful socialization. The male and female versions of reality are socially recognized, and this recognition, too, is transmitted in primary socialization. Thus there is a predefined dominance of the male version for the male child and of the female version for the female. The child will *know* the version appertaining to the other sex, to the extent that it has been mediated to him by the significant others of the other sex, but he will not *identify* with this version. Even minimal distribution of knowledge posits specific jurisdictions for the different versions of the common reality. In the above case the female version is socially defined as having no jurisdiction over the male child. Normally, this definition of the 'proper place' of the reality of the other sex is internalized by the child, who 'properly' identifies with the reality to which he has been assigned.

However, 'abnormality' becomes a biographical possibility if a certain competition exists between reality-definitions, raising the possibility of choosing between them. For a variety of biographical reasons the child may make the 'wrong choice'. For example, a male child may internalize 'improper' elements of the female world because his father is absent during the crucial period of primary socialization and it is administered exclusively by his mother and three older sisters. They may mediate the 'proper' jurisdictional definitions to the little boy so that he *knows* he is not supposed to live in the women's world. But he may nevertheless *identify* with it. His resulting 'effeminacy' may be either 'visible' or 'invisible'. In either case, there will be asymmetry between his social identity-assignment and his subjectively real identity.[36]

Obviously a society will supply therapeutic mechanisms to take care of such 'abnormal' cases. We need not reiterate here what has been said about therapy, except to stress that the need for therapeutic mechanisms increases in proportion to the structurally given potentiality for unsuccessful socialization. In the example just discussed, at the very least the successfully socialized children will put pressure on the 'wrong' ones. As long as there is no fundamental conflict between the mediated definitions of reality, but only differences between versions of the same common reality, the chances for successful therapy are good.

Unsuccessful socialization may also result from the mediation of acutely discrepant worlds by significant others during primary socialization. As the distribution of knowledge becomes more complex, discrepant worlds become available and may be mediated by different significant others in primary socialization. This happens less frequently than the situation just discussed, in which versions of the same common world are distributed among the socializing personnel, because individuals (say, a married couple) sufficiently cohesive as a group to take on the task of primary socialization are likely to have concocted some sort of common world between them. It does occur, however, and is of considerable theoretical interest.

For example, a child may be raised not only by his parents but also by a nurse recruited from an ethnic or class sub-society. The parents mediate to the child the world of, say, a conquering aristocracy of one race; the nurse mediates the world of a subjugated peasantry of another race. It is even pos-sible that the two mediations employ completely different languages, which the child learns simultaneously but which the parents and the nurse find mutually unintelligible. In such a case, of course, the parental world will have dominance by predefinition. The child will be recognized by all concerned and by himself as belonging to his parents' group and not his nurse's. All the same, the predefinition of the respective juris-dictions of the two realities may be upset by various bio-graphical accidents, just as it may in the first situation dis-cussed, except that now unsuccessful socialization entails the possibility of alternation internalized as a permanent feature of the individual's subjective self-apprehension. The choice potentially available to the child now is more profiled, involv-ing different worlds rather than different versions of the same world. Needless to say, in practice there will be many grada-tions between the first and second situations.

When acutely discrepant worlds are mediated in primary socialization, the individual is presented with a choice of pro-filed identities apprehended by him as genuine biographical possibilities. He may become a man as understood by race *A* or as understood by race *B*. This is when the possibility of a truly hidden identity, not readily recognizable in accordance with the objectively available typifications, appears. In other words, there may be a socially concealed asymmetry between 'public' and 'private' biography. As far as the parents are concerned, the child is now ready for the preparatory phase of knighthood. Unknown to them, but sustained by the plausi-bility structure supplied by his nurse's sub-society, the child himself is 'only playing at' this process, while 'really' prepar-ing himself for initiation into the higher religious mysteries of the subjugated group. Similar discrepancies occur in con-temporary society between the socialization processes in the family and in the peer group. As far as the family is concerned, the child is ready for graduation from junior high school. As far as the peer group is concerned, he is ready for his first serious test of courage by stealing an automobile. It goes without saying that such situations are fraught with possibilities of internal conflict and guilt.

Presumably all men, once socialized, are potential 'traitors to themselves'. The internal problem of such 'treason', however, becomes much more complicated if it entails the further problem of *which* 'self' is being betrayed at any particular moment, a problem posited as soon as identification with different significant others includes different generalized others. The child is betraying his parents as he prepares for the mysteries and his nurse as he trains for knighthood, just as he betrays his peer group by being a 'square' young scholar and his parents by stealing an automobile, with each betrayal concomitant with 'treason to himself' in so far as he has identified with the two discrepant worlds. We have discussed the various options open to him in our previous analysis of alternation, although it will be clear that these options have a different subjective reality when they are already internalized in primary socialization. It is safe to assume that alternation remains a lifelong threat to whatever subjective reality emerges from such conflict as the result of whatever options, a threat posited once and for all with the introduction of the alternating possibility into primary socialization itself.

The possibility of 'individualism' (that is, of individual choice between discrepant realities and identities) is directly linked to the possibility of unsuccessful socialization. We have argued that unsuccessful socialization opens up the question of 'Who am I?' In the social-structural context in which unsuccessful socialization becomes so recognized, the same question arises for the *successfully* socialized individual by virtue of his reflection about the unsuccessfully socialized. He will sooner or later encounter those with 'hidden selves', the 'traitors', those who have alternated or are alternating between discrepant worlds. By a kind of mirror effect the question may come to apply to himself, first according to the formula 'There, but for the grace of God, go I', eventually perhaps by the formula 'If they, why not I?' This opens a Pandora's box of 'individualistic' choices, which eventually become generalized regardless of whether one's biographical course was determined by the 'right' or the 'wrong' choices. The 'individualist' emerges as a specific social type who has at least the potential to migrate between a number of available worlds and who has deliberately and awarely constructed a self out of the 'material' provided by a number of available identities.

A third important situation leading to unsuccessful socialization arises when there are discrepancies between primary and secondary socialization. The unity of primary socialization is maintained, but in secondary socialization, alternative realities and identities appear as subjective options. The options are, of course, limited by the social-structural context of the individual. For example, he may want to become a knight, but his social position makes this a foolish ambition. When secondary socialization has been differentiated to the point where subjective disidentification from one's 'proper place' in society becomes possible, and when at the same time the social structure does not permit the realization of the subjectively chosen identity, an interesting development occurs. The subjectively chosen identity becomes a fantasy identity, objectified within the individual's consciousness as his 'real self'. It may be assumed that people always have dreams of impossible wish-fulfilment, and the like. The peculiarity of this particular fantasy lies in the objectification, on the level of imagination, of an identity other than the one objectively assigned and previously internalized in primary socialization. It is obvious that any wider distribution of this phenomenon will introduce tensions and unrest into the social structure, threatening the institutional programmes and their taken-for-granted reality.

Another very important consequence when there is discrepancy between primary and secondary socialization is the possibility that the individual may have a relationship to discrepant worlds qualitatively different from the relationships in the previously discussed situations. If discrepant worlds appear in primary socialization, the individual has the option of identifying with one of them as against the others, a process that, because it occurs in primary socialization, will be affectively charged to a high degree. Identification, disidentification and alternation will all be accompanied by affective crises, since they will invariably depend upon the mediation of significant others. The appresentation of discrepant worlds in secondary socialization produces an entirely different configuration. In secondary socialization, internalization need *not* be accompanied by affectively charged identification with significant others; the individual may internalize different realities *without* identifying with them. Therefore, if an alternative world appears in secondary socialization, the individual may opt for it in a manipulative manner. One could speak here of 'cool' alternation. The individual internalizes the new reality, but instead of its being *his* reality, it is a reality to be used by him for specific purposes. In so far as this involves the performance of certain roles, he retains subjective detachment *vis-à-vis* them – he 'puts them on' deliberately and purposefully. If this phenomenon becomes widely distributed, the institutional order as a whole begins to take on the character of a network of reciprocal manipulations.[37]

A society in which discrepant worlds are generally available on a market basis entails specific constellations of subjective reality and identity. There will be an increasingly general consciousness of the relativity of *all* worlds, including one's own, which is now subjectively apprehended as '*a* world', rather than '*the* world'. It follows that one's own institutionalized conduct may be apprehended as 'a role' from which one may detach oneself in one's own consciousness, and which one may 'act out' with manipulative control. For example, the aristocrat no longer simply *is* an aristocrat, but he *plays at being* an aristocrat, and so forth. The situation, then, has a much more far-reaching consequence than the possibility of individuals playing at being what they are *not* supposed to be. They also play at being what they *are* supposed to be – a quite different matter. This situation is increasingly typical of contemporary industrial society, but it would obviously transcend the scope of our present considerations to enter further into a sociology-of-knowledge and social-psychological analysis of this constellation.[38] What should be stressed is that such a situation cannot be understood unless it is ongoingly related to its social-structural context, which follows logically from the necessary relationship between the social division of labour (with its consequences for social structure) and the social distribution of knowledge (with its consequences for the social objectivation of reality). In the contemporary situation this entails the analysis of both reality and identity pluralism with reference to the structural dynamics of industrialism, particularly the dynamics of the social stratification patterns produced by industrialism.[39]

3. Theories about Identity

Identity is, of course, a key element of subjective reality and, like all subjective reality, stands in a dialectical relationship with society. Identity is formed by social processes. Once crystallized, it is maintained, modified, or even reshaped by social relations. The social processes involved in both the formation and the maintenance of identity are determined by the social structure. Conversely, the identities produced by the interplay of organism, individual consciousness and social structure react upon the given social structure, maintaining it, modifying it, or even reshaping it. Societies have histories in the course of which specific identities emerge; these histories are, however, made by men with specific identities.

If one is mindful of this dialectic one can avoid the misleading notion of 'collective identities' without having recourse to the uniqueness, *sub specie aeternitatis*, of individual existence.[40] Specific historical social structures engender identity *types*, which are recognizable in individual cases. In this sense one may assert that an American has a different identity than a Frenchman, a New Yorker than a Midwesterner, an executive than a hobo, and so forth. As we have seen, orientation and conduct in everyday life depend upon such typifications. This means that identity types can be observed in everyday life and that assertions like the ones above can be verified – or refuted – by ordinary men endowed with common sense. The American who doubts that the French are different can go to France and find out for himself. Clearly the status of such typifications is not comparable to that of the constructs of the social sciences, nor do the verification and refutation follow the canons of scientific method. We must leave aside the methodological problem of what the precise relationship is between everyday-life typifications and scientific constructs (a Puritan knew himself to be a Puritan and was recognized as one by, say, Anglicans without much deliberation; the social scientist, however, who wishes to check Max Weber's thesis about the Puritan ethic must follow somewhat different and more complex procedures in order to 'recognize' the empirical referents of the Weberian ideal type). The point of interest in the present context is that identity types are 'observable' and 'verifiable' in pre-theoretical, and thus pre-scientific experience.

Identity is a phenomenon that emerges from the dialectic between individual and society. Identity *types*, on the other hand, are social products *tout court*, relatively stable elements of objective social reality (the degree of stability being, of course, socially determined in its turn). As such, they are the topic of some form of theorizing in any society, even if they are stable and the formation of individual identities is relatively unproblematic. Theories about identity are always embedded in a more general interpretation of reality; they are 'built into' the symbolic universe and its theoretical legitimations, and vary with the character of the latter. Identity remains unintelligible unless it is located in a world. Any theorizing about identity – and about specific identity types – must therefore occur within the framework of the theoretical interpretations within which it and they are located. We will return to this point presently.

It should be stressed again that we are here referring to theories about identity as a social phenomenon; that is, without prejudice as to their acceptability to modern science. Indeed, we will refer to such theories as 'psychologies' and will include any theory about identity that claims to explain the empirical phenomenon in a comprehensive fashion, whether or not such an explanation is 'valid' for the contemporary scientific discipline of that name.

If theories about identity are always embedded in the more comprehensive theories about reality, this must be understood in terms of the logic underlying the latter. For example, a psychology interpreting certain empirical phenomena as possession by demoniacal beings has as its matrix a mythological theory of the cosmos, and it is inappropriate to interpret it in a non-mythological framework. Similarly, a psychology interpreting the same phenomena in terms of electrical disturbances of the brain has as its background an overall scientific theory of reality, both human and non-human, and derives its consistency from the logic underlying this theory. Put simply, psychology always presupposes cosmology.

This point can be well illustrated by reference to the much used psychiatric term 'reality-oriented'.[41] A psychiatrist trying to diagnose an individual whose psychological status is in doubt asks him questions to determine the degree of his 'reality-orientedness'. This is quite logical; from a psychiatric viewpoint there is obviously something problematic about an individual who does not know what day of the week it is or who readily admits he has talked with departed spirits. Indeed, the term 'reality-oriented' itself can be useful in such a context. The sociologist, however, has to ask the additional question '*Which* reality?' Incidentally, this addition is not irrelevant psychiatrically. The psychiatrist will certainly take it into account, when an individual does not know the day of the week, if he has just arrived by jet plane from another continent. He may not know the day of the week simply because he is still 'on another time' – Calcutta time, say, instead of Eastern Standard Time. If the psychiatrist has any sensitivity to the socio-cultural context of psychological conditions he will also arrive at different diagnoses of the individual who converses with the dead, depending on whether such an individual comes from, say, New York City or from rural Haiti. The individual could be 'on another reality' in the same socially objective sense that the previous one was 'on another time'. In other words, questions of psychological status cannot be decided without recognizing the reality-definitions that are taken for granted in the social situation of the individual. To put it more sharply, psychological status is relative to the social definitions of reality in general and is itself socially defined.[42]

The emergence of psychologies introduces a further dialectical relationship between identity and society – the relationship between psychological theory and those elements of subjective reality it purports to define and explain. The level of such theorizing may, of course, vary greatly, as in the case of all theoretical legitimations. What has been said previously about the origins and phases of legitimating theories applies here with equal validity, but with one not unimportant difference. Psychologies pertain to a dimension of reality that is of the greatest and most continuous subjective relevance for all individuals. Therefore the dialectic between theory and reality affects the individual in a palpably direct and intensive manner.

When psychological theories attain a high degree of intellectual complexity they are likely to be administered by personnel specially trained in this body of knowledge. Whatever the social organization of these specialists may be, psychological theories re-enter everyday life by providing the interpretative schemes for disposing of problematic cases. Problems arising out of the dialectic between either subjective identity and social identity-assignments, or identity and its biological substratum (of which more later), can be classified according to theoretical categories – which is, of course, the presupposition for any therapy. The psychological theories then serve to legitimate the identity-maintenance and identity-repair procedures established in the society, providing the theoretical linkage between identity and world, as these are both socially defined and subjectively appropriated.

Psychological theories may be empirically adequate or inadequate, by which we do *not* mean their adequacy in terms of the procedural canons of empirical science, but rather, as interpretative schemes applicable by the expert or the layman to empirical phenomena in everyday life. For example, a psychological theory positing demoniacal possession is unlikely to be adequate in interpreting the identity problems of middle-class, Jewish intellectuals in New York City. These people simply do not have an identity capable of producing phenomena that could be so interpreted. The demons, if such there are, seem to avoid them. On the other hand, psychoanalysis is unlikely to be adequate for the interpretation of identity problems in rural Haiti, while some sort of Voudun psychology might supply interpretative schemes with a high degree of empirical accuracy. The two psychologies demonstrate their empirical adequacy by their applicability in therapy, but neither thereby demonstrates the ontological status of its categories. Neither the Voudun gods nor libidinal energy may exist outside the world defined in the respective social contexts. But in these contexts they do exist by virtue of social definition and are internalized as realities in the course of socialization. Rural Haitians *are* possessed and New York intellectuals *are* neurotic. Possession and neurosis are thus constituents of both objective and subjective reality *in these contexts*. This reality is empirically available in everyday life. The respective psychological theories are empirically adequate in precisely the same sense. The problem of whether or how psychological theories could be developed to transcend this socio-historical relativity need not concern us here.

In so far as psychological theories are adequate in this sense, they are capable of empirical verification. Again, what is at issue is not verification in the scientific sense, but testing in the experience of everyday social life. For example, it may be proposed that individuals born on certain days of the month are likely to be possessed, or that individuals with domineering mothers are likely to be neurotic. Such propositions are empirically verifiable to the extent that they belong to adequate theories, in the afore-mentioned sense. Such verification may be undertaken by participants as well as by outside observers of the social situations in question. A Haitian ethnologist can empirically discover New York neurosis, just as an American ethnologist can empirically discover Voudun possession. The presupposition for such discoveries is simply that the outside observer is willing to employ the conceptual machinery of the indigenous psychology for the inquiry at hand. Whether he is also willing to accord that psychology a more general epistemological validity is irrelevant to the immediate empirical investigation.

Another way of saying that psychological theories are adequate is to say that they reflect the psychological reality they purport to explain. But if this were the whole story, the relationship between theory and reality here would not be a dialectical one. A genuine dialectic is involved because of the *realizing* potency of psychological theories. In so far as psychological theories are elements of the social definition of reality, their reality-generating capacity is a characteristic they share with other legitimating theories; however, their realizing potency is particularly great because it is actualized by emotionally charged processes of identity-formation. If a psychology becomes socially established (that is, becomes generally recognized as an adequate interpretation of objective reality), it tends to realize itself forcefully in the phenomena it purports to interpret. Its internalization is accelerated by the fact that it pertains to internal reality, so that the individual realizes it in the very act of internalizing it. Again, since a psychology by definition pertains to identity, its internalization is likely to be accompanied by identification, hence is *ipso facto* likely to be identity-forming. In this close nexus between internalization and identification, psychological theories differ considerably from other types of theory. Not surprisingly, since problems of unsuccessful socialization are most conducive to this kind of theorizing, psychological theories are more apt to have socializing effects. This is not the same thing as saying that psychologies are self-verifying. As we have indicated, verification comes by confronting psychological theories and psychological reality as empirically available. Psychologies produce a reality, which in turn serves as the basis for their verification. In other words, we are dealing here with dialectics, not tautology.

The rural Haitian who internalizes Voudun psychology will become possessed as soon as he discovers certain well-defined signs. Similarly, the New York intellectual who internalizes Freudian psychology will become neurotic as soon as he diagnoses certain well-known symptoms. Indeed, it is possible that, given a certain biographical context, signs or symptoms will be produced by the individual himself. The Haitian will, in that case, produce not symptoms of neurosis but signs of possession, while the New Yorker will construct his neurosis in conformity with the recognized symptomatology. This has nothing to do with 'mass hysteria', much less with malingering, but with the imprint of societal identity types upon the individual subjective reality of ordinary people with common sense. The degree of identification will vary with the conditions of internalization, as previously discussed, depending, for instance, on whether it takes place in primary or secondary socialization. The social establishment of a psychology, which also entails the accordance of certain social roles to the personnel administering the theory and its therapeutic application, will naturally depend upon a variety of socio-historical circumstances.[43] But the more socially established it becomes, the more abundant will be the phenomena it serves to interpret.

If we posit the possibility that certain psychologies come to be adequate in the course of a realizing process, we imply the question of why as-yet-inadequate theories (as they would have to be in the earlier stages of this process) arise in the first place. Put more simply, why should one psychology replace another in history? The general answer is that such change occurs when identity appears as a problem, for whatever reasons. The problem may arise out of the dialectic of psychological reality and social structure. Radical changes in the social structure (such as, for instance, the changes brought about by the Industrial Revolution) may result in concomitant changes in the psychological reality. In that case, new psychological theories may arise because the old ones no longer adequately explain the empirical phenomena at hand. Theorizing about identity will then seek to take cognizance of the transformations of identity that have actually occurred, and will be itself transformed in the process. On the other hand, identity may become problematic on the level of theory itself, that is, as a result of intrinsic theoretical developments. In that case, psychological theories will be concocted 'before the fact', so to speak. Their *subsequent* social establishment, and concomitant reality-generating potency, may be brought about by any number of affinities between the theorizing personnel and various social interests. Deliberate ideological manipulation by politically interested groups is one historical possibility.

4. Organism and Identity

We discussed much earlier the organismic presuppositions and limitations of the social construction of reality. It is important to stress now that the organism continues to affect each phase of man's reality-constructing activity and that the organism, in turn, is itself affected by this activity. Put crudely, man's animality is transformed in socialization, but it is not abolished. Thus man's stomach keeps grumbling away even as he is about his business of world-building. Conversely, events in this, his product, may make his stomach grumble more, or less, or differently. Man is even capable of eating and theorizing at the same time. The continuing coexistence of man's animality and his sociality may be profitably observed at any conversation over dinner.

It is possible to speak of a dialectic between nature and society.[44] This dialectic is given in the human condition and manifests itself anew in each human individual. For the individual, of course, it unfolds itself in an already structured socio-historical situation. There is an ongoing dialectic, which comes into being with the very first phases of socialization and continues to unfold throughout the individual's existence in society, between each human animal and its socio-historical situation. Externally, it is a dialectic between the individual animal and the social world. Internally, it is a dialectic between the individual's biological substratum and his socially produced identity.

In the external aspect, it is still possible to say that the organism posits limits to what is socially possible. As English constitutional lawyers have said, Parliament can do anything except make men bear children. If Parliament tried, its project would founder on the hard facts of human biology. Biological factors limit the range of social possibilities open to any individual, but the social world, which is pre-existent to each individual, in its turn imposes limits on what is biologically possible to the organism. The dialectic manifests itself in the *mutual* limitation of organism and society.

A pointed illustration of society's limitation of the organism's biological possibilities is longevity. Life expectancy varies with social location. Even in contemporary American society there is considerable discrepancy between the life expectancies of lower-class and upper-class individuals. Furthermore, both the incidence and the character of pathology vary with social location. Lower-class individuals are ill more frequently than upper-class individuals; in addition they have different illnesses. In other words, society determines how long and in what manner the individual organism shall live. This determination may be institutionally programmed in the operation of social controls, as in the institution of law. Society can maim and kill. Indeed, it is in its power over life and death that it manifests its ultimate control over the individual.

Society also directly penetrates the organism in its functioning, most importantly in respect to sexuality and nutrition. While both sexuality and nutrition are grounded in biological drives, these drives are extremely plastic in the human animal. Man is driven by his biological constitution to seek sexual release and nourishment. But his biological constitution does not tell him *where* he should seek sexual release and *what* he should eat. Left to himself, man may attach himself sexually to just about any object and is perfectly capable of eating things that will kill him. Sexuality and nutrition are channelled in specific directions socially rather than biologically, a channelling that not only imposes limits upon these activities, but directly affects organismic functions. Thus the successfully socialized individual is incapable of functioning sexually with the 'wrong' sexual object and may vomit when confronted with the 'wrong' food. As we have seen, the social channelling of activity is the essence of institutionalization, which is the foundation for the social construction of reality. It may be said then that social reality determines not only activity and consciousness but, to a considerable degree, organismic functioning. Thus such intrinsically biological functions as orgasm and digestion are socially structured. Society also determines the manner in which the organism is used in activity; expressivity, gait and gesture are socially structured. The possibility of a sociology of the body that this raises need not concern us here.[45] The point is that society sets limits to the organism, as the organism sets limits to society.

In the internal aspect, the dialectic manifests itself as the resistance of the biological substratum to its social moulding.[46] This is, of course, most obvious in the process of primary socialization. The difficulties in first socializing a child cannot be accounted for simply in terms of intrinsic problems of learning. The little animal fights back, so to speak. The fact that it is fated to lose the battle does not eliminate its animality's resistance to the ever more penetrating influence of the social world. For example, the child resists the imposition of the temporal structure of society on the natural temporality of his organism.[47] He resists eating and sleeping by the clock rather than by the biologically given demands of the organism. The resistance is progressively broken in the course of socialization, but perpetuates itself as frustration on every occasion when society forbids the hungry individual to eat and the sleepy individual to go to bed. Socialization inevitably involves this sort of biological frustration. Social existence depends upon the continuing subjugation of biologically grounded resistance in the individual, which entails legitimation as well as institutionalization. Thus society provides the individual with various explanations as to why he should eat three times a day, and not whenever he is hungry, and with even stronger explanations as to why he should not sleep with his sister. Similar problems of fitting the organism into the socially constructed world exist in secondary socialization, although, of course, the degree of biological frustration is likely to be less acute.

In the fully socialized individual there is a continuing internal dialectic between identity and its biological substratum.[48] The individual continues to experience himself as an organism, apart from and sometimes set against the socially derived objectifications of himself. Often this dialectic is apprehended as a struggle between a 'higher' and a 'lower' self, respectively equated with social identity and pre-social, possibly antisocial animality. The 'higher' self must repeatedly assert itself over the 'lower', sometimes in critical tests of strength. For example, a man must overcome his instinctive fear of death by courage in battle. The 'lower' self here is whipped into submission by the 'higher', an assertion of dominance over the biological substratum that is necessary if the social identity of warrior is to be maintained, both objectively and subjectively. Similarly, a man may force himself to perform sexually against the inert resistance of physiological satiety in order to maintain his identity as a paragon of virility. Again, the 'lower' self is pressed into service for the sake of the 'higher'. The victory over fear and the victory over sexual prostration both illustrate the manner in which the biological substratum resists and is overcome by the social self within man. It goes without saying that there are many lesser victories routinely undertaken in the course of everyday life, as indeed there are both lesser and greater defeats.

Man is biologically predestined to construct and to inhabit a world with others. This world becomes for him the dominant and definite reality. Its limits are set by nature, but, once constructed, this world acts back upon nature. In the dialectic between nature and the socially constructed world the human organism itself is transformed. In this same dialectic man produces reality and thereby produces himself.

Conclusion

The Sociology of Knowledge
and Sociological Theory

In the foregoing we have tried to present a general and systematic account of the role of knowledge in society. It is obvious that our analyses are not exhaustive. But we hope that our attempt to develop a systematic theory for the sociology of knowledge will stimulate both critical discussion and empirical investigations. Of one thing we are confident. A redefinition of the problems and tasks of the sociology of knowledge was long overdue. We hope that our analysis indicates the way along which further work might fruitfully proceed.

However, our conception of the sociology of knowledge also contains some general implications for sociological theory and the sociological enterprise at large, and furnishes a different perspective on a number of specific areas of sociological interest.

The analyses of objectivation, institutionalization and legitimation are directly applicable to the problems of the sociology of language, the theory of social action and institutions, and the sociology of religion. Our understanding of the sociology of knowledge leads to the conclusion that the sociologies of language and religion cannot be considered peripheral specialities of little interest to sociological theory as such, but have essential contributions to make to it. This insight is not new. Durkheim and his school had it, but it was lost for a variety of theoretically irrelevant reasons. We hope we have made it clear that the sociology of knowledge presupposes a sociology of language, and that a sociology of knowledge without a sociology of religion is impossible (and vice versa). Furthermore, we believe that we have shown how the theoretical positions of Weber and Durkheim can be combined in a comprehensive theory of social action that does not lose the inner logic of either. Finally, we would contend that the linkage we have been led to make here between the sociology of knowledge and the theoretical core of the thought of Mead and his school suggests an interesting possibility for what might be called a sociological psychology, that is, a psychology that derives its fundamental perspectives from a sociological understanding of the human condition. The observations made here point to a programme that seems to carry theoretical promise.

More generally, we would contend that the analysis of the role of knowledge in the dialectic of individual and society, of personal identity and social structure, provides a crucial complementary perspective for all areas of sociology. This is certainly not to deny that purely structural analyses of social phenomena are fully adequate for wide areas of sociological inquiry, ranging from the study of small groups to that of large institutional complexes, such as the economy or politics. Nothing is further from our intentions than the suggestion that a sociology-of-knowledge 'angle' ought somehow to be injected into all such analyses. In many cases this would be unnecessary for the cognitive goal at which these studies aim. We are suggesting, however, that the integration of the findings of such analyses into the body of sociological theory requires more than the casual obeisance that might be paid to the 'human factor' behind the uncovered structural data. Such integration requires a systematic accounting of the dialectical relation between the structural realities and the human enterprise of constructing reality – in history.

We have no polemic interest in writing this book. It would be foolish to deny, however, that our enthusiasm for the present state of sociological theory is markedly restrained. For one thing, we have tried to show, by our analysis of the interrelations between institutional processes and the legitimating symbolic universes, why we must consider the standard versions of functionalist explanations in the social sciences a theoretical legerdemain. Furthermore, we hope we have shown cause for our conviction that a purely structural sociology is endemically in danger of reifying social phenomena. Even if it begins by modestly assigning to its constructs merely heuristic status, it all too frequently ends by confusing its own conceptualizations with the laws of the universe.

In contrast to some of the dominant fashions of theorizing in contemporary sociology, the ideas we have tried to develop posit *neither* an ahistorical 'social system' *nor* an ahistorical 'human nature'. The approach we have employed here is both non-sociologistic and non-psychologistic. We cannot agree that sociology has as its object the alleged 'dynamics' of social and psychological 'systems', placed *post hoc* into a dubious relationship (incidentally, the intellectual itinerary of these two terms is worthy of a case study in the empirical sociology of knowledge).

The insight into the dialectic between social reality and individual existence in history is by no means new. It was, of course, most powerfully introduced into modern social thought by Marx. What is needed, however, is to bring to bear a dialectical perspective upon the theoretical orientation of the social sciences. Needless to say, we do not have in mind some doctrinaire introduction of Marxian ideas into sociological theory. Nor is there any point in the mere assertion that the afore-mentioned dialectic, in fact and generally, does exist. What is needed is to proceed from such an assertion to a specification of the dialectical processes in a conceptual framework that is congruent with the great traditions of sociological thought. Mere rhetoric about dialectics, such as is commonly engaged in by doctrinaire Marxists, must appear to the sociologist as just another form of obscurantism. And yet we are convinced that only an understanding of what Marcel Mauss called the 'total social fact' will protect the sociologist against the distortive reifications of both sociologism and psychologism. It is against the background of an intellectual situation in which this double danger is very real that we wish our treatise to be understood.

Our undertaking has been theoretical. Yet theory, in any empirical discipline, must be relevant in a double fashion to the 'data' defined as pertinent to that discipline. It must be congruent with them, and it must be geared to further empirical inquiry. There is a vast area of empirical problems that opens up for the sociology of knowledge. This is not the place to provide a catalogue of what we consider to be the most interesting of these problems, even less to propound specific hypotheses. We have given some indications of what we have in mind in some of the illustrations of our theoretical argument. We would add here only that, in our view, empirical research in the relation of institutions to legitimating symbolic universes will greatly enhance the sociological understanding of contemporary society. The problems here are numerous. They are more obscured than clarified by speaking about contemporary society in terms of 'secularization', of a 'scientific age', of 'mass society', or, conversely, of the 'autonomous individual', of the 'discovery of the unconscious', and so forth. These terms indicate only the immensity of the problem requiring scientific clarification. It may readily be conceded that contemporary Western men, by and large, live in a world vastly different from any preceding one. Yet just what this means in terms of the reality, objective and subjective, in which these men conduct their everyday lives and in which their crises occur is very far from clear. Empirical research into these problems, as distinct from more or less intelligent speculation, has barely begun. We would hope that the clarification of the theoretical perspective of the sociology of knowledge we have attempted here points to problems for such research that are easily ignored in other theoretical perspectives. To give but one example, the present interest on the part of social scientists in theories derived from psychoanalysis would take on a very different coloration as soon as these theories were not regarded, positively or negatively, as propositions of 'science', but analysed as legitimations of a very peculiar and probably highly significant construction of reality in modern society. Such analysis, of course, would bracket the question of the 'scientific validity' of these theories and simply look upon them as data for an understanding of the subjective and objective reality from which they emerged and which, in turn, they influence.

We have expressly refrained from following up the methodological implications of our conception of the society of knowledge. It should be clear, however, that our approach is non-positivistic, if positivism is understood as a philosophical position defining the object of the social sciences in such a way as to legislate away their most important problems. All the same, we do not underestimate the merit of 'positivism', broadly understood, in redefining the canons of empirical investigation for the social sciences.

The sociology of knowledge understands human reality as

socially constructed reality. Since the constitution of reality has traditionally been a central problem of philosophy, this understanding has certain philosophical implications. In so far as there has been a strong tendency for this problem, with all the questions it involves, to become trivialized in contemporary philosophy, the sociologist may find himself, to his surprise perhaps, the inheritor of philosophical questions that the professional philosophers are no longer interested in considering. In various sections of this treatise, especially in the analysis of the foundations of knowledge in everyday life and in the discussion of objectivation and institutionalization in relation to the biological presuppositions of human existence, we have given some indication of the contributions sociologically oriented thought may make to philosophical anthropology.

In sum, our conception of the sociology of knowledge implies a specific conception of sociology in general. It does *not* imply that sociology is not a science, that its methods should be other than empirical, or that it cannot be 'value-free'. It *does* imply that sociology takes its place in the company of the sciences that deal with man *as* man; that it is, in that specific sense, a humanistic discipline. An important consequence of this conception is that sociology must be carried on in a continuous conversation with both history and philosophy or lose its proper object of inquiry. This object is society as part of a human world, made by men, inhabited by men, and, in turn, making men, in an ongoing historical process. It is not the least fruit of a humanistic sociology that it rewakens our wonder at this astonishing phenomenon.

Notes

Notes

Introduction: The Problem of the Sociology of Knowledge

1. cf. Max Scheler, *Die Wissensformen und die Gesellschaft* (Bern: Francke, 1960). This volume of essays, first published in 1925, contains the basic formulation of the sociology of knowledge in an essay entitled '*Probleme einer Soziologie des Wissens*', which was originally published a year earlier.

2. cf. Wilhelm Windelband and Heinz Heimsoeth, *Lehrbuch der Geschichte der Philosophie* (Tübingen: Mohr, 1950), pp. 605 ff.

3. cf. Albert Salomon, *In Praise of Enlightenment* (New York: Meridian Books, 1963); Hans Barth, *Wahrheit und Ideologie* (Zurich: Manesse, 1945); Werner Stark, *The Sociology of Knowledge* (Chicago: Free Press of Glencoe, 1958; London: Routledge & Kegan Paul), pp. 46 ff.; Kurt Lenk, ed., *Ideologie* (Neuwied/Rhein: Luchterhand, 1961), pp. 13 ff.

4. *Pensées* v. 294.

5. cf. Karl Marx, *Die Frühschriften* (Stuttgart: Kröner, 1953). The *Economic and Philosophical Manuscripts of 1844* will be found on pp. 225 ff.

6. On Marx's *Unterbau/Ueberbau* scheme, cf. Karl Kautsky, '*Verhältnis von Unterbau und Ueberbau*', in Iring Fetscher, ed., *Der Marxismus* (Munich: Piper, 1962), pp. 160 ff.; Antonio Labriola, '*Die Vermittlung zwischen Basis und Ueberbau*', ibid., pp. 167 ff.; Jean-Yves Calvez, *La Pensée de Karl Marx* (Paris: Éditions du Seuil, 1956), pp. 424 ff. The most important twentieth-century reformulation of the problem is that by György Lukács, in his *Geschichte und Klassenbewusstsein* (Berlin, 1923), today more readily accessible in the French translation, *Histoire et conscience de classe* (Paris: Éditions de Minuit, 1960). Lukács's understanding of Marx's concept of dialectics is all the more remarkable as it antedated by almost a decade the rediscovery of the *Economic and Philosophical Manuscripts of 1844*.

7. The most important works of Nietzsche's for the sociology of knowledge are *The Genealogy of Morals* and *The Will to Power*. For secondary discussions, cf. Walter A. Kaufmann, *Nietzsche* (New

York: Meridian Books, 1956); Karl Löwith, *From Hegel to Nietzsche* (New York: Holt, Rinehart and Winston, 1964).

8. One of the earliest and most interesting applications of Nietzsche's thought to a sociology of knowledge is Alfred Seidel's in *Bewusstsein als Verhängnis* (Bonn: Cohen, 1927). Seidel, who had been a student of Weber's, tried to combine both Nietzsche and Freud with a radical sociological critique of consciousness.

9. One of the most suggestive discussions of the relationship between historicism and sociology is Carlo Antoni's in *Dallo storicismo alla sociologia* (Florence, 1940). Also, cf. H. Stuart Hughes, *Consciousness and Society* (New York: Knopf, 1958; London: Macgibbon & Kee), pp. 183 ff. The most important work of Wilhelm Dilthey's for our present considerations is *Der Aufbau der geschichtlichen Welt in den Geisteswissenschaften* (Stuttgart: Teubner, 1958).

10. For an excellent discussion of Scheler's conception of the sociology of knowledge, cf. Hans-Joachim Lieber, *Wissen und Gesellschaft* (Tübingen: Niemeyer, 1952), pp. 55 ff. See also Stark, op. cit., *passim*.

11. For the general development of German sociology during this period, cf. Raymond Aron, *La Sociologie allemande contemporaine* (Paris: Presses Universitaires de France, 1950). For important contributions from this period concerning the sociology of knowledge, cf. Siegfried Landshut, *Kritik der Soziologie* (Munich, 1929); Hans Freyer, *Soziologie als Wirklichkeitswissenschaft* (Leipzig, 1930); Ernst Grünwald, *Das Problem der Soziologie des Wissens* (Vienna, 1934); Alexander von Schelting, *Max Webers Wissenschaftslehre* (Tübingen, 1934). The last-named work, still the most important discussion of Weber's methodology, must be understood against the background of the debate on the sociology of knowledge, then centring on both Scheler's and Mannheim's formulations.

12. Karl Mannheim, *Ideology and Utopia* (London: Routledge & Kegan Paul, 1936); *Essays on the Sociology of Knowledge* (New York: O.U.P., 1952); *Essays on Sociology and Social Psychology* (New York: O.U.P., 1953); *Essays on the Sociology of Culture* (New York: O.U.P., 1956). A compendium of Mannheim's most important writings in the sociology of knowledge, compiled and with a useful introduction by Kurt Wolff, is Karl Mannheim, *Wissenssoziologie* (Neuwied/Rhein: Luchterhand, 1964). For secondary discussions of Mannheim's conception of the sociology of knowledge, cf. Jacques J. Maquet, *Sociologie de la connaissance* (Louvain: Nauwelaerts, 1949); Aron, op. cit.; Robert K. Merton, *Social Theory and Social Structure* (Chicago: Free Press of Glencoe,

1957; London: Collier-Macmillan), pp. 489 ff.; Stark, op. cit.; Lieber, op. cit.

13. This characterization of the two original formulations of the discipline was made by Lieber, op. cit.

14. cf. Merton, op. cit., pp. 439 ff.

15. cf. Talcott Parsons, 'An Approach to the Sociology of Knowledge', *Transactions of the Fourth World Congress of Sociology* (Louvain: International Sociological Association, 1959), vol. IV, pp. 25 ff.; 'Culture and the Social System', in Parsons *et al.*, eds., *Theories of Society* (New York: Free Press, 1961; London: Collier-Macmillan), vol. II, pp. 963 ff.

16. cf. Talcott Parsons, *The Social System* (Glencoe, Ill.: Free Press, 1951; London: Tavistock), pp. 326 ff.

17. cf. C. Wright Mills, *Power, Politics and People* (New York: Ballantine Books, 1963), pp. 453 ff.

18. cf. Theodor Geiger, *Ideologie und Wahrheit* (Stuttgart: Humboldt, 1953); *Arbeiten zur Soziologie* (Neuwied/Rhein: Luchterhand, 1962), pp. 412 ff.

19. cf. Ernst Topitsch, *Vom Ursprung und Ende der Metaphysik* (Vienna: Springer, 1958); *Sozialphilosophie zwischen Ideologie und Wissenschaft* (Neuwied/Rhein: Luchterhand, 1961). An important influence on Topitsch is the Kelsen school of legal positivism. For the implications of the latter for the sociology of knowledge, cf. Hans Kelsen, *Aufsätze zur Ideologiekritik* (Neuwied/Rhein: Luchterhand, 1964).

20. cf. Daniel Bell, *The End of Ideology* (New York: Free Press of Glencoe, 1960; London: Collier-Macmillan); Kurt Lenk, ed., *Ideologie*; Norman Birnbaum, ed., *The Sociological Study of Ideology* (Oxford: Blackwell, 1962).

21. cf. Stark, op. cit.

22. Alfred Schutz, *Collected Papers*, vol. I (The Hague: Nijhoff, 1962), p. 149. Italics ours.

23. Ibid., vol. II (1964), p. 121.

24. For discussions of the implications of Durkheimian sociology for the sociology of knowledge, cf. Gerard L. DeGré, *Society and Ideology* (New York: Columbia University Bookstore, 1943), pp. 54 ff.; Merton, op. cit.; Georges Gurvitch, '*Problèmes de la sociologie de la connaissance*', *Traité de sociologie* (Paris: Presses Universitaires de France, 1960), vol. II, pp. 103 ff.

25. The closest approach, to our knowledge, of symbolic-interactionism to the problems of the sociology of knowledge may be found in Tamotsu Shibutani, '*Reference Groups and Social Control*', in Arnold Rose, ed., *Human Behavior and Social Processes* (Boston: Houghton Mifflin, 1962; London: Routledge & Kegan

Paul), pp. 128 ff. The failure to make the connexion between Meadian social psychology and the sociology of knowledge, on the part of the symbolic-interactionists, is of course related to the limited 'diffusion' of the sociology of knowledge in America, but its more important theoretical foundation is to be sought in the fact that both Mead himself and his later followers did not develop an adequate concept of social structure. Precisely for this reason, we think, is the integration of the Meadian and Durkheimian approaches so very important. It may be observed here that, just as the indifference to the sociology of knowledge on the part of American social psychologists has prevented the latter from relating their perspectives to a macro-sociological theory, so is the total ignorance of Mead a severe theoretical defect of neo-Marxist social thought in Europe today. There is considerable irony in the fact that, of late, neo-Marxist theoreticians have been seeking a liaison with Freudian psychology (which is fundamentally incompatible with the anthropological presuppositions of Marxism), completely oblivious of the existence of a Meadian theory of the dialectic between society and the individual that would be immeasurably more congenial to their own approach. For a recent example of this ironic phenomenon, cf. Georges Lapassade, *L'Entrée dans la vie* (Paris: Éditions de Minuit, 1963), an otherwise highly suggestive book that, as it were, cries out for Mead on every page. The same irony, albeit in a different context of intellectual segregation, pertains to the recent American efforts for a *rapprochement* between Marxism and Freudianism. One European sociologist who has drawn heavily and successfully upon Mead and the Meadian tradition in the construction of sociological theory is Friedrich Tenbruck. Cf. his *Geschichte und Gesellschaft (Habilitationsschrift*, University of Freiburg, to be published shortly), especially the section entitled *'Realität'*. In a different systematic context from ours, but in a manner quite congenial to our own approach to the Meadian problematic, Tenbruck discusses the social origin of reality and the social-structural bases for the maintenance of reality.

26. Talcott Parsons, *The Structure of Social Action* (Chicago: Free Press, 1949; London: Allen & Unwin), p. v.

27. Emile Durkheim, *The Rules of Sociological Method* (Chicago: Free Press, 1950; London: Collier-Macmillan), p. 14.

28. Max Weber, *The Theory of Social and Economic Organization* (New York: O.U.P., 1947), p. 101.

One. The Foundation of Knowledge in Everyday Life ❋

1. This entire section of our treatise is based on Alfred Schutz and Thomas Luckmann, *Die Strukturen der Lebenswelt,* now being prepared for publication. In view of this, we have refrained from providing individual references to the places in Schutz's published work where the same problems are discussed. Our argument here is based on Schutz, as developed by Luckmann in the afore-mentioned work, *in toto.* The reader wishing to acquaint himself with Schutz's work published to date may consult Alfred Schutz, *Der sinnhafte Aufbau der sozialen Welt* (Vienna: Springer, 1960); *Collected Papers,* vols. I and II. The reader interested in Schutz's adaptation of the phenomenological method to the analysis of the social world may consult especially his *Collected Papers,* vol. I, pp. 99 ff., and Maurice Natanson, ed., *Philosophy of the Social Sciences* (New York: Random House, 1963), pp. 183 ff.

Two. Society as Objective Reality ❋

1. On recent biological work concerning the peculiar position of man in the animal kingdom, cf. Jakob von Uexküll, *Bedeutungslehre* (Hamburg: Rowohlt, 1958); F. J. J. Buytendijk, *Mensch und Tier* (Hamburg: Rowohlt, 1958); Adolf Portmann, *Zoologie und das neue Bild vom Menschen* (Hamburg: Rowohlt, 1956). The most important evaluations of these biological perspectives in terms of a philosophical anthropology are those by Helmuth Plessner (*Die Stufen des Organischen und der Mensch,* 1928 and 1965) and Arnold Gehlen (*Der Mensch, seine Natur und seine Stellung in der Welt,* 1940 and 1950). It was Gehlen who further developed these per-spectives in terms of a sociological theory of institutions (especially in his *Urmensch und Spätkultur,* 1956). For an introduction to the latter, cf. Peter L. Berger and Hansfried Kellner, 'Arnold Gehlen and the Theory of Institutions', *Social Research* 32: 1, pp. 110 ff. (1965).

2. The term 'species-specific environment' is taken from von Uexküll.

3. The anthropological implications of the term 'world-openness' were developed by both Plessner and Gehlen.

4. The peculiarity of the human organism as ontogenetically

grounded was shown particularly in the investigations of Portmann.

5. The suggestion that the foetal period in man extends through the first year of life was made by Portmann, who called this year the 'extrauterine Frühjahr'.

6. The term 'significant others' is taken from Mead. For Mead's theory of the ontogenesis of the self, cf. his *Mind, Self and Society* (Chicago: University of Chicago Press, 1934). A useful compendium of Mead's writings is Anselm Strauss, ed., *George Herbert Mead on Social Psychology* (Chicago: University of Chicago Press, 1964). For a suggestive secondary discussion, cf. Maurice Natanson, *The Social Dynamics of George H. Mead* (Washington: Public Affairs Press, 1956).

7. There is a fundamental dichotomy between the conception of man as a self-producing being and a conception of 'human nature'. This constitutes a decisive anthropological difference between Marx and any properly sociological perspective on the one hand (especially one that is grounded in Meadian social psychology), and Freud and most non-Freudian psychological perspectives on the other. A clarification of this difference is very important if there is to be any meaningful conversation between the fields of sociology and psychology today. Within sociological theory itself it is possibl: to distinguish between positions in terms of their closeness to the 'sociological' and the 'psychological' poles. Vilfredo Pareto probably expresses the most elaborate approach to the 'psychological' pole within sociology itself. Incidentally, acceptance or rejection of the 'human nature' presupposition also has interesting implications in terms of political ideologies, but this point cannot be developed here.

8. The work of Bronislaw Malinowski, Ruth Benedict, Margaret Mead, Clyde Kluckhohn and George Murdock may be cited in this connexion.

9. The view here presented on the sexual plasticity of man has an affinity with Freud's conception of the originally unformed character of the libido.

10. This point is explicated in Mead's theory of the social genesis of the self.

11. The term 'eccentricity' is taken from Plessner. Similar perspectives can be found in Scheler's later work on philosophical anthropology. Cf. Max Scheler, *Die Stellung des Menschen im Kosmos* (Munich: Nymphenburger Verlagshandlung, 1947).

12. The social character of man's self-production was formulated most sharply by Marx in his critique of Stirner, in *The German Ideology*. Jean-Paul Sartre's development from his earlier

existentialism to its later Marxist modification, that is, from *L'Être et le néant* to the *Critique de la raison dialectique*, is the most impressive example in contemporary philosophical anthropology of the achievement of this sociologically crucial insight. Sartre's own interest in the 'mediations' between the macroscopic socio-historical processes and individual biography would be greatly served, once more, through a consideration of Meadian social psychology.

13. The inextricable connexion between man's humanity and his sociality was most sharply formulated by Durkheim, especially in the concluding section of the *Formes élémentaires de la vie religieuse*.

14. In insisting that social order is not based on any 'laws of nature' we are not *ipso facto* taking a position on a metaphysical conception of 'natural law'. Our statement is limited to such facts of nature as are empirically available.

15. It was Durkheim who insisted most strongly on the character *sui generis* of social order, especially in his *Règles de la méthode sociologique*. The anthropological necessity of externalization was developed by both Hegel and Marx.

16. The biological foundation of externalization and its relationship to the emergence of institutions was developed by Gehlen.

17. The term 'stock of knowledge' is taken from Schutz.

18. Gehlen refers to this point in his concepts of *Triebüberschuss* and *Entlastung*.

19. Gehlen refers to this point in his concept of *Hintergrundserfüllung*.

20. The concept of the definition of the situation was formed by W. I. Thomas and developed throughout his sociological work.

21. We are aware of the fact that this concept of institution is broader than the prevailing one in contemporary sociology. We think that such a broader concept is useful for a comprehensive analysis of basic social processes. On social control, cf. Friedrich Tenbruck, '*Soziale Kontrolle*', *Staatslexikon der Goerres-Gesellschaft* (1962), and Heinrich Popitz, '*Soziale Normen*', *European Journal of Sociology*.

22. The term 'taking the role of the other' is taken from Mead. We are here taking Mead's paradigm of socialization and applying it to the broader problem of institutionalization. The argument combines key features of both Mead's and Gehlen's approaches.

23. Simmel's analysis of the expansion from the dyad to the triad is important in this connexion. The following argument combines Simmel's and Durkheim's conceptions of the objectivity of social reality.

24. In Durkheim's terms this means that, with the expansion of

the dyad into a triad and beyond, the original formations become geniune 'social facts', that is, they attain *choséité*.

25. Jean Piaget's concept of infantile 'realism' may be compared here.

26. For an analysis of this process in the contemporary family, cf. Peter L. Berger and Hansfried Kellner, 'Marriage and the Construction of Reality', *Diogenes* 46 (1964), pp. 1 ff.

27. The preceding description closely follows Durkheim's analysis of social reality. This does *not* contradict the Weberian conception of the meaningful character of society. Since social reality always originates in meaningful human actions, it continues to carry meaning even if it is opaque to the individual at a given time. The original may be *reconstructed*, precisely by means of what Weber called *Verstehen*.

28. The term 'objectivation' is derived from the Hegelian/ Marxian *Versachlichung*.

29. Contemporary American sociology tends towards leaving out the first moment. Its perspective on society thus tends to be what Marx called a reification (*Verdinglichung*), that is, an undialectical distortion of social reality that obscures the latter's character as an ongoing human production, viewing it instead in thing-like categories appropriate only to the world of nature. That the dehumanization implicit in this is mitigated by values deriving from the larger tradition of the society is, presumably, morally fortunate, but is irrelevant theoretically.

30. Pareto's analysis of the 'logic' of institutions is relevant here. A point similar to ours is made by Friedrich Tenbruck, op. cit. He too insists that the 'strain towards consistency' is rooted in the meaningful character of human action.

31. This, of course, is the fundamental weakness of any functionalistically oriented sociology. For an excellent critique of this, cf. the discussion of Bororo society in Claude Lévi-Strauss, *Tristes Tropiques* (New York: Atheneum, 1964), pp. 183 ff.

32. The term 'recipe knowledge' is taken from Schutz.

33. The term 'objectification' is derived from the Hegelian *Vergegenständlichung*.

34. The term 'sedimentation' is derived from Edmund Husserl. It was first used by Schutz in a sociological context.

35. This is meant by the term 'monothetic acquisition' of Husserl's. It was also used extensively by Schutz.

36. On the 'social self' confronting the self in its totality, cf. Mead's concept of the 'me' with Durkheim's concept of *homo duplex*.

37. Although our argument uses terms foreign to Mead, our

conception of the role is very close to his and intends to be an expansion of Meadian role theory in a broader frame of reference, namely one that includes a theory of institutions.

38. The term 'representation' is closely related here to the Durkheimian usage, but broader in scope.

.39. This process of 'binding together' is one of the central concerns of Durkheimian sociology – the integration of society through the fostering of solidarity.

40. The symbolic representations of integration are what Durkheim called 'religion'.

41. The concept of the social distribution of knowledge is derived from Schutz.

42. The term 'mediation' has been used by Sartre, but without the concrete meaning that role theory is capable of giving to it. The term serves well to indicate the general nexus between role theory and the sociology of knowledge.

43. This question could be designated as concerning the 'density' of the institutional order. However, we have been trying to avoid introducing new terms and have decided not to use this term, although it is suggestive.

44. This is what Durkheim referred to as 'organic solidarity'. Lucien Lévy-Bruhl gives further psychological content to this Durkheimian concept when he speaks of 'mystic participation' in primitive societies.

45. Eric Voegelin's concepts of 'compactness' and 'differentiation' may be compared here. See his *Order and History*, vol. I (Baton Rouge, La: Louisiana State University Press, 1956; Oxford: O.U.P.). Talcott Parsons has spoken of institutional differentiation in various parts of his work.

46. The relationship between the division of labour and institutional differentiation has been analysed by Marx, Durkheim, Weber, Ferdinand Tönnies and Talcott Parsons.

47. It may be said that, despite different interpretations in detail, there is a high degree of consensus on this point throughout the history of sociological theory.

48. The relationship between 'pure theory' and economic surplus was first pointed out by Marx.

49. The tendency of institutions to persist was analysed by Georg Simmel in terms of his concept of 'faithfulness'. Cf. his *Soziologie* (Berlin: Duncker und Humblot, 1958), pp. 438 ff.

50. This concept of de-institutionalization is derived from Gehlen.

51. The analysis of de-institutionalization in the private sphere is a central problem of Gehlen's social psychology of modern

society. Cf. his *Die Seele im technischen Zeitalter* (Hamburg: Rowohlt, 1957).

52. If one were willing to put up with further neologisms, one could call this the question about the degree of 'fusion' or 'segmentation' of the institutional order. On the face of it, this question would seem to be identical with the structural-functional concern about the 'functional integration' of societies. The latter term, however, presupposes that the 'integration' of a society can be determined by an outside observer who investigates the external functioning of the society's institutions. We would contend, on the contrary, that both 'functions' and 'disfunctions' can only be analysed by way of the level of meaning. Consequently, 'functional integration', if one wants to use this term at all, means the integration of the institutional order by way of various legitimating processes. In other words, *the integration lies not in the institutions but in their legitimation.* This implies, as against the structural-functionalists, that an institutional order cannot adequately be understood as a 'system'.

53. This problem is related to that of 'ideology', which we discuss later in a more narrowly defined context.

54. Weber repeatedly refers to various collectivities as 'carriers' (*Träger*) of what we have called here sub-universes of meaning, especially in his comparative sociology of religion. The analysis of this phenomenon is, of course, related to Marx's *Unterbau/Ueberbau scheme.*

55. The pluralistic competition between sub-universes of meaning is one of the most important problems for an empirical sociology of knowledge of contemporary society. We have dealt with this problem elsewhere in our work in the sociology of religion, but see no point in developing an analysis of this in the present treatise.

56. This proposition can be put into Marxian terms by saying that there is a dialectical relationship between substructure (*Unterbau*) and superstructure (*Ueberbau*) – a Marxian insight that has been widely lost in main-line Marxism until very recently. The problem of the possibility of socially detached knowledge has, of course, been a central one for the sociology of knowledge as defined by Scheler and Mannheim. We are not giving it such a central place for reasons inherent in our general theoretical approach. The important point for a theoretical sociology of knowledge is the dialectic between knowledge and its social base. Questions such as Mannheim's concerning the 'unattached intelligentsia' are applications of the sociology of knowledge to concrete historical and empirical phenomena. Propositions about these will have to be made on a level of much lesser theoretical generality than interests

us here. Questions concerning the autonomy of social-scientific knowledge, on the other hand, should be negotiated in the context of the methodology of the social sciences. This area we have excluded in our definition of the scope of the sociology of knowledge, for theoretical reasons stated in our introduction.

57. This is the phenomenon commonly called 'cultural lag' in American sociology since Ogburn. We have avoided this term because of its evolutionistic and implicitly evaluative connotation.

58. Reification (*Verdinglichung*) is an important Marxian concept, particularly in the anthropological considerations of the *Frühschriften*, then developed in terms of the 'fetishism of commodities' in *Das Kapital*. For more recent developments of the concept in Marxist theory, cf. György Lukács, *Histoire et conscience de classe*, pp. 109 ff.; Lucien Goldmann, *Recherches dialectiques* (Paris: Gallimard, 1959), pp. 64 ff.; Joseph Gabel, *La Fausse Conscience* (Paris: Éditions de Minuit, 1962), and *Formen der Entfremdung* (Frankfurt: Fischer, 1964). For an extensive discussion of the applicability of the concept within a non-doctrinaire sociology of knowledge, cf. Peter L. Berger and Stanley Pullberg, 'Reification and the Sociological Critique of Consciousness', *History and Theory* IV: 2, pp. 198 ff. (1965). In the Marxian frame of reference the concept of reification is closely related to that of alienation (*Entfremdung*). The latter concept has been confused in recent sociological writing with phenomena ranging from *anomie* to neurosis, almost beyond the point of terminological retrieval. In any case, we have felt that this is not the place to attempt such a retrieval and have, therefore, avoided the use of the concept.

59. Recent French critics of Durkheimian sociology, such as Jules Monnerot (*Les Faits sociaux ne sont pas des choses*, 1946) and Armand Cuvillier ('*Durkheim et Marx*', *Cahiers internationaux de sociologie*, 1948), have accused it of a reified view of social reality. In other words, they have argued that Durkheim's *choséité* is *ipso facto* a reification. Whatever one may say about this in terms of Durkheim exegesis, it is possible in principle to assert that 'social facts are things', and to intend thereby no more than the objectivity of social facts *as human products*. The theoretical key to the question is the distinction between objectivation and reification.

60. Compare here Sartre's concept of the 'practico-inert', in *Critique de la raison dialectique*.

61. For this reason Marx called reifying consciousness a *false* consciousness. This concept may be related to Sartre's 'bad faith' (*mauvaise foi*).

62. The work of Lucien Lévy-Bruhl and Jean Piaget may be taken as basic for an understanding of protoreification, both phylo-

and ontogenetically. Also, cf. Claude Lévi-Strauss, *La Pensée sauvage* (Paris: Plon, 1962).

63. On the parallelism between 'here below' and 'up above', cf. Mircea Eliade, *Cosmos and History* (New York: Harper, 1959). A similar point is made by Voegelin, op. cit., in his discussion of 'cosmological civilizations'.

64. On the reification of identity, compare Sartre's analysis of anti-Semitism.

65. On conditions for dereification, cf. Berger and Pullberg, loc. cit.

66. The term 'legitimation' is derived from Weber, where it is developed particularly in the context of his political sociology. We have given it a much broader use here.

67. On legitimations as 'explanations', compare Pareto's analysis of 'derivations'.

68. Both Marx and Pareto were aware of the possible autonomy of what we have called legitimations ('ideology' in Marx, 'derivations' in Pareto).

69. Our concept of 'symbolic universe' is very close to Durkheim's 'religion'. Schutz's analysis of 'finite provinces of meaning' and their relationship to each other, and Sartre's concept of 'totalization', have been very relevant for our argument at this point.

70. The term 'marginal situation' (*Grenzsituation*) was coined by Karl Jaspers. We are using the term in a manner quite different from Jaspers's.

71. Our argument here is influenced by Durkheim's analysis of *anomie*. We are more interested, though, in the *nomic* rather than the *anomic* processes in society.

72. The paramount status of everyday reality was analysed by Schutz. Cf. especially the article 'On Multiple Realities', *Collected Papers*, vol. I, pp. 207 ff.

73. The precariousness of subjective identity is already implied in Mead's analysis of the genesis of the self. For developments of this analysis, cf. Anselm Strauss, *Mirrors and Masks* (New York: Free Press of Glencoe, 1959; London: Collier-Macmillan); Erving Goffmann, *The Presentation of Self in Everyday Life* (Garden City, N.Y.: Doubleday-Anchor, 1959).

74. Heidegger gives the most elaborate analysis in recent philosophy of death as the marginal situation *par excellence*. Schutz's concept of the 'fundamental anxiety' refers to the same phenomenon. Malinowski's analysis of the social function of funerary ceremonialism is also relevant at this point.

75. The use of certain perspectives on 'anxiety' (*Angst*) de-

veloped by existential philosophy makes it possible to place Durkheim's analysis of *anomie* in a broader anthropological frame of reference.

76. cf. Lévi-Strauss, op. cit.

77. On collective memory, cf. Maurice Halbwachs, *Les Cadres sociaux de la mémoire* (Paris: Presses Universitaires de France, 1952). Halbwachs also developed his sociological theory of memory in *La Mémoire collective* (1950) and in *La Topographie légendaire des Evangiles en Terre Sainte* (1941).

78. The concepts of 'predecessors' and 'successors' are derived from Schutz.

79. The conception of the transcending character of society was especially developed by Durkheim.

80. The conception of 'projection' was first developed by Feuerbach, then, albeit in greatly different directions, by Marx, Nietzsche and Freud.

81. Compare again Weber's concept of 'carrier' (*Träger*).

82. The analyses of 'culture contact' in contemporary American cultural anthropology are relevant here.

83. Compare the concept of 'culture shock' in contemporary American cultural anthropology.

84. Marx developed in considerable detail the relationship between material power and 'conceptual success'. Cf. the well-known formulation of this in *The German Ideology*: '*Die Gedanken der herrschenden Klasse sind in jeder Epoche die herrschenden Gedanken*' (*Frühschriften*, Kröner edition, p. 373).

85. Pareto comes closest to the writing of a history of thought in sociological terms, which makes Pareto important for the sociology of knowledge regardless of reservations one may have about his theoretical frame of reference. Cf. Brigitte Berger, *Vilfredo Pareto and the Sociology of Knowledge* (unpublished doctoral dissertation, New School for Social Research, 1964).

86. This may be reminiscent of Auguste Comte's 'law of the three stages'. We cannot accept this, of course, but it may still be useful in suggesting that consciousness develops in historically recognizable stages, though they cannot be conceived of in Comte's manner. Our own understanding of this is closer to the Hegelian/Marxian approach to the historicity of human thought.

87. Both Lévy-Bruhl and Piaget suggest that mythology constitutes a necessary stage in the development of thought. For a suggestive discussion of the biological roots of mythological/magical thought, cf. Arnold Gehlen, *Studien zur Anthropologie und Soziologie* (Neuwied/Rhein: Luchterhand, 1963), pp. 79 ff.

88. Our conception of mythology here is influenced by the work

of Gerardus van der Leeuw, Mircea Eliade and Rudolf Bultmann.

89. On the continuity between social and cosmic orders in mythological consciousness, compare again the work of Eliade and Voegelin.

90. It will be clear from our theoretical presuppositions that we cannot here go in any detail into the questions of the 'sociology of intellectuals'. In addition to Mannheim's important work in this area (to be found especially in *Ideology and Utopia* and *Essays on the Sociology of Culture*), cf. Florian Znaniecki, *The Social Role of the Man of Knowledge* (New York: Columbia University Press, 1940); Theodor Geiger, *Aufgaben und Stellung der Intelligenz in der Gesellschaft* (Stuttgart, 1949); Raymond Aron, *L'Opium des intellectuals* (Paris, 1955); George B. de Huszar, ed., *The Intellectuals* (New York: Free Press of Glencoe, 1960; London: Allen & Unwin).

91. On ultimate legitimations strengthening institutional 'inertia' (Simmel's 'faithfulness'), compare both Durkheim and Pareto.

92. It is precisely at this point that any functionalist interpretation of institutions is weakest, tending to look for practicalities that are not in fact existing.

93. On the Brahman/Kshatriya conflict, compare Weber's work on the sociology of religion in India.

94. On the social validation of propositions that are hard to validate empirically, cf. Leon Festinger, *A Theory of Cognitive Dissonance* (Evanston, Ill.: Row, Peterson and Co., 1957; London: Tavistock).

95. The term 'affinity' (*Wahlverwandschaft*) is derived from Scheler and Weber.

96. On monopolistic definitions of reality in primitive and archaic societies, compare both Durkheim and Voegelin.

97. The work of Paul Radin suggests that scepticism is possible even in such monopolistic situations.

98. The term 'guest peoples' (*Gastvölker*) is derived from Weber.

99. On the affinity between politically conservative forces and religious monopolies ('churches'), compare Weber's analysis of hierocracy.

100. The term 'ideology' has been used in so many different senses that one might despair of using it in any precise manner at all. We have decided to retain it, in a narrowly defined sense, because it is useful in the latter and preferable to a neologism. There is no point here in discussing the transformations of the term in the history of both Marxism and of the sociology of knowledge. For a useful overview, cf. Kurt Lenk, ed., *Ideologie*.

101. On the relationship of Christianity to bourgeois ideology,

see both Marx and Veblen. A useful overview of the former's treatment of religion may be obtained from the anthology *Marx and Engels on Religion* (Moscow: Foreign Languages Publishing House, 1957).

102. cf. Thomas Luckmann, *Das Problem der Religion in der modernen Gesellschaft* (Freiburg: Rombach, 1963).

103. Our conception of the intellectual as the 'unwanted expert' is not very different from Mannheim's insistence on the marginality of the intellectual. In a definition of the intellectual that will be sociologically useful it is important, we think, to set off this type clearly from the 'man of knowledge' in general.

104. On the marginality of intellectuals, compare Simmel's analysis of the 'objectivity' of the stranger and Veblen's of the intellectual role of the Jews.

105. cf. Peter L. Berger, 'The Sociological Study of Sectarianism', *Social Research*, Winter 1954, pp. 467 ff.

106. Compare Mannheim's analysis of revolutionary intellectuals. For the Russian prototype of the latter, cf. E. Lampert, *Studies in Rebellion* (New York: Frederick A. Praeger, 1957; London: Routledge & Kegan Paul).

107. The transformation of revolutionary intellectuals into legitimators of the *status quo* can be studied in practically 'pure' form in the development of Russian Communism. For a sharp critique of this process from a Marxist viewpoint, cf. Leszek Kolakowski, *Der Mensch ohne Alternative* (Munich, 1960).

Three. Society as Subjective Reality ✳

1. Our conception of 'understanding the other' is derived from both Weber and Schutz.

2. Our definitions of socialization and its two sub-types closely follow current usage in the social sciences. We have only adapted the wording to conform to our overall theoretical framework.

3. Our description here, of course, leans heavily on the Meadian theory of socialization.

4. The concept of 'mediation' is derived from Sartre, who lacks, however, an adequate theory of socialization.

5. The affective dimension of early learning has been especially emphasized by Freudian child psychology, although there are various findings of behaviouristic learning theory that would tend

to confirm this. We do not imply acceptance of the theoretical presuppositions of either psychological school in our argument here.

6. Our conception of the reflected character of the self is derived from both Cooley and Mead. Its roots may be found in the analysis of the 'social self' by William James (*Principles of Psychology*).

7. Although this could not be developed here, enough may have been said to indicate the possibility of a genuinely dialectical social psychology. The latter would be equally important for philosophical anthropology as for society. As far as the latter is concerned, such a social psychology (fundamentally Meadian in orientation, but with the addition of important elements from other streams of social-scientific thought) would make it unnecessary to seek theoretically untenable alliances with either Freudian or behaviouristic psychologism.

8. On nomenclature, cf. Claude Lévi-Strauss, *La Pensée sauvage*, pp. 253 ff.

9. The concept of the 'generalized other' is used here in a fully Meadian sense.

10. Compare Georg Simmel on the self-apprehension of man as both inside and outside society. Plessner's concept of 'eccentricity' is again relevant here.

11. Compare Piaget on the massive reality of the child's world.

12. Compare Lévy-Bruhl on the phylogenetic analogue to Piaget's infantile 'realism'.

13. cf. Philippe Ariès, *Centuries of Childhood* (New York: Knopf, 1962; London: Jonathan Cape).

14. Compare here the cultural-anthropological analyses of 'rites of passage' connected with puberty.

15. The concept of 'role distance' is developed by Erving Goffman, particularly in *Asylums* (Garden City, N.Y.: Doubleday-Anchor, 1961). Our analysis suggests that such distance is *only* possible with regard to realities internalized in secondary socialization. If it extends to the realities internalized in primary socialization, we are in the domain of what American psychiatry calls 'psychopathy', which implies a deficient formation of identity. A very interesting further point suggested by our analysis concerns the structural limits within which a 'Goffmanian model' of social interaction may be viable – to wit, societies so structured that decisive elements of objectivated reality are internalized in secondary socialization processes. This consideration, incidentally, should make us careful not to equate Goffman's 'model' (which is very useful, let it be added, for the analysis of important features of modern industrial society) with a 'dramatic model' *tout court*. There

have been other dramas, after all, than that of the contemporary organization man bent on 'impression management'.

16. The studies in the sociology of occupations, as developed particularly by Everett Hughes, offer interesting material on this point.

17. cf. Talcott Parsons, *Essays in Sociological Theory, Pure and Applied* (Chicago: Free Press, 1949; London: Collier-Macmillan), pp. 233 ff.

18. Hans H. Gerth and C. Wright Mills, in *Character and Social Structure* (New York: Harcourt, Brace, 1953; London: Routledge & Kegan Paul), suggest the term 'intimate others' for significant others engaged in reality-maintenance in later life. We prefer not to use this term because of its similarity to that of *Intimsphäre*, which has been employed a lot in recent German-speaking sociology and which has a considerably different connotation.

19. Compare Goffman again on this point, as well as David Riesman.

20. The concepts of 'primary group' and 'secondary group' are derived from Cooley. We are following current usage in American sociology here.

21. On the concept of the 'conversational apparatus', cf. Peter L. Berger and Hansfried Kellner, 'Marriage and the Construction of Reality', *Diogenes* 46 (1964), pp. 1 ff. Friedrich Tenbruck (op. cit.) discusses in some detail the function of communicative networks in maintaining common realities.

22. On correspondence, cf. Georg Simmel, *Soziologie*, pp. 287 ff.

23. The concept of 'reference group' is relevant in this connexion. Compare Merton's analysis of this, in his. *Social Theory and Social Structure*.

24. cf. Peter L. Berger, *Invitation to Sociology* (Garden City, N.Y.: Doubleday-Anchor, 1963; Harmondsworth: Penguin Books), pp. 54 ff.

25. The psycho-analytic concept of 'transference' refers precisely to this phenomenon. What the psycho-analysts who use it do not understand, of course, is that the phenomenon can be found in *any* process of re-socialization with its resultant identification with the significant others who are in charge of it, so that no conclusions can be drawn from it concerning the cognitive validity of the 'insights' occurring in the psychoanalytic situation.

26. This is what Durkheim referred to in his analysis of the inevitably social character of religion. We would not use, however, his term 'church' for the 'moral community' of religion, because it

is appropriate only to a historically specific case in the institutionalization of religion.

27. The studies of Chinese Communist 'brainwashing' techniques are highly revealing of the basic patterns of alternation. Cf., for instance, Edward Hunter, *Brainwashing in Red China* (New York: Vanguard Press, 1951). Goffman, in his *Asylums*, comes close to showing the procedural parallel to group psychotherapy in America.

28. Again, compare Festinger for the avoidance of discrepant definitions of reality.

29. cf. Thomas Luckmann and Peter L. Berger, 'Social Mobility and Personal Identity', *European Journal of Sociology* V, pp. 331 ff. (1964).

30. Riesman's concept of 'other-direction' and Merton's of 'anticipatory socialization' are relevant at this point.

31. cf. the essays on medical sociology by Eliot Freidson, Theodor J. Litman and Julius A. Roth in Arnold Rose, ed., *Human Behavior and Social Processes*.

32. Our argument implies the necessity of a macro-sociological background for analyses of internalization, that is, of an understanding of the *social structure* within which internalization occurs. American social psychology today is greatly weakened by the fact that such a background is widely lacking.

33. cf. Gerth and Mills, op. cit. Also cf. Tenbruck, op. cit., who assigns a prominent place to the structural bases of personality in his typology of primitive, traditional and modern societies.

34. This has the important implication that most psychological models, including those of contemporary scientific psychology, have limited socio-historical applicability. It further implies that a sociological psychology will at the same time have to be a *historical psychology*.

35. cf. Erving Goffman, *Stigma* (Englewood Cliffs, N. J.: Prentice-Hall, 1963). Also, cf. A. Kardiner and L. Ovesey, *The Mark of Oppression* (New York: Norton, 1951).

36. cf. Donald W. Cory, *The Homosexual in America* (New York: Greenberg, 1951).

37. We would stress here once more the social-structural conditions for the applicability of a 'Goffmanian model' of analysis.

38. Helmut Schelsky has coined the suggestive term 'permanent reflectiveness' (*Dauerreflektion*) for the psychological cognate of the contemporary 'market of worlds' ('*Ist die Dauerreflektion institutionalisierbar?*', *Zeitschrift für evangelische Ethik*, 1957). The theoretical background of Schelsky's argument is Gehlen's general theory of 'subjectivization' in modern society. It

was developed further in terms of the sociology of contemporary religion by Luckmann, op. cit.

39. cf. Luckmann and Berger, loc. cit.

40. It is inadvisable to speak of 'collective identity' because of the danger of false (and reifying) hypostatization. The *exemplum horribile* of such hypostatization is the German 'Hegelian' sociology of the 1920s and 1930s (such as the work of Othmar Spann). The danger is present in greater or lesser degree in various works of the Durkheim school and the 'culture and personality' school in American cultural anthropology.

41. What is implied here, of course, is a sociological critique of the Freudian 'reality principle'.

42. cf. Peter L. Berger, 'Towards a Sociological Understanding of Psychoanalysis', *Social Research*, Spring 1965, pp. 26 ff.

43. cf. ibid.

44. The dialectic between nature and society here discussed is in no way to be equated with the 'dialectic of nature', as developed by Engels and later Marxism. The former underlines that man's relationship to his own body (as to nature in general) is itself a specifically human one. The latter, on the contrary, projects specifically human phenomena into non-human nature and then proceeds to theoretically dehumanize man by looking upon him as but the object of natural forces or laws of nature.

45. For this possibility of a discipline of 'sociosomatics', cf. Georg Simmel, op. cit., pp. 483 ff. (the essay on the 'sociology of the senses'); Marcel Mauss, *Sociologie et anthropologie* (Paris: Presses Universitaires de France, 1950), pp. 365 ff. (the essay on the 'techniques of the body'); Edward T. Hall, *The Silent Language* (Garden City, N.Y.: Doubleday, 1959). The sociological analysis of sexuality would probably provide the richest empirical material for such a discipline.

46. This was understood very well in Freud's conception of socialization. It was greatly underestimated in the functionalist adaptations of Freud, from Malinowski on.

47. Compare here Henri Bergson (especially his theory of *durée*), Maurice Merleau-Ponty, Alfred Schutz and Jean Piaget.

48. Compare here both Durkheim and Plessner, as well as Freud.

Indexes

Subject Index

Name Index for Introduction and Notes

Antoni, Carlo 216 n. 9
Ariès, Philippe, 230 n. 13
Aron, Raymond, 216 n. 11, n. 12, 228 n. 90

Barth, Hans, 215 n. 3
Bell, Daniel, 217 n. 20
Benedict, Ruth, 220 n. 8
Berger, Brigitte, 227 n. 85
Berger, Peter L., 219 n. 1, 222 n. 26, 225 n. 58, 226 n. 65, 229 n. 105, 231 n. 21, n. 24, 232 n. 29, 233 n. 39, n. 42
Bergson, Henri, 233 n. 47
Birnbaum, Norman, 217 n. 20
Bultmann, Rudolf, 228 n. 88
Buytendijk, F. J. J., 219 n. 1

Calvez, Jean-Yves, 215 n. 6
Cooley, Charles Horton, 230 n. 6, 231 n. 20
Cory, Donald W., 232 n. 36
Cuvillier, Armand, 225 n. 59

DeGré, Gerard L., 217 n. 24
Dilthey, Wilhelm, 19, 22, 216 n. 9
Durkheim, Emile, 18, 28, 30, 218 n. 27, 221 n.13, n. 15, n. 23, n. 24, 222 n. 27, 223 n. 38, n. 39, n. 40, n. 44, n. 46, 225 n. 59, 226 n. 69, n. 71,
227 n. 75, n. 79, 228 n. 91, n. 96, 231 n. 26, 233 n. 48

Eliade, Mircea, 226 n. 63, 228 n. 88, n.89
Engels, Friedrich, 233 n. 44

Festinger, Leon, 228 n. 94, 232 n. 28
Fetscher, Iring, 215 n. 6
Feuerbach, Ludwig, 227 n. 80
Freidson, Eliot, 232 n. 31
Freud, Sigmund, 216 n. 8, 220 n. 9, 227 n. 80, 233 n. 46, n. 48
Freyer, Hans, 216 n. 11

Gabel, Joseph, 225 n. 58
Gehlen, Arnold, 28, 219 n. 1, n. 3, 221 n. 16, n. 18, n. 19, n. 22, 223 n. 50, n. 51, 227 n. 87, 232 n. 38
Geiger, Theodor, 23-4, 217 n. 18, 228 n. 90
Gerth, Hans H., 231 n. 18, 232 n. 33
Goffman, Erving, 226 n. 73, 230 n. 15, 231 n. 19, 232 n. 27, n. 35
Goldmann, Lucien, 225 n. 58
Grünwald, Ernst, 216 n.11
Gurvitch, Georges, 217 n. 24

247

READ MORE IN PENGUIN

In every corner of the world, on every subject under the sun, Penguin represents quality and variety – the very best in publishing today.

For complete information about books available from Penguin – including Puffins, Penguin Classics and Arkana – and how to order them, write to us at the appropriate address below. Please note that for copyright reasons the selection of books varies from country to country.

In the United Kingdom: Please write to *Dept. JC, Penguin Books Ltd, FREEPOST, West Drayton, Middlesex UB7 OBR*

If you have any difficulty in obtaining a title, please send your order with the correct money, plus ten per cent for postage and packaging, to *PO Box No. 11, West Drayton, Middlesex UB7 OBR*

In the United States: Please write to *Penguin USA Inc., 375 Hudson Street, New York, NY 10014*

In Canada: Please write to *Penguin Books Canada Ltd, 10 Alcorn Avenue, Suite 300, Toronto, Ontario M4V 3B2*

In Australia: Please write to *Penguin Books Australia Ltd, 487 Maroondah Highway, Ringwood, Victoria 3134*

In New Zealand: Please write to *Penguin Books (NZ) Ltd,182–190 Wairau Road, Private Bag, Takapuna, Auckland 9*

In India: Please write to *Penguin Books India Pvt Ltd, 706 Eros Apartments, 56 Nehru Place, New Delhi 110 019*

In the Netherlands: Please write to *Penguin Books Netherlands B.V., Keizersgracht 231 NL–1016 DV Amsterdam*

In Germany: Please write to *Penguin Books Deutschland GmbH, Friedrichstrasse 10–12, W–6000 Frankfurt/Main 1*

In Spain: Please write to *Penguin Books S. A., C. San Bernardo 117–6° E–28015 Madrid*

In Italy: Please write to *Penguin Italia s.r.l., Via Felice Casati 20, I–20124 Milano*

In France: Please write to *Penguin France S. A., 17 rue Lejeune, F–31000 Toulouse*

In Japan: Please write to *Penguin Books Japan, Ishikiribashi Building, 2–5–4, Suido, Tokyo 112*

In Greece: Please write to *Penguin Hellas Ltd, Dimocritou 3, GR–106 71 Athens*

In South Africa: Please write to *Longman Penguin Southern Africa (Pty) Ltd, Private Bag X08, Bertsham 2013*

FOR THE BEST IN PAPERBACKS, LOOK FOR THE 🐧

PENGUIN PSYCHOLOGY

Introduction to Jung's Psychology Frieda Fordham

'She has delivered a fair and simple account of the main aspects of my psychological work. I am indebted to her for this admirable piece of work' – C. G. Jung in the Foreword

Child Care and the Growth of Love John Bowlby

His classic 'summary of evidence of the effects upon children of lack of personal attention ... it presents to administrators, social workers, teachers and doctors a reminder of the significance of the family' – *The Times*

The Anatomy of Human Destructiveness Erich Fromm

What makes men kill? How can we explain man's lust for cruelty and destruction? 'If any single book could bring mankind to its senses, this book might qualify for that miracle' – Lewis Mumford

Sanity, Madness and the Family R. D. Laing and A. Esterson

Schizophrenia: fact or fiction? Certainly not fact, according to the authors of this controversial book. Suggesting that some forms of madness may be largely social creations, *Sanity, Madness and the Family* demands to be taken very seriously indeed.

The Social Psychology of Work Michael Argyle

Both popular and scholarly, Michael Argyle's classic account of the social factors influencing our experience of work examines every area of working life – and throws constructive light on potential problems.

Check Your Own I.Q. H. J. Eysenck

The sequel to his controversial bestseller, containing five new standard (omnibus) tests and three specifically designed tests for verbal, numerical and visual–spatial ability.

PENGUIN POLITICS AND SOCIAL SCIENCES

Political Ideas David Thomson (ed.)

From Machiavelli to Marx – a stimulating and informative introduction to the last 500 years of European political thinkers and political thought.

On Revolution Hannah Arendt

Arendt's classic analysis of a relatively recent political phenomenon examines the underlying principles common to all revolutions, and the evolution of revolutionary theory and practice. 'Never dull, enormously erudite, always imaginative' – *Sunday Times*

The Apartheid Handbook Roger Omond

The facts behind the headlines: the essential hard information about how apartheid actually works from day to day.

The Social Construction of Reality Peter Berger and Thomas Luckmann

Concerned with the sociology of 'everything that passes for knowledge in society' and particularly with that which passes for common sense, this is 'a serious, open-minded book, upon a serious subject' – *Listener*

The Care of the Self Michel Foucault
The History of Sexuality Vol 3

Foucault examines the transformation of sexual discourse from the Hellenistic to the Roman world in an inquiry which 'bristles with provocative insights into the tangled liaison of sex and self' – *The Times Higher Educational Supplement*

A Fate Worse than Debt Susan George

How did Third World countries accumulate a staggering trillion dollars' worth of debt? Who really shoulders the burden of reimbursement? How should we deal with the debt crisis? Susan George answers these questions with the solid evidence and verve familiar to readers of *How the Other Half Dies*.

FOR THE BEST IN PAPERBACKS, LOOK FOR THE 🐧

PENGUIN POLITICS AND SOCIAL SCIENCES

Comparative Government S. E. Finer

'A considerable *tour de force* ... few teachers of politics in Britain would fail to learn a great deal from it ... Above all, it is the work of a great teacher who breathes into every page his own enthusiasm for the discipline' – Anthony King in *New Society*

Karl Marx: Selected Writings in Sociology and Social Philosophy T. B. Bottomore and Maximilien Rubel (eds.)

'It makes available, in coherent form and lucid English, some of Marx's most important ideas. As an introduction to Marx's thought, it has very few rivals indeed' – *British Journal of Sociology*

Post-War Britain A Political History Alan Sked and Chris Cook

Major political figures from Attlee to Thatcher, the aims and achievements of governments and the changing fortunes of Britain in the period since 1945 are thoroughly scrutinized in this readable history.

Inside the Third World Paul Harrison

From climate and colonialism to land hunger, exploding cities and illiteracy, this comprehensive book brings home a wealth of facts and analysis on the often tragic realities of life for the poor people and communities of Asia, Africa and Latin America.

Housewife Ann Oakley

'A fresh and challenging account' – *Economist*. 'Informative and rational enough to deserve a serious place in any discussion on the position of women in modern society' – *The Times Educational Supplement*

The Raw and the Cooked Claude Lévi-Strauss

Deliberately, brilliantly and inimitably challenging, Lévi-Strauss's seminal work of structural anthropology cuts wide and deep into the mind of mankind, as he finds in the myths of the South American Indians a comprehensible psychological pattern.

PENGUIN PHILOSOPHY

I: The Philosophy and Psychology of Personal Identity Jonathan Glover

From cases of split brains and multiple personalities to the importance of memory and recognition by others, the author of *Causing Death and Saving Lives* tackles the vexed questions of personal identity. 'Fascinating ... the ideas which Glover pours forth in profusion deserve more detailed consideration' – Anthony Storr

Minds, Brains and Science John Searle

Based on Professor Searle's acclaimed series of Reith Lectures, *Minds, Brains and Science* is 'punchy and engaging ... a timely exposé of those woolly-minded computer-lovers who believe that computers can think, and indeed that the human mind is just a biological computer' – *The Times Literary Supplement*

Ethics Inventing Right and Wrong J. L. Mackie

Widely used as a text, Mackie's complete and clear treatise on moral theory deals with the status and content of ethics, sketches a practical moral system and examines the frontiers at which ethics touches psychology, theology, law and politics.

The Penguin History of Western Philosophy D. W. Hamlyn

'Well-crafted and readable ... neither laden with footnotes nor weighed down with technical language ... a general guide to three millennia of philosophizing in the West' – *The Times Literary Supplement*

Science and Philosophy: Past and Present Derek Gjertsen

Philosophy and science, once intimately connected, are today often seen as widely different disciplines. Ranging from Aristotle to Einstein, from quantum theory to renaissance magic, Confucius and parapsychology, this penetrating and original study shows such a view to be both naive and ill-informed.

The Problem of Knowledge A. J. Ayer

How do you *know* that this is a book? How do you *know* that you know? In *The Problem of Knowledge* A. J. Ayer presented the sceptic's arguments as forcefully as possible, investigating the extent to which they can be met. 'Thorough ... penetrating, vigorous ... readable and manageable' – *Spectator*